My Country is
the Whole World

'. . . as a woman I have no country.
As a woman I want no country. As a
woman my country is the whole world.'

Virginia Woolf, *Three Guineas*

My Country is the Whole World

An Anthology of Women's Work on Peace and War

Cambridge Women's Peace Collective

PANDORA PRESS

London, Boston, Melbourne and Henley

First Published in 1984
by Pandora Press
(Routledge & Kegan Paul plc)
39 Store Street, London WC1E 7DD,
9 Park Street, Boston, Mass. 02108, USA,
464 St Kilda Road, Melbourne,
Victoria 3004, Australia and
Broadway House, Newtown Road,
Henley-on-Thames, Oxon RG9 1EN
Set in Palatino by
Rowland Phototypesetting
Bury St Edmunds, Suffolk
and printed in Great Britain by
Unwin Brothers Ltd
Old Woking, Surrey

Library of Congress Cataloging in Publication Data

My country is the whole world.
Bibliography: p.
1. Women and peace – addresses, essays, lectures.
2. Peace – addresses, essays, lectures. 3. War –
addresses, essays, lectures. I. Cambridge Women's
Peace Collective.
JX1965.M9   1984   327.1'72'088042   83-17201

ISBN 0-86358-004-1

Contents

Contents

Contents

Contents

Contents

Contents

Contents

Illustrations

Illustrations

Introduction

The suggestion that a group of us should compile this anthology was first made in March 1981 at a meeting in Cambridge of Women Oppose the Nuclear Threat (WONT). WONT groups had been forming in different parts of Britain since autumn 1980 as the outcome of an international workshop on feminism and non-violence that year. The groups were expressing an urgent desire on the part of women to search for ways of stopping the proliferation of nuclear weapons. A book which celebrates the courage and makes heard the voices of women speaking out for peace is our way of working for that end ourselves.

Our purpose is to reveal the long history of women's protests against war and of their efforts to suggest other ways of resolving conflict. Men indeed have a history of seeking non-violent solutions and of expressing their horror of war. Their words are better known, but women's words, once spoken, have had a way of quickly becoming inaudible. In uncovering this history we have been surprised and moved to find just how extensive it has been. We have also been forced to face the complexity of the questions which arise. Do women, through their loyalty to men, through their economic dependence on them, and through their silence, collude in war? Are we in some way less aggressive than men? Is blaming men, as some writing on patriarchy seems to do, a way of avoiding our share of the responsibility? How do we advocate non-violence without lapsing into a weak passivity? We explore these issues more fully later in the introduction, but first it might be helpful to explain the structure and scope of the anthology.

The extracts are presented within a broadly chronological framework. This enables the reader to sense the historical extent of women's involvement. It also reveals a remarkable continuity in women's thinking and at the same time makes it possible to discern shifts and changes in the analysis of the causes of war and in the styles of opposing it. We should make it clear that we do not see the anthology as a definitive collection. We see it as providing an impressionistic view. We have tried to weave together material from very different kinds of sources in a way which is intended to stimulate and provoke. Diaries, letters, speeches, poems, songs, political tracts, paintings, petitions, cartoons have been chosen for their intrinsic merit and to highlight or challenge each other. Though we have tried to show the dilemmas which arise for women in wartime, we have not given much space to those who chose to support war.

Brief biographical details and, where necessary, a short introduction accompany the extracts. No period or country has been studied exhaustively. The greater part of the material comes from the twentieth century, and most of the written pieces are in English though there is some work in translation. All original work is by women, but some translating and editing is by men. We have largely excluded historical or biographical writing which provides a commentary on past events rather than speaking with the immediacy of the voice of the time. Where such pieces are included they are usually placed, not at the time when they were written, but at the time to which they refer. We are sure that we must have missed many powerful and important voices, and even more certain that many intimate ones remain hidden or lost.

Since we see the anthology partly as a source book, we have given full references to the most accessible edition of each extract so that the reader may follow up those pieces which particularly inspire or puzzle her or him. We have drawn up a chronological table which gives an outline of some of the main events referred to. In addition, there is a list of further reading containing the works which we suggest provide a powerful development of the themes which this anthology merely touches on. Finally, there are names and addresses of peace organisations which can give up-to-date information on local, national and international peace actions by women's and mixed groups.

Women's Relationship to Peace and War

Why an anthology of *women's* writings on peace and war? This is of course not a question people ask when collections of work exclusively by men appear. It is important to pinpoint what it is that women have to say that is distinct from what men have said both now and in the past. Throughout recorded history, women's relationship to war has differed from that of men. War has rarely been a tool which women have used directly. It has been a method used ostensibly on their behalf, for their defence. It has been something from which they have suffered, through death, rape, starvation, injury, loss of loved ones. It has been something they have endured with great courage and resourcefulness. It has been something from which they have apparently gained in that they won the vote and the opportunity to work outside the home. In the First and Second World Wars women were needed to replace men in the factories and on the land, and some child care was provided. After the wars they were coerced out of their jobs and back into the home to make way for the returning men, and the nurseries were closed down.

The relationship between women and war, their experience of it, has been complex and obscure. Out of this lack of clarity has developed a line of thought which suggests that women are somehow less aggressive than men. It is partly an argument from biology: women give birth, as mothers they know the cost of human flesh, they are therefore by nature unwilling to kill (see Olive Schreiner, p.81). The positive energy women can gain from taking responsibility for children gives them a concern for peace. However, the assumption that women, whether they have children or not, are more suited to caring roles than men can also restrict their energies and put them in a passive position which hinders their attempts to campaign effectively (see Elise Boulding, p.199 and Ann Nicol, p.267). Those who define men as aggressors point to the strong evidence that men commit more violence on each other and on women than women do, but it should not be concluded that men's biological destiny is to rape and kill. It may be that women are more peace-loving than men but they will not be able to demonstrate this effectively until they acquire genuine equality.

All forms of violence and the problem as to what both men and women do with their aggression are related. Aggression as an element of both sexuality and militarism is an accepted part of male behaviour. But from women overtly aggressive behaviour, even physical strength, is not expected and their repressed anger has often been turned destructively against themselves and their immediate circle. The extract by Barbara Deming (p.194) deals magnificently with this issue. What women must now learn is, she says, to stop turning their anger in on themselves and to use it positively in the cause of non-violence. This kind of statement goes to the paradoxical heart of the matter: how to outlaw war and other forms of violence without using violence oneself and thus perpetuating the very system which needs radical change. It is in the light of this paradox that the position of women in countries fighting for liberation is so painful: are women in El Salvador and Afghanistan, Northern Ireland and Palestine justified in using force against military oppressors? Is there any such thing as a just war? What is the difference between small countries fighting to acquire or maintain their independence and large powers – usually using much more lethal and sophisticated equipment – trying to extend their power?

Clearly, no simple definition of war or of peace can cover the ideas raised in an anthology like this. War as armed conflict between nations shades into civil war and wars of liberation and then into violence and its control in society, and finally into individual violence. Similarly, peace is something more than mere absence of war. Peace has to be sought actively. For instance, until children are encouraged to value co-operation and non-violence above competitiveness it is unlikely that war will be outlawed (see Mrs Auckland, p.64, Bertha von Suttner, p.68 and Brenda Thomson p.211). Because peace is an unknown concept, it is one that is difficult to talk about or imagine. Several writers, instead of trying to make abstract definitions of peace, attempt to suggest peaceful ways of bringing about change. Maude Royden (p. 86) points out that it is useless to try and stop people being violent by violence. The women at Greenham Common Peace Camp (p.262) have specifically rejected belligerence as a method of protest and they and other peace camps have tried to organise without hierarchies.

Women's Implication in War

Women are still largely defined in terms of their relationships with men. Those who have achieved sufficient independence to speak their own minds have been few, and surviving records belong mostly to the middle and upper classes. What they say cannot necessarily be taken to represent a 'women's view'. And their voices have not proved to be united against war. Some condoned and encouraged war; many suffragettes offered white feathers, denoting cowardice, to those British men not active during the First World War (see Helen Hamilton, p.101). Women have traditionally been seen as weak and defenceless. They have been proud and willing to be protected by men or armies doing violence on their behalf and have greeted them like heroes on their return from battle. Their adoption of such a role offers to the fighters some justification for the hideous destruction of war. Until women disclaim this role, they are implicated. Some women rulers too, both past and present, have been war-mongers. Women have been and are active in the armed forces: Israel, for example, conscripts them. And they are fighting throughout the world in liberation and guerilla armies. Some of the most vicious men have been loyally supported by wives and lovers (see Jill Tweedie, p.153). Women have also been naive in their welcoming of peace without questioning what exploitation or tyranny it restores or bolsters.

We are not sufficiently informed about the extent to which governments, the military, the arms companies and the rest of the economy are linked. Major world powers which increasingly promote the growth of arms industries by funding military research and by extravagant armaments purchasing are in effect perpetually subsidising the arms trade. Women as workers and consumers participate in the system by paying taxes, directly or indirectly, to governments which squander large sums on 'defence' (see Dorothy Day, p.187). Arms spending contributes to an erosion of essential state services in industrial countries and to underdevelopment in poorer countries.

Women's History of Opposing War
The earliest writings in the anthology focus simply on the moral and religious views of war, and they sound the note of lamentation which runs right through to the present. To begin with the voices are solitary. One of the earliest groups to oppose war actively was a religious one, the Society of Friends (Quakers), in the seventeenth century. Within their organisation they gave a more equal voice to women than was common at the time, and unlike many other Christians they took the New Testament teaching of non-violence literally. In 1660 a group of English Quakers including a woman, Elizabeth Streater, was imprisoned for fifteen days for refusing to pay towards the cost of the county militia (see also Mary Fisher and Elizabeth Williams, p.18). Other small Christian groups which refused to carry or contribute towards the cost of arms were the Plymouth Brethren, Christadelphians, New Lighters and the French Hinschinists. The New Lighters were started in the 1820s by, among others, a Dutch woman called Maria Leer, and the

Hinschinists were founded by Marguerite Coraly Hinsch in the 1840s.

The first secular peace organisation was probably one started in New York in 1815. The London Peace Society was founded the following year. While it had no women officers initially, women did become members and the eighth of their published tracts was by an anonymous Lady (see p.42). In 1820 a group of women in Cincinnati, USA, founded a women's peace society and during the second half of the nineteenth century such groups existed in Europe, often linked to suffragist ones, although in the American Civil War many suffragists did actively support the Northern anti-slavery side (see Cady Stanton, p.58). In 1876 British women organised a petition against war in Turkey and collected over 43,000 women's signatures in three weeks. At the Paris Peace Conference of 1878 five women actually spoke and one of them, Hubertine Auclert, asked for equal places for her sex on councils of arbitration (see cartoon by her, p.67). An anti-war congress in England in the same year invited delegates from women's suffrage organisations. In Europe, Bertha von Suttner's writings had a huge influence from the 1880s onwards (see p.68). Priscilla Peckover set up numerous (mixed) peace associations and edited the journal *Peace and Goodwill* from 1882 to her death in 1931. Many women actively protested against the First World War, both by organising peace groups and by supporting conscientious objectors (see Emma Goldman, p.73 and Margaret Hobhouse, p.104.).

In 1915 members of the International Suffrage Alliance managed, against extraordinary odds, to arrange an international women's congress at The Hague, attended by over 1,000 delegates. The Congress set up the International Committee of Women for Permanent Peace and asked the neutral nations to help mediate. The committee sent delegates to the heads of state of the fighting nations to inform them personally of the Congress's resolutions for peace. In 1919 the committee became known as the Women's International League for Peace and Freedom (WILPF), the name by which it is known today. WILPF's main aim is to remove the causes of war, rather than try to mitigate its effects, although it has helped in the reconstruction work which followed the two World Wars.

Women continued to work through formal organisations. Emily Balch with the League of Nations and Alvar Myrdal through the special sessions on disarmament of the United Nations tried to use existing institutions to foster international peace-keeping. More recently women have pointed out just how dangerous to us all is the domination of men over women and the subsequent polarisation of so-called male and female characteristics. If the qualities of caring and nurturing are ascribed to those in society who have no political power, and the influence of those qualities banned from international relations, the opposite attributes of forcefulness and competitiveness rule unhindered. The feminist peace movement which re-emerged in the 1970s seeks to heal this split between what is valued at home and what is valued in the conference chamber. It is clearly facile for women to maintain that all men are more aggressive than all women; but there is much in the claim that the power relationship between men and women is out of balance in such a way as to make war more likely (see Joan Cavanagh, p.257 and Petra Kelly, p.258).

Perhaps even more since Hiroshima and the realisation that modern warfare destroys vast civilian populations as well as those technically fighting, women have been active in both conventional and more radical protest. Partly because of an increased confidence gained from claiming greater control over their lives through the women's movement, they are now influential both in mixed and women-only groups working to prevent the spread of nuclear weapons (see Women's Pentagon Action, p.243, Peace Camps at Greenham Common and Molesworth, pp.262 and 265).

Men *seem* to have the power to control or destroy the world. Trying to break into their power circle, trying to make a case – and a space – for our view that peace is the responsibility of everyone, is an upward struggle. What emerges from our attempts to uncover women's work on peace is how so many women have had a vision of a better world, and have tried to communicate this to their contemporaries. Most of their dreams have not yet been realised. Having wondered why, we are left with the pressing question of our present significance in the peace movement and in international politics. We want to make room for our vision. The national and international decision-making processes should involve us all. This anthology is an expression of our urge to take part. We hope that women and men who read this anthology will be inspired to find whatever ways they can to work together for peace.

The Making of the Anthology

The anthology has been compiled by a group of ten women working together collectively over a period of twenty months. We undertook the work in the spirit of experiment, committed as feminists to working collectively on a project designed to further peace, and yet very well aware of the possibilities for conflict among us, both over the issues involved and over ways of working.

We had none of us produced a book before (though one of us is a publisher's editor and two others have worked as printers); neither were we able to work full-time on the anthology but took it on in addition to the other commitments we all had. This has meant that most of the time we have been working under pressure on material which is, in itself, often deeply distressing. Within the group there is a great variety in the relation of individuals to both the women's movement and to pacifism and to the thought and action of the peace movement. All this has meant inevitable disagreements and conflicts, some of which we have deliberately allowed to remain unresolved in the interests of bringing out the book. We see it as a positive part of working co-operatively that we can publish the book without every detail of it having to have our unanimous support. Because of our inexperience, both of working collectively and of the technicalities of producing an anthology, we sometimes dealt with making decisions by shelving them. This seemed to be a very reasonable strategy since it recognised the absence of right answers to so many questions, both technical and ideological. But it did expose us to uncertainty about how we were progressing and we certainly had our moments of panic about finishing on time, so that occasionally we did not deal very inventively with the problems that remained. Sometimes we were 'forced' to make decisions by time limits. We did not challenge the timetable within which we were working, and in the end used it as a goad that enabled us to finish what could have been an interminable project. We have all of us been very moved and exhilarated by the shared experience of searching out the material and working together to make a whole out of the fragments. We know that not one of us would have produced the book if she had tried alone.

For the gathering of the material we worked in historical sections, alone, or in groups of two or three, though in fact we were often drawing each other's attention to pieces we found from outside 'our' section. We would then bring extracts to regular meetings and discuss our reasons for choosing or rejecting them. In this way what might be called an editorial policy evolved. This policy was never static: new material repeatedly challenged us to elaborate our thinking. For example, the two issues of women's collusion in war and women's supposed natural opposition to war recurred in new disguises throughout the project, and made the establishment of strict criteria for selection very difficult. Final decisions about the overall balance, for example between mourning and political argument, and about visual appearance were made by us all together. A draft of this introduction was drawn up by one of us, edited and expanded by a group of three, and submitted to the whole group whose comments and criticisms were then assimilated. Arduous jobs like the obtaining of permission to use all the material still in copyright, the compiling of the chronological and other lists, and the typing were done by individuals or small groups.

We should like to thank Philippa Brewster, Harriet Griffey and Lesley Stewart of Routledge & Kegan Paul for their willingness to respect our collective working methods.

We should also like to thank those people who have given us their generous help: Peter van den Dungen and Josephine Eglin of the Bradford School of Peace Studies for their suggestions for material, and their encouragement of the project; Cynthia Enloe, and Priscilla Eckhart and Lynn Jones for help in finding material and for their enthusiasm; Judith Hayward, Diane Kenny and Peter Rickard for translations; Janet Bragg, Richard Keeble, Frida Knight, Wendy Mulford and Lucy Munby for their extensive comments on the typescript; Chris Scarles for advice on copyright, and Moira Maconachie for reading the introduction. The librarians at the Fawcett Library have given generously to us of their time and knowledge, and the staff of the University Library in Cambridge have helped us to make full use of its resources.

Finally, we should like to thank very specially those who have supported us personally during the making of this book: our friends and lovers, our children and babysitters, our families and colleagues.

Cambridge Women's Peace Collective

Frances Connelly	Elspeth Owen
Kate Ivy	Elizabeth Jane Rickard
Jenny Lyon	Liz Rothschild
Judith Milner	Diane Speakman
Carol Naughton	Bobbie Wells

SAPPHO (7th–6th c. BC) Greek. Poet, respected and famous in her time. Work was largely destroyed by the church in 1073 and all that remains are fragments and quotations.

Untitled Poem

Some say cavalry and others claim
infantry or a fleet of long oars
is the supreme sight on the black earth.
I say it is
the one you love . . .

these things remind me now
of Anaktoria who is far,
and I
for one

would rather see her warm supple step
and the sparkle of her face than watch
all the dazzling chariots and armoured
hoplites of Lydia.

TS'AI YEN (*c.* AD 200) Chinese. Considered the first great woman poet of China. Captured by Huns (Tartars) after her husband's death and taken to the north.

from **Eighteen Verses Sung to a Tartar Reed Whistle**

1

I was born in a time of peace,
But later the mandate of Heaven
Was withdrawn from the Han Dynasty.

Heaven was pitiless.
It sent down confusion and separation.
Earth was pitiless.
It brought me to birth in such a time.
War was everywhere. Every road was dangerous.

Soldiers and civilians everywhere
Fleeing death and suffering.
Smoke and dust obscured the land
Overrun by the ruthless Tartar bands.
Our people lost their will power and integrity.
I can never learn the ways of the barbarians.
I am daily subject to violence and insult.
I sing one stanza to my lute and a Tartar horn.
But no one knows my agony and grief.

2

A Tartar chief forced me to become his wife,
And took me far away to Heaven's edge.
Ten thousand clouds and mountains
Bar my road home.
And whirlwinds of dust and sand
Blow for a thousand miles.
Men here are as savage as giant vipers,
And strut about in armour, snapping their bows.
As I sing the second stanza I almost break the lutestrings,
Will broken, heart broken, I sing to myself.

AL-KHANSÂ (7th c.) Pre-Islamic Arab. Name given to four pre-Islamic poets. This poem is an example of the ritual lament, traditionally composed by women.

For her Brother

Weep! Weep! Weep!
These tears are for my brother,
Henceforth that veil which lies between us,
That recent earth,
Shall not be lifted again.
You have gone down to the bitter water
Which all must taste,
And you went pure, saying:
'Life is a buzz of hornets about a lance point.'

But my heart remembers, O son of my father and mother,
I wither like summer grass,
I shut myself in the tent of consternation.

He is dead, who was the buckler of our tribe
And the foundation of our house,
He has departed in calamity.

He is dead, who was the lighthouse of courageous men,
Who was for the brave
As fires lighted upon the mountains.

(cont'd overleaf)

Rasamandala by the women of Mithila, traditional

This depicts Krishna making the world dance and wheel of life turn. Symbol of eternal return, the circle is also an image of Karma, the divine law according to which we enjoy in this life the reward of good actions in past lives or punishment for wickedness.

He is dead, who rode costly horses,
Shining in his garments.
The hero of the long shoulder belt is dead,
The young man of valiance and beauty breathes no more;
The right hand of generosity is withered,
And the beardless king of our tribe shall breathe no more.

Let the stars go out,
Let the sun withdraw his rays,
He was our star and sun.

Who now will gather in the strangers at dusk
When the sad North whistles with her winds?

While you have tears, O daughters of the Solamides,
Weep! Weep! Weep!

YÜ HSÜAN-CHI *c.* **843–68)** Chinese. Worked as a courtesan until she became a concubine. Abandoned by her lover, she became a Taoist nun.

To the Minister Liu

The Board of War has quelled the mutiny:
Songs fill the streets again.

Now there are spring rains on Fen River.
Flowers on the banks of the Chin.

The jails are long locked and empty,
Spears dusty.

Scholars and monks watch Midnight sing,
We travelers are drunk, on scarlet cushions.

Pen and inkstone close at hand,
Odes and *History* surround my seat;

For now, in happy times like these,
Even small talents live at ease.

CHRISTINE de PISAN (1364-*c*.1430) French. Lived at the court of Charles V. Widowed at 25 and with three children to maintain, she became a writer and produced many important works, including *The City of Women* and *The Book of Peace*. Her book on the conduct of battle was consulted in many European courts.

The following extract is from *Le Livre de la Paix [The Book of Peace]*, addressed to the Duke of Guyenne, grandson of the deceased Charles V, and then in power. The work is part of a literary tradition which outlines the qualities befitting the ideal ruler.

Every kingdom divided against itself shall be destroyed and every city and house divided against its own good cannot endure, for Holy Scripture attests this on the strength of, and by mentioning, many relevant examples, such as those of Troy, Rome, and other cities and several countries, which I omit for brevity's sake, which were formerly of such great power that the whole world could not have harmed them if they had all been united; but which perished through discord. We may furthermore, most awesome Prince, magnify your achievement of this worthy peace, for since it is a fact that any kingdom in which there is dissent must perish, it is certain that it is saved and preserved by the opposite – namely peace and love. Thus you, in your wisdom and good counsel, could have found no better wisdom nor so sovereign a remedy to preserve from destruction this noble realm which is your heritage, than by establishing peace within it. In this way you have saved your kingdom and thereby acquired much in heaven and earth, for so says the Scripture: Blessed and holy are the peacemakers, for they shall be called the Sons of God. And, similarly, there is advantage to you on earth, as the same scripture says that the glory of the ruler, that is to say the lord, is powerfully enhanced when his subjects are at peace without warlike occupation. . . .

David said, 'Seek out peace and follow it', and surely you have done this well, for you sought it diligently until you found it. And you must so pursue it that you persist therein steadfastly in accordance with the Scriptural precept. It is highly praiseworthy in a Prince when he is so well able to apply the benefits of peace that it redounds to the advantage of all and is harmful to none but is loved by all. You must continue in this endeavour with great wisdom; you must, namely, wisely bring about and maintain all things relevant to the preservation of peace and which are appropriate to it for sound reasons by removing all things prejudicial to it, so that no harmful incident occurring through lack of foresight can prevent it or disturb it. . . .

You must be for your subjects at all times the means of guiding them in the ways of peace, with such great gentleness, and not simply for a mere month or two, but always, that you soften and win their hearts so completely that, both for the love of you and of your gentleness and for their own good, the gnawing of past rancour may be completely obliterated and converted into love, benevolence and unity.

Le Livre de la Paix [The Book of Peace]

MARGARET PASTON (d. 1484) English. Was in charge of the family house in Gresham, Norfolk, until expelled by force in 1449. Between 1459 and 1466 managed the family estates in Norfolk in her husband's absence, with great courage and fortitude, during which time the Pastons suffered further violent attacks.

This is part of one of her many letters to her husband.

27th October

Right worshipful husband, I recommend me to you . . . I was at Haylesdon upon Thursday last passed and saw the place there, and in good faith there will no creature think how foully and horribly it is arrayed but if they had seen it. There cometh much people daily to wonder thereupon, both of Norwich and of other places, and they speak shamefully thereof. The Duke had been better a thousand pounds that it had never been done, and you have the more good will of the people that it is so foully done. And they made your tenants of Haylesdon and Drayton, with others, to help to break down the walls of the place and the lodge both, God knoweth full evil against their wills, but that they dare no otherwise have done for fear. I have spoken with your tenants of Haylesdon and Drayton both, and put them in comfort as well as I can.

The Duke's men ransacked the church and bare away all the goods that were left there, both of ours and of the tenants, and left not so much but that they stood upon the high altar and ransacked the images, and took away such as they might find, and put away the parson out of the church till they had done, and ransacked every man's house in the town 5 or 6 times. And the chief masters of robbing was the bailey of Eye, the bailey of Stradbroke, Thomas Slyford; and Slyford was the chief robber of the church, and he hath most of the robbery next the bailey of Eye. And as for lead, brass, pewter, iron, doors, gates, and other stuff of the house, men of Costessy and Causton have it, and that they might not carry they have hewn it asunder in the most dispiteous wise. If it might be, I would some men of worship might be sent from the King to see how it is, both there and at the lodge before any snows come, that they may make report of the truth; else it shall no more be seen so plainly as it may now.

And at the reverence of God, speed your matters now, for it is too horrible a cost and trouble that we have now daily, and must till it be otherwise; and your men dare not go about to gather up your rents, and we keep here daily more than 30 persons for salvation of us and the place, for in very truth if the place had not been kept strongly the Duke would have come hither.

Letter to John Paston

ST TERESA OF AVILA (1515–82) Spanish. Against opposition from the Church, reformed the Carmelite order of nuns. Was the author of several religious works.

Our Lord asks but two things of us: love for Him and for our neighbour. . . . I think the most certain sign that we keep these two commandments is that we have a genuine love for others. We cannot know whether we love God although there may be strong reasons for thinking so, but there can be no doubt about whether we love our neighbour or no. Be sure that in proportion as you advance in fraternal charity, you are increasing in your love of God.

The Interior Castle

PETITION in favour of Lilburne's release.

John Lilburne was the popular leader of the Levellers, a republican group at the time of the English Civil War, who demanded universal suffrage and extensive reform of the law.

[Women] appeare so despicable in your eyes as to be thought unworthy to petition or represent our grievances. . . . Can you imagine us to be so sottish or stupid, as not to perceive, or not to be sensible when daily those strong defences of our Peace and Welfare are broken down and trod underfoot by force or arbitrary power? Would you have us keep at home in our houses while men . . . are fetched out of their beds and forced from their houses by souldiers, to the affrighting and undoing of themselves, and their wives, children and families. . . . Shall we sit still and keep at home?

Quoted in *Women, Resistance and Revolution*, by Sheila Rowbotham

MARY FISHER and ELIZABETH WILLIAMS, two English Puritan women, visited the fens in the autumn of 1653 to preach the gospel. After complaints from Cambridge students, the two women were brought before the Mayor for questioning.

They answered that they were Strangers, and knew not the Name of the Place, but paid for what they had and came away. He asked their names: They replied, their Names were written in the Book of Life. He demanded their husbands' names. They told him: they had no Husband but Jesus Christ, and he sent them. Upon this the Mayor grew angry, called them Whores, and issued his Warrant to the Constable to whip them at the Market-Cross till the Blood ran down their Bodies: and ordered three of his Serjeants to see that Sentence, equally cruel and lawless, severely executed.

The poor Women, kneeling down, in Christian Meekness besought the Lord to forgive him, for that he knew not what he did. So they were led to the Market-Cross, calling upon God to strengthen their faith. The Executioner commanded them to put off their Clothes, which they refused. Then he stripped them naked to the Waste, put their Arms into the Whipping-Post, and executed the Mayor's Warrant far more cruelly than is usually done to the worst of Malefactors, so that their

Flesh was miserably cut and torn. The Constancy and Patience which they expressed under this barbarous Usage was astonishing to the Beholders, for they endured the cruel Torture without the least Change of Countenance or Appearance of Uneasiness, and in the midst of their Punishment sang and rejoiced.

Quoted in *Quaker Women 1650–1690*, by Mabel Richmond Brailsford

MARGARET CAVENDISH, DUCHESS OF NEWCASTLE (1623–73)

English. One of the first women in England to publish her work, which included poetry, plays, biography, letters, philosophical works and scientific treatises. This extract comes from *Sociable Letters*, a fictional series designed to 'Express the Humours of Mankind and the Actions of Man's Life'.

Madam,

I hope I have given the Lady D.A. no cause to believe I am not her friend. For though she has been of P[arliament]'s and I of K[ing]'s side, yet I know no reason why that should make a difference between us as to make us enemies; no more than cases of conscience in religion, for one may be my very good friend, and yet not of my opinion. Everyone's conscience in religion is between God and themselves, and it belongs to none other. 'Tis true, I should be glad my friend were of my opinion, or if I thought my friend's opinion were better than mine, I would be of the same. But it should be no breach of friendship if our opinions were different, since God is only to be the judge.

And as for the matter of governments, we women understand them not; yet if we did, we are excluded from intermeddling therewith, and almost from being subject thereto. We are not tied nor bound to state or Crown. We are free, not sworn to allegiance, nor do we take the Oath of Supremacy. We are not made citizens of the commonwealth. We hold no offices, nor bear we any authority therein. We are accounted neither useful in peace, nor serviceable in war. And if we be not citizens in the commonwealth, I know no reason we should be subjects to the commonwealth. And the truth is we are no subjects, unless it be to our husbands, and not always to them, for sometimes we usurp their authority, or else by flattery we get their good wills to govern. But

19

if nature had not befriended us with beauty and other good graces to help us to insinuate ourselves into men's affections, we should have been more enslaved than any other of nature's creatures she has made. But nature be thanked, she has been so bountiful to us as we oftener enslave men than men enslave us. They seem to govern the world, but we really govern the world in that we govern men. For what man is he that is not governed by a woman, more or less? None, unless some dull stoic, or an old miserable usurer, or a cold, old, withered bachelor, or a half-starved hermit, and such like persons, which are but here and there one. And not only wives and mistresses have prevalent power with men, but mothers, daughters, sisters, aunts, cousins, nay, maid-servants have many times a persuasive power with their masters, and a landlady with her lodger, or a she-hostess with her he-guest. Yet men will not believe this, and 'tis the better for us, for by that we govern as it were by an insensible power, so as men perceive not how they are led, guided, and ruled by the feminine sex.

But howsoever, Madam, the disturbance in this country has made no breach of friendship between us, for though there has been a civil war in the kingdom, and a general war amongst the men, yet there has been none amongst the women. They have not fought pitched battles, and if they had there has been no particular quarrel between her and me, for her Ladyship is the same in my affection, as if the kingdom had been in a calm peace. In which friendship I shall always remains hers, as also,

> *Your Ladyship's*
> *Most humble and devoted S.*

Sociable Letters

APHRA BEHN (1640–89) English. One of the first women in England to make a living writing plays, poetry and novels. Worked for a time as an English spy in Flanders.

from **The Golden Age**

I

Blest Age! when ev'ry Purling Stream
    Ran undisturb'd and clear,
When no scorn'd Shepherds on your Banks were seen,
Tortur'd by Love, by Jealousie, or Fear;
When an Eternal Spring drest ev'ry Bough,
And Blossoms fell, by new ones dispossest;
These their kind Shade affording all below,
And those a Bed where all below might rest.
The Groves appear'd all drest with Wreaths of Flowers,
And from their Leaves dropt Aromatick Showers,
Whose fragrant Heads in Mystick Twines above,
Exchang'd their Sweets, and mix'd with thousand Kisses,
    As if the willing Branches strove
    To beautifie and shade the Grove
    Where the young wanton Gods of Love
Offer their Noblest Sacrifice of Blisses.

IV

    Then no rough sound of Wars Alarms,
Had taught the World the needless use of Arms:
    Monarchs were uncreated then,
Those Arbitrary Rulers over men:
Kings that made Laws, first broke 'em, and the Gods
By teaching us Religion first, first set the World at Odds:
    Till then Ambition was not known,
That Poyson to Content, Bane to Repose;
Each Swain was Lord o'er his own will alone,
His Innocence Religion was, and Laws.

Nor needed any troublesome defence
   Against his Neighbours Insolence.
Flocks, Herds, and every necessary good
Which bounteous Nature had design'd for Food,
Whose kind increase o'er-spread the Meads and Plaines,
Was then a common Sacrifice to all th'agreeing Swaines.

V

Right and Property were words since made,
   When Power taught Mankind to invade:
When Pride and Avarice became a Trade;
   Carri'd on by discord, noise and wars,
   For which they barter'd wounds and scarrs;
And to Inhaunce the Merchandize, miscall'd it, Fame,
   And Rapes, Invasions, Tyrannies,
   Was gaining of a Glorious Name:
Stiling their savage slaughters, Victories;
   Honour, the Error and the Cheat
   Of the Ill-natur'd Bus'ey Great,
   Nonsense, invented by the Proud,
   Fond Idol of the slavish Crowd,
   Thou wert not known in those blest days
Thy Poyson was not mixt with our unbounded Joyes;
Then it was glory to pursue delight,
And that was lawful all, that Pleasure did invite,
Then 'twas the Amorous world injoy'd its Reign;
And Tyrant Honour strove t' usurp in Vain.

VII

The Lovers thus, thus uncontroul'd did meet,
Thus all their Joyes and Vows of Love repeat:
   Joyes which were everlasting, ever new
   And every Vow inviolably true:
Not kept in fear of Gods, no fond Religious cause,
Nor in obedience to the duller Laws.
Those Fopperies of the Gown were then not known,

Those vain, those Politick Curbs to keep man in,
Who by a fond mistake Created that a Sin;
Which freeborn we, by right of Nature claim our own.
  Who but the Learned and dull moral Fool
Could gravely have forseen, man ought to live by Rule?

MARIE de SÉVIGNÉ (1626–86) French. Member of intellectual circle at Hôtel Rambouillet, Paris. Renowned as brilliant conversationalist. Famed for prolific letters.
  This extract is from a letter to her daughter written in August 1675.

Let me tell you something which I feel is very fine: I get the impression that I am reading Roman history. It would appear that Saint-Hilaire, Lieutenant-General of the Artillery, made M. de Turenne who had been galloping all the way, stop so that he could show him a battery: it's as if he had said to him: Sir, pause a little, this is where you are to be killed. The cannon shot was fired, and shot away Saint-Hilaire's arm, extended to point out the battery, and killed M. de Turenne. Saint-Hilaire's son rushed to his father, shouting and weeping. 'Be quiet, child,' he said; and pointing to M. de Turenne lying stiff and dead: 'Look, that is what you must lament eternally, that is what cannot be undone'; and without caring at all for himself, he started to weep over that great loss. M. de La Rochefoucauld himself wept in admiration at the nobility of his feelings.

Lettres Choisies de Mme de Sévigné [Selected Letters of Mme de Sévigné]

ANNE FINCH, COUNTESS OF WINCHELSEA (1661–1720) English.
Wrote many works often about women. Challenged her contemporaries'
prejudice against women writers.

The Soldier's Death

Trail all your pikes, dispirit every drum,
March in a slow procession from afar,
Ye silent, ye dejected men of war!
Be still the hautboys, and the flute be dumb!
Display no more, in vain, the lofty banner.
For see! where on the bier before ye lies,
The pale, the fall'n, th'untimely sacrifice
To your mistaken shrine, to your false idol Honour.

ANON. Irish song. About the 'Wild Geese', the emigrant Irish who went to
fight for foreign armies (mainly French) after the Treaty of Limerick of 1691.

Shule Agra

With fife and drum he marched away,
He would not heed what I did say,
He'll not come back for many a day,
My Johnny has gone for a soldier.

Chorus: Shule, shule, shule agra.
His pick and shovel's laid awa',
He's gone away to fight the war,
My Johnny has gone for a soldier.

Me oh my I loved him so,
And I often asked him not to go,
But only time will heal my woe,
My Johnny has gone for a soldier.

But now my love has gone to France
To try his fortune to advance,
If he comes back 'tis but a chance,
My Johnny has gone for a soldier.

His hair was black, his eye was blue,
His arm was stout, his word was true,
I wish in my heart I was with you,
My Johnny has gone for a soldier.

I'll sell my rock, I'll sell my reel,
Likewise I'll sell my spinning wheel,
To buy my love a coat of steel,
My Johnny has gone for a soldier.

I'll dye my petticoat, dye it red,
And through the world I'll beg my bread,
He'll not come back alive or dead,
My Johnny has gone for a soldier.

I'll go and sit on yonders hill,
Who can blame me cry my fill,
And every tear would turn a mill,
My Johnny has gone for a soldier.

MARY DAVYS (1674–1732) English. After her husband's death she opened a coffee house in Cambridge, and made her living by writing.
   Familiar Letters is an early example of the novel written in the form of letters.

To Artander

You sent me to the *English* Annals for a Cure of *Whiggism*, and (as if Heaven had design'd me for what I am) I insensibly found myself in Queen *Mary's* Reign, where I had so many Objects of Cruelty presented to my view, that I was ready to creep into myself at the dreadful Reflection. How many brave Men, courageous Women, and innocent Children did I see butcher'd, to do God good Service? Our Bishops burning both with Fire and Zeal, to confirm the Reformation so happily begun; while its Enemies, set on by Hell's chief Engineer, depress'd its Growth, and trod it under foot. From thence, I went to the *Irish* Rebellion, where I saw more than three hundred thousand Souls murder'd in cold Blood, the Clergy's Mouths cut from Ear to Ear, their

Tongues pull'd out and thrown to the Dogs, then bid to go preach up Heresy; Men's Guts pull'd out and ty'd to each other's Waists, then whipp'd different ways; some stabb'd, burnt, drowned, impal'd and flea'd alive; Children ripp'd out of their Mother's Womb, and thrown to the Dogs, or dash'd against the Stones; crying, *Nits will become Lice, destroy Root and Branch*: with a thousand other Barbarities, too tedious as well as too dreadful to repeat, beside what has been transacted abroad. And now, *Artander*, if those things be true, as we have the same Authority for, that you have for your martyr'd King, tell me, to use your own Words, *Whether it be not every true Churchman's Business, to dread and crush the like Proceedings?* . . .

I think there is more Reason to bury one Fault in Oblivion, than to keep it up with a Spirit of Malice, to foment and heighten those unhappy Feuds which are already begun.

Familiar Letters betwixt a Gentleman and a Lady

LADY MARY WORTLEY MONTAGU (1689–1762) English. Well known for collections of her letters. Introduced smallpox vaccination to England from Turkey.

Whether Women are naturally qualified for military offices, or not

I must confess, I cannot find how the oddity would be greater, to see a lady with a truncheon in her hand, than with a crown on her head; or why it should create more surprise, to see her preside in a council of war, than in a council of state. Why may she not be as capable of heading an army as a parliament; or of commanding at sea as of reigning at land? What should hinder her from holding the helm of a fleet with the same safety and steadiness as that of a nation? And why may she not exercise her soldiers, draw up her troops in battle array, and divide her forces into battalions at land, squadrons at sea, &c. with the same pleasure she would have in seeing or ordering it to be done? The military art has no mystery in it beyond others, which Women cannot attain to. . . . Persuasion, heat, and example are the soul of victory: And *Women* can shew as much eloquence, intrepidity, and warmth, where their honour is at stake, as is requisite to attack or defend a town.

There can be no real difference pointed out between the inward or outward constitution of *Men* and *Women*, excepting what merely tends to giving birth to posterity. And the differences thence arising are no ways sufficient to argue more natural strength in the one than in the other, to qualify them more for military labours. Are not the *Women* of different degrees of strength, like the *Men*? Are there not strong and weak of both sexes? *Men* educated in sloth and softness are weaker than *Women;* and *Women,* become hardened by necessity, are often more robust than *Men. . . .*

What has greatly helped to confirm the *Men* in the prejudiced notion of *Women's* natural weakness, is the common manner of expression which this very vulgar error gave birth to. When they mean to stigmatise a *Man* with want of courage they call him *effeminate,* and when they would praise a *Woman* for her courage they call her *manly.* But as these, and such like expressions, are merely arbitrary and but a fulsome compliment which the *Men* pass on themselves, they establish no truth. The real truth is, That humanity and integrity, the character-istics of our sex, make us abhor unjust slaughter, and prefer honour-able peace to unjust war. And therefore to use these expressions with propriety, when a *Man* is possest of our virtues he should be called *effeminate* by way of the highest praise of his good nature and justice; and a *Woman* who should depart from our sex by espousing the injustice and cruelty of the *Men's* nature, should be called a *Man:* that is, one whom no sacred ties can bind to the observation of just treaties, and whom no blood-shed can deter from the most cruental violence and rapin.

But be this as it may, certain it is, that bare strength intitles the *Men* to no superiority above *us,* as I have already remark'd. Otherwise brutes wou'd deserve the pre-eminence of them. And among themselves, the strongest man ought to be the chief in power. Whereas we plainly see that, generally speaking, the strongest are only fit to make drudges to the rest; and particularly in armies, they who have most of brutal vigour are often useful only for fascines to men much weaker than themselves to mount a breach. On the other hand men who have less strength have very often the most brains.

It is quite idle then to insist so much on bodily strength, as a necessary qualification to military employments. And it is full as idle to imagine that *Women* are not naturally as capable of *courage* and *resolu-*

27

tion as the *Men*. We are indeed charged, without any exception, with being timorous, and incapable of defence. But is this universally true? Are there not *Men* as void of courage as the most heartless of our sex? And yet it is known that the most timorous *Women* often make a virtue of necessity and sacrifice their own fears for the safety of a husband, a son, or a brother. Fearful and weak as they are, they often behave more courageously than the *Men* under pains, sickness, want, and the terrors of death itself.

Fear is almost an inseparable attendant on virtue. The virtuous are ever timid more or less; their own inoffensive disposition and the knowledge they have how much vice abounds among *Men*, are sufficient to incline them to fear on every appearance of danger. 'Tis a passion natural to all: Princes fear the rebellion of their subjects; generals the surprize of an enemy; and the very man who draws a sword to resent an injury, fears the shame of it, fears his adversary, and fears the law.

But fear is ever greatest in those who know themselves incapable of resisting what they fear; and is only blameable in such as have the power to repel the evil which threatens them. The manner *Women* are bred in, gives them room to apprehend every thing. They are admitted no share of the exercises which wou'd qualify them to attack or defend. They see themselves helplessly exposed to the outrages of a sex enslaved to the most brutal transports; and find themselves victims of contempt to wretches whose prevalent strength is often exerted against them, with more fury and cruelty than beasts practise towards one another. Can our fear then be imputed to want of courage? Is it a defect? Or ought it not rather to be alleged as a proof of our sense: Since it wou'd be rather fool-hardiness than courage to withstand brutes, who want the sense to be overcome by reason, and whom we want vigour to repel by force of arms?

And yet it is far from being true that all *Women* want courage, strength, or conduct to lead an army to triumph; any more than it is that all *Men* are endow'd with them: There are many of our sex as intrepid as the *Men*; and I myself cou'd, with more ease and less repugnance, dare the frowns and fury of an already victorious army, which I had forces to resist, then I cou'd stoop to court the smiles of a corrupt minister, whom I had reason to despise.

Thus far I think it evidently appears, that there is no *science, office*, or *dignity*, which *Women* have not an equal right to share in with the *Men*: Since there can be no superiority, but that of brutal strength, shewn in the *latter*, to entitle them to engross all *power* and *prerogative* to themselves: nor any incapacity proved in the *former*, to disqualify them of their right, but what is owing to the unjust oppression of the *Men*, and might be easily removed. With regard however to war-like employments, it seems to be a disposition of *Providence* that custom has exempted us from them. As sailors in a storm throw overboard their more useless lumber, so it is but fit that the *Men* shou'd be exposed to the dangers and hardships of war, while we remain in safety at home. They are, generally speaking, good for little else but to be our bulwarks: and our smiles are the most noble rewards which the bravest of them all ought to desire, or can deserve, for all the hazards they encounter, and for all the labours they go thro' for our defence, in the most tedious campaign.

Woman Not Inferior to Man

ELLEN WEETON (1776–*c*.1851) British. Writer of essays, poetry, a journal and seven volumes of letters. Kept a school to earn her living.

I have heard my mother tell all she heard of my father's last moments, when my brother and I on a winter's evening have drawn our little seats close on each side of hers, and leaning our arms on her lap, and our faces almost meeting, we have looked up to hers and wept as she wept, whilst she spoke. He had done so much injury to the enemy by the number of prizes he had taken during the American War, that a vessel was sent out, of superior force, with express orders to take my father wherever they could find him. They met with him – and a most severe engagement took place. My father's vessel was much inferior in size and number of men. Notwithstanding, when he was summoned to strike, and perceiving the Captain to be an old school-fellow of his, he exclaimed: 'No! he would shed the last drop of his blood before he would strike to a traitor, a rebel to his country.' A dreadful cannonading began. The American vessel was so large that her guns could not be brought to bear upon the hull of its opponent, but wrought execution upon the masts and rigging, dropping all the poor fellows stationed there. The English vessel directed all her fire to the hull of the American, between wind and water, so successfully that she was soon in a sinking state, and struck. The instant before, a chain shot came sweeping past my father, who was speaking with a trumpet to the men in the shrouds, and took off one side of his face. He dropped; the American made off, and my father was taken by his crew to Jamaica, near where the battle had taken place. He lived a few days, and then died at about 34 years of age. 'He that liveth by the sword shall die by the sword.' The warrior is not in the sight of God a man of honour and glory, whatever his fellow men may think. It is a dreadful life, a dreadful death; and such the Almighty deems it when he speaks to us in the above language. How glad should I be could I be assured that the universal Judge would pity those men who are educated in error and whose lives are destroyed in consequence.

Journal of a Governess

MARY WOLLSTONECRAFT (1759–97) British. Kept a school with her sister. Wrote *A Vindication of the Rights of Women* in 1792 as a courageous reply to a speech by Edmund Burke. Also wrote, among other things, an account of *The Origin and Progress of the French Revolution* (1794).

I may be accused of arrogance; still I must declare, what I firmly believe, that all the writers who have written on the subject of female education and manners . . . have contributed to render women more artificial, weaker characters, than they would otherwise have been; and, consequently, more useless members of society. . . . It is first necessary to observe, that my objection extends to the whole purport of those books, which tend, in my opinion, to degrade one half of the human species, and render women pleasing at the expense of every solid virtue.

It is wandering from my present subject, perhaps, to make a political remark; but as it was produced naturally by the train of my reflections, I shall not pass it silently over.

Standing armies can never consist of resolute, robust men; they may be well disciplined machines, but they will seldom contain men under the influence of strong passions or with very vigorous faculties. And as for any depth of understanding, I will venture to affirm, that it is as rarely to be found in the army as amongst women; and the cause I maintain, is the same. It may be further observed, that officers are also particularly attentive to their persons, fond of dancing, crowded rooms, adventures, and ridicule. Like the *fair* sex, the business of their lives is gallantry. They were taught to please, and they only live to please. Yet they do not lose their rank in the distinction of sexes, for they are still reckoned superior to women, though in what their superiority consists, beyond what I have just mentioned, it is difficult to discover.

The great misfortune is this, that they both acquire manners before morals, and a knowledge of life before they have from reflection, any acquaintance with the grand ideal outline of human nature. The consequence is natural; satisfied with common nature, they become a prey to prejudices, and taking all their opinions on credit, they blindly submit to authority. So that if they have any sense, it is a kind of instinctive glance, that catches proportions, and decides with respect to manners; but fails when arguments are to be pursued below the surface or opinions analyzed.

May not the same remark be applied to women? Nay, the argument may be carried still further, for they are both thrown out of a useful station by the unnatural distinctions established in civilized life. Riches and hereditary honours have made cyphers of women to give consequence to the numerical figure; and idleness has produced a mixture of gallantry and despotism in society, which leads the very men who are the slaves of their mistresses, to tryrannize over their sisters, wives and daughters. This is only keeping them in rank and file, it is true. Strengthen the female mind by enlarging it, and there will be an end to blind obedience; but, as blind obedience is ever sought for by power, tyrants and sensualists are in the right when they endeavour to keep women in the dark, because the former only want slaves, and the latter a play-thing. The sensualist, indeed, has been the most dangerous of tyrants, and women have been duped by their lovers, as princes by their ministers, whilst dreaming that they reigned over them.

A Vindication of the Rights of Women

Sampler, by Mary Ann Body, 1789

ANNA LAETITIA BARBAULD (1743–1825) British. Prolific and successful writer and poet. Educated at her father's school. Ran a number of schools with her husband.

War is a state in which all our feelings and our duties suffer a total and strange inversion; a state, in which

Life dies, Death lives, and Nature breeds
Perverse, all monstrous, all prodigious things.

A state in which it becomes our business to hurt and annoy our neighbour by every possible means; instead of building, to pull down; instead of peopling, to depopulate; a state in which we drink the tears, and feed upon the misery of our fellow-creatures; such a state, therefore, requires the extremest necessity to justify it; it ought not to be the common and usual state of society. As both parties *cannot* be in the right, there is always an equal chance, at least, to either of them, of being in the wrong; but as both parties *may* be to blame, and most commonly are, the chance is very great indeed against its being entered into from any adequate cause; yet war may be said to be, with regard to nations, the sin which most easily besets them. We, my friends, in common with other nations, have much guilt to repent of from this cause, and it ought to make a large part of our humiliations on this day. When we carry our eyes back through the long records of our history, we see wars of plunder, wars of conquest, wars of religion, wars of pride, wars of succession, wars of idle speculation, wars of unjust interference, and hardly among them one war of necessary self-defence in any of our essential or very important interests. Of late years, indeed, we have known none of the calamities of war in our own country but the wasteful expence of it; and sitting aloof from those circumstances of personal provocation, which in some measure might excuse its fury, we have calmly voted slaughter and merchandized destruction – so much blood and tears for so many rupees, or dollars, or ingots. Our wars have been wars of cool calculating interest, as free from hatred as from love of mankind; the passions which stir the blood have had no share in them. We devote a certain number of men to perish on land and sea, and the rest of us sleep sound, and, protected in our usual occupations, talk of the events of war as what diversifies the flat uniformity of life.

We should, therefore, do well to *translate* this word war in language more intelligible to us. When we pay our army and our navy estimates, let us set down – so much for killing, so much for maiming, so much for making widows and orphans, so much for bringing famine upon a district, so much for corrupting citizens and subjects into spies and traitors, so much for ruining industrious tradesmen and making bankrupts (of that species of distress at least, we *can* form an idea,) so much for letting loose the daemons of fury rapine and lust within the fold of cultivated society, and giving to the brutal ferocity of the most ferocious, its full scope and range of invention. We shall by this means know what we have paid our money for, whether we have made a good bargain, and whether the account is likely to pass – elsewhere. We must take in too, all those concomitant circumstances which make war, considered as battle, the least part of itself, *pars minima sui.* We must fix our eyes, not on the hero returning with conquest, nor yet on the gallant officer dying in the bed of honour, the subject of picture and of song, but on the private soldier, forced into the service, exhausted by camp-sickness and fatigue; pale, emaciated, crawling to an hospital with the prospect of life, perhaps a long life, blasted, useless and suffering. We must think of the uncounted tears of her who weeps alone, because the only being who shared her sentiments is taken from her; no martial music sounds in unison with her feelings; the long day passes and he returns not. She does not shed her sorrows over his grave, for she has never learnt whether he ever had one. If he had returned, his exertions would not have been remembered individually, for he only made a small imperceptible part of a human machine, called a Regiment. We must take in the long sickness which no glory soothes, occasioned by distress of mind, anxiety and ruined fortunes. – These are not fancy pictures, and if you please to heighten them, you can every one of you do it for yourselves. We must take in the consequences, felt perhaps for ages, before a country which has been completely desolated, lifts its head again; like a torrent of lava, its worst mischief is not the first overwhelming ruin of towns and palaces, but the long sterility to which it condemns the track it has covered with its stream. Add the danger to regular governments which are changed by war, sometimes to anarchy, and sometimes to despotism. Add all these, and then let us think when a General performing these exploits is saluted with, 'well done good and faithful servant', whether the plaudit is likely to be echoed in another place.

In this guilty business there is a circumstance which greatly aggravates its guilt, and that is the impiety of calling upon the Divine Being to assist us in it. Almost all nations have been in the habit of mixing with their bad passions a shew of religion, and of prefacing these their murders with prayers, and the solemnities of worship. When they send out armies to desolate a country, and destroy the fair face of nature, they have the presumption to hope that the sovereign of the universe will condescend to be their auxiliary, and to enter into their petty and despicable contests. Their prayer, if put into plain language, would run thus: God of love, father of all the families of the earth, we are going to tear in pieces our brethren of mankind, but our strength is not equal to our fury, we beseech thee to assist us in the work of slaughter. Go out we pray thee with our fleets and armies; we call them christian, and we have interwoven in our banners and the decorations of our arms the symbols of a suffering religion, that we may fight under the cross upon which our Saviour died. Whatever mischief we do, we shall do it in thy name; we hope, therefore, thou wilt protect us in it. Thou, who hast made of one blood all the dwellers upon the earth, we trust thou wilt view us alone with partial favour, and enable us to bring misery upon every other quarter of the globe – Now if we really expect such prayers to be answered, we are the weakest, if not, we are the most hypocritical of beings.

Sins of Government, Sins of the Nation

MARY WOLLSTONECRAFT (For biographical note, see p.30.)

Havre July 8th'94
. . . my God, how many victims fall beneath the sword and the guillotine! My blood runs cold, and I sicken at thoughts of a Revolution which costs so much blood and bitter tears.

Adieu!
Yours sincerely
Mary

Letter to Ruth Barlow

CAROLINE WALKER
To Mrs Kearsley of Welch's Female Pills, Fleet Street, London

Madam,
I am the unfortunate daughter of an officer in the army, who fell in his country's cause, by which means his family are left in a situation that it is necessary each should endeavour to provide for themselves which, from indisposition, I was intirely incapacitated from, till an intimate friend recommended your PILLS, which have in a wonderful manner restored me to health . . .

Your much obliged
and very humble servant
Exeter, Aug. 4, 1799   Caroline Walker

The Cambridge Intelligencer

DOROTHY WORDSWORTH (1771–1855) British. Writer of journals and letters, sister of the poet and his collaborator. She had published two books – *Recollections of a Tour Made in Scotland* (1803) and *Journal of a Tour on the Continent* (1820) before a nervous breakdown incapacitated her in 1829.

In this piece, she introduces a young sailor, press-ganged at least once into the Royal Navy, probably during the wars with France, who has also seen bad days in the merchant fleet.

[1802, March 15th] *Monday Morning* . . . a sailor who was travelling from Liverpool to Whitehaven called. . . . He had been at sea since he was 15 years old. He was by trade a sail-maker. His last voyage was to the coast of Guinea. He had been on board a slave ship, the captain's name Maxwell, where one man had been killed, a boy put to lodge with the pigs and was half eaten, one boy set to watch in the hot sun till he dropped down dead. He had been cast away in North America and had travelled thirty days among the Indians, where he had been well treated. He had twice swum from a King's ship in the night and escaped. He said he would rather be in hell than be pressed. He was now going to wait in England to appear against Captain Maxwell. 'O he's a Rascal, Sir, he ought to be put in the papers!'

Journals of Dorothy Wordsworth

ANNA LAETITIA BARBAULD (For biographical note, see p.33.)
The battles of Crécy and Poitiers – in which the English overcame the French – took place in 1346 and 1356 respectively.

[Letter to Mrs J. Taylor]   *1806*
I am now reading Mr Johnes's Froissart, and I think I never was more struck with the horrors of war, – simply because *he* seems not at all struck with them; and I feel ashamed at my heart having ever beat with pleasure at the names of Cressy and Poitiers. He tells you the English marched into such a district; the barns were full, and cattle and corn plentiful; they burned and destroyed all the villages, and laid the country bare; such an English earl took a town, and killed men, women, and little children; – and he never makes a remark, but shows he looks upon it as the usual mode of proceeding.

The Works of Anna Laetitia Barbauld

MARIA EDGEWORTH (1767–1849) British. Collaborated with her father on *Practical Education* (1788) and *Essay on Irish Bulls* (1802). First novel, *Castle Rackrent* (1800), was followed by many others for adults and children.
Maria Edgeworth is referring to an incident in the Peninsular War.

To Mrs Ruxton   *Edgeworthstown, Oct. 26, 1812*
Lord Longford told us of Colonel Hercules Pakenham, at the siege of Badajos, walking with an engineer. A bomb whizzed over their heads and fell among the soldiers, as they were carrying off the wounded. When the Colonel expressed some regret, the engineer said, 'I wonder you have not steeled your mind to these things. These men are carried to the hospital, and others come in their place. Let us go to the depot.' Here the engineer had his wheelbarrows all laid out in nice order, and his pickaxes arranged in stars and various shapes; but, just as they were leaving the depot, a bomb burst in the midst of them. 'Oh, heavenly powers, my picks!' cried the engineer, with clasped hands, in despair.

The Life and Letters of Maria Edgeworth

In the Reign of Terror, 1891, by Jessie McGregor

LUCY AIKIN (1781–1864) British. The niece of Anna Laetitia Barbauld and, like her, the author of works in various forms – poems, a novel, essays, historical memoirs and a voluminous correspondence.

Necessity

The battle roars, the day is won,
Exulting Fortune crowns her son:
Sickening I turn on yonder plain
To mourn the widows and the slain;
To mourn the woes, the crimes of man,
To search in vain the eternal plan,
In outraged nature claim a part,
And ponder, desolate of heart.

FANNY BURNEY (1752–1840) British. Novelist, diarist. Her novel, *Evelina*, published anonymously in 1778, later made her famous. Her novels achieved greater success than her dramatic pieces. Married a French refugee in 1793, and lived in France from 1802 to 1812. In 1815, she wrote from Brussels:

For more than a week from this time I never approached my window but to witness sights of wretchedness. Maimed, wounded, bleeding, multilated, tortured victims of this exterminating contest passed by every minute: the fainting, the sick, the dying, and the dead, on brancards, in carts, in wagons, succeeded one another without inter-mission. There seemed to be a whole and large army of disabled or lifeless soldiers! All that was intermingled with them bore an aspect of still more poignant horror; for the Bonapartian prisoners, who were now poured into the city by hundreds, had a mien of such ferocious desperation, where they were marched on, uninjured, from having been taken by surprise, or overpowered by numbers; or faces of such anguish, where they were drawn on in open vehicles, the helpless victims of gushing wounds or horrible dislocations, that to see them without commiseration for their sufferings, or admiration for the heroic, however misled enthusiasm, to which they were martyrs, must have demanded an apathy dead to all feeling but what is personal, or a rancour too ungenerous to yield even to the view of defeat.

Fanny Burney's Diary

'MILL', the writer, goes to call on an old acquaintance . . .

In the course of conversation – we were unaccountably chatty that afternoon – she spoke of something as being a custom in France. 'France,' I said, 'you haven't been there, surely!'

She gave a most undeniable French shrug, and then shaking her head, sighed out with a strange sort of smile – that rare smile that only very old people ever manage, a gleam of sunshine on an autumn landscape – 'I should think I *had* been in France, but oh! it's *long* ago!'

'*Do* tell me about it, Mrs L.; you know I love to hear anything like a story, – How came you there?'

She drew herself up, crossed her arms in a nice old-fashioned way she had, and began, –

'I dare say, miss, you've heard tell of a *place called Waterloo*, where there was a battle once.'

Now I hate war. I've often tried to feel a proper amount of reverence for the heroes of a 'hundred fights' without attaining it to any very great extent; nevertheless, I am English enough to experience a certain straightening of my person at the sound of that word, and I believe the Iron Duke himself would have smiled a grim approval of my prompt response.

'*Waterloo!* heard of WATERLOO! of *course* I have, – well, go on.'

'Well, miss, my first husband was a soldier, and he was in that battle. I was then young, and living with my sister and my little baby in the West of England, and I wanted sorely to go to my husband. My sister wasn't willing for me to go at all, and did everything to dissuade me, but I didn't like being beholden to her, and I thought as I could get to him easily, and so I set off along with another young woman, whose husband was out there too; but if we had but have known what we was to go thro', and what treatment we should get, I question whether we shouldn't have stopped in Old England.'

'Where did you land?'

'At a place called – let me see, I forget them foreign names so now – why Ostend I think it was, and there we met with some other women going to the camp. . . . It was just three days after the battle as we got to the place. It was just before harvest, and the field they told me was all waving ripe corn when they reached it. When I saw it, it was as flat all over as if it had been rolled.'

'And the dead bodies, were they all gone?'

'Oh! they don't leave them unburied lying about, miss, they're put underground directly. There was plenty of wounded poor creatures I saw, and the remains of a shed where a many were lying at the close of the battle, as their comrades had dragged in for protection, and would you believe it, as them cruel wretches fired at the shed, full of wounded men, till it was all of a blaze? and them who had strength enough crawled out, and the dying or helpless was suffocated. My husband saw that himself. Oh! no wonder the people hated the French, but the French was quite as bitter against the English.'

'But you didn't find them *all* so, surely, you found *some* kind hearts there!'

She gave me the pleasant old smile again, and leaning forward, said very gently –

'Kind hearts! Oh dear, yes! I tell ye what it is, miss, I found it in France the same as it is in England, and it's my belief it's the same all over the world, – if you treat people well, and keep a kind heart yourself, no fear as you won't meet with kindness too. People is *very often what we makes 'em.*'

'A Place Called Waterloo: Experiences of a Soldier's Wife'

LADY MORGAN, née SYDNEY OWENSON (born c.1776) British. On father's bankruptcy, resolved to become self-supporting through writing and working as governess. Reputation established by her novel, *The Wild Irish Girl*. Visited France after revolution as sympathiser but not admirer of Napoleon.

Here, she observes the driver of a cart bound for market giving a lift to some soldiers from a nearby garrison.

In this singular and intimate association of the natives of two countries so long opposed by

'Contumelious, beastly, mad-brain'd war,'

there was something extremely gracious to the feelings; and the horrible and sanguinary details which filled up the interval from the moment the British troops first entered France, were all forgotten in the contemplation of this little scene of reciprocal good-will. The English soldier no longer tracked his progress with blood, nor carried desolation to the hearth of the French peasant: the French peasant no longer fled in fear, nor execrated in indignation the 'armipotent soldier' of a rival country. Oh, why should nations, so closely associated by natural position, be ever opposed in sanguinary conflict; and, assisting the wild ambition of their rulers, discover too late that they are but the dupes of their own national prejudice; the victims of a policy, which works on them for its own views!

France, 1817: the Aftermath of War

A LADY

Defensive warfare is . . . objectionable, not only on the general principle that all war is unlawful, but because the admittance of this exception has been in fact the base of the greatest proportion of offensive wars.

We call upon all, who are capable of discerning the mischief and ultimate inutility of War, to unite in diffusing those sentiments which will lead to the discovery of some better means of adjusting differences – some 'more dignified tribunal' than the field of battle. Why should there not be a congress of nations to combine the energies of all in the promotion of one common interest? Let us urge home to the conscience and understanding of every rational creature, the necessity of an adherence to fixed principles. Half the mischief in the world arises from man's forsaking those grand general rules of Christianity which are calculated to secure the greatest eventual sum of good, to go in quest of temporary expedients. It is this which fills our streets with beggars – it is this which overspreads the earth with slaughter. . . . When every single nation is determined on the preservation of peace, there will be an end to contest.

An Examination of the Principles which are Considered to Support the Practice of War

CLAIRE MARY JANE CLAIRMONT (1798–1879) British. Stepsister of Mary (Godwin) Shelley. She never married, and after working as a governess in Europe and Russia, retired to Florence in 1849.

In her journal for Sunday 13 September 1823, she writes of her former lover, Byron, who has joined the insurgents in Greece. (He died in 1824 at Missolonghi.)

After breakfast, in a mood hopeless of good and careless utterly of my future fate, the newspapers were put by Catherine Ivanovna into my mind – I glanced over them hastily as is my custom to see if there is any thing about Greece. I saw my dear friend's name. I did not dare to read, yet notwithstanding with a horrible feeling of dread & yet hope – I read – that he was well and still in his cavern. Who shall describe the happiness I felt. This sudden relief from horrible inquietude to all the sweet certainty of his being well. I went then instantly into the garden and sat myself on the balcony to enjoy all the fullness of my happiness. The whole sky was dark and portentous; the grove was agitated by a rushing wind which poured thro' its bared form and shook the dying leaves to the ground in showers. Not a single bird was heard, the whole grove was solitary its leaves abandoned it and were strewed on the plain. But I in this wasted scene was full of joy & life. I spent the whole day in silent happiness.

The Journals of Claire Clairmont

FRANCES ANNE (FANNY) KEMBLE (1809–93) British. Born into famous acting family. Poet, actor, dramatist and memoir writer. First stage appearance at 20 as Juliet. Toured USA in 1833 and married Pierce Butler, a Georgia planter. Divorced 1848. In 1877 she returned to England permanently.

[*February 28–March 2, 1839*]

Dear E[lizabeth].

. . . I detained Louisa, whom I had never seen but in the presence of her old grandmother, whose version of the poor child's escape to, and hiding in the woods, I had a desire to compare with the heroine's own story.

She told it very simply, and it was most pathetic. She had not finished her task one day, when she said she felt ill, and unable to do so, and had been severely flogged by driver Bran, in whose 'gang' she then was. The next day, in spite of this encouragement to labor, she had again been unable to complete her appointed work; and Bran having told her that he'd tie her up and flog her if she did not get it done, she had left the field and run into the swamp.

'Tie you up, Louisa!' said I; 'what is that?'

She then described to me that they were fastened up by their wrists to a beam or a branch of a tree, their feet barely touching the ground, so as to allow them no purchase for resistance or evasion of the lash, their clothes turned over their heads, and their backs scored with a leather thong, either by the driver himself, or, if he pleases to inflict their punishment by deputy, any of the men he may choose to summon to the office; it might be father, brother, husband, or lover, if the overseer so ordered it. I turned sick, and my blood curdled listening to these details from the slender young slip of a lassie, with her poor piteous face and murmuring, pleading voice.

Journal of a Residence on a Georgian Plantation in 1838–1839

MARGARET ARMSTRONG on Fanny Kemble

States Rights meant nothing to her [Fanny Kemble]; if slavery had meant as little she might have hesitated to take an active part. But twenty-two years had not been able to wipe out her memories of Georgia. After the [American Civil] war began, she wrote exultingly to Henry Greville: 'When I used to stand in utter despondency listening to the waves breaking on the beach at the river's mouth, and watching the revolving light that warned the vessels from the dangerous bar, not seldom crying with bitter tears, "How long, O Lord, how long!" I little thought to see the day when Northern vessels would ride along that coast, bringing freedom to the land of bondage.' Fanny was as sure as were her country neighbors, the Puritan New England farmers whom she considered the most intelligent men of their class in the world, that the war was being fought to free the slaves, that freedom for the slaves was a magnificent battle-cry, and that the North would win in the end.

So she did her share; she handed out swords and pistols to volunteers in New York and Philadelphia; she gave readings for the benefit of 'sanitary fairs;' she tried to keep up her enthusiasm by recalling a conversation with Welcker, the German archeologist, who had insisted that no nation could achieve greatness without 'a great heroic war,' and hoped and prayed that Welcker was right. But in her heart she hated the war; she was too imaginative and too just. She could not give a sword to some young volunteer whom she remembered as a little boy in a round jacket without a shudder, and both sides boasted unduly of their victories; she was thankful that she was not personally involved, no one near and dear to her could be drawn into the conflict.

Margaret Armstrong, *Fanny Kemble: a Passionate Victorian*

HARRIET MARTINEAU (1802–76) British. Writer on social and economic reform, history, politics and religion. Also wrote children's stories, novels and serious journalism for *Edinburgh Review* and *Daily News*.

How did we become involved in an Affgan [*sic*] war, which cost us a deluge of blood and tears, of which the loss of fifteen millions of treasure is only the bare material record? . . .

After an anxious summer [1841], during which the gathering of the storm was watched by the wise and made a jest of by the sanguine, the day of doom was drawing near. The best officers were the most depressed, because most aware of the necessity of good command under the approaching crisis, and of the utter imbecility of the commander. . . .

The British, half starved and without ammunition, looking in vain for help from below and behind, and distant a mile and a half from the citadel, which should have been their grand bulwark, were 'advised' by the enemy to go back to India; and on the 6th of January, 1842, they set out. Their doom was clear before five miles were over. Of the 4,500 soldiers, 1,200 camp followers and a great body of women and children, only one individual accomplished the march. At the first halt, they saw the glare from their burning cantonments as they sat in the snow. The women were pillaged of everything but the scanty clothing they wore; the children were lost in the hubbub; and the snow was soaked with the blood and strewn with the corpses of our soldiers till there was not one left. The camp followers, frost-bitten and be-

(cont'd p.47)

After the Battle of Prestonpans, 1849, by Fanny McIan

Showing the camp followers of General John Cope of the 5th Regiment of Foot Soldiers. It is the only known surviving picture by this artist.

The Remnants of an Army, Jellalabad, 13th January 1842, 1879, by Elizabeth Thompson

Painted in 1879 this refers to the first Afghan War (1938–42), showing Dr William Brydon, surgeon of the Army Medical Corps and the sole survivor of the disastrous retreat of the 16,500 strong British garrison from Kabul, arriving at Jellalabad.

numbed, lay down in the road, or crawled among the rocks, to die of cold or hunger.

The generals did not appear, because they were obstructed below, and had enough to do to save our military reputation. That reputation *was* saved, the errors of the Affganistan war being attributed to the weakness of civilians, who laid themselves open to irresponsible military importunities . . . large reinforcements were sent . . . our flag was planted on the citadel at Cabul, and the bazaar – a work of Aurungzebe's – was burnt. . . .

Lord Ellenborough by proclamation commanded the evacuation of Affganistan, declaring to the astonishment of the Affgans, that it is contrary to British principles and policy to force a ruler on a reluctant people. It was for the Affgans and all India to argue whether the British were perfidious, or simply infirm; and we are now suffering the practical consequences of the speculation.

British Rule in India

CHARLOTTE BRONTË (1816–55) British. Lived at Haworth, where father was curate. Like sisters Anne and Emily, she achieved success as a writer, drawing on unhappy experiences as pupil of Cowan Bridge School and as governess. She attended Miss Wooler's school at Roe Head in 1831.

The year 1848 was one of agitation throughout Europe: in the last three lines, Charlotte Brontë is probably referring to a worker uprising in Paris; revolutionary activities in Ireland, partly as a result of the potato famine; the 'March days in Berlin', when soldiers had to clear the streets of people demanding reform; and the 'five days of Milan' (18–22 March), another episode marking popular dissatisfaction with Austrian rule.

Haworth, March 31st, 1848

My dear Miss Wooler, . . .

I remember well wishing my lot had been cast in the troubled times of the late war, and seeing in its exciting incidents a kind of stimulating charm which it made my pulse beat fast only to think of – I remember even, I think, being a little impatient that you would not fully sympath- ise with my feelings on this subject, that you heard my aspirations and speculations very tranquilly, and by no means seemed to think the flaming sword could be any pleasant addition to the joys of paradise. I have now outlived youth; and, though I dare not say that I have outlived all its illusions, that the romance is quite gone from life, the veil fallen from truth, and that I see both in naked reality, yet, certainly, many things are not to me what they were ten years ago; and amongst the rest, 'the pomp and circumstance of war' have quite lost in my eyes their factitious glitter. I have still no doubt that the shock of moral earthquakes wakens a vivid sense of life both in nations and individuals; that the fear of dangers on a broad national scale diverts men's minds momentarily from brooding over small private perils, and, for the time, gives them something like largeness of views; but, as little doubt have I that convulsive revolutions put back the world in all that is good, check civilisation, bring the dregs of society to its surface – in short, it appears to me that insurrections and battles are the acute diseases of nations, and that their tendency is to exhaust by their violence the vital energies of the countries where they occur. That England may be spared the spasms, cramps, and frenzy-fits now contorting the Continent and threatening Ireland, I earnestly pray!

With the French and Irish I have no sympathy. With the Germans and Italians I think the case is different – as different as the love of freedom is from the lust of license.

The Brontës and their Circle

GEORGE SAND, pseudonym of AMANTINE AURORE LUCILE DUPIN, BARONNE DUDEVANT (1804–76) French. Married 1822, separated 1831. She earned her living in Paris, translating, drawing and writing for *Le Figaro*. Prolific novelist, close friend of Chopin. Here she appeals to Louis Napoleon.

Prince, my family is scattered and flung to the four corners of the earth. Friends of my childhood and my old age, brothers and adopted children, are in dungeons or in exile. Your wrath has descended on all those who take, accept or even tolerate the title of socialist republican. . . . I would not presume to discuss politics with you, it would be laughable of me to do so; but from the depth of my ignorance and fallibility I beg of you with tears in my eyes and with blood streaming from my heart: Stay your hand, conqueror! Spare the strong as well as the weak, have mercy for the women who weep as well as for the men who do not. Be merciful and humane. . . . Amnesty, amnesty, and soon, my prince.

Nohant, 20 January 1852

Calling the Roll after an Engagement, Crimea, 1874, by Elizabeth Thompson
This painting shows the Grenadier Guards after the battle of Inkerman,
1854. It was approved for accuracy by Florence Nightingale and made the
artist's reputation.

War, 1883, by Anna Lea Merritt

. . . Her efforts bore results. Sick prisoners were released; four young soldiers sentenced to death were reprieved; some well-known socialists had their deportation sentences commuted to exile into a country of their own choice. Some of George's protégés felt she could have done more for them, others viewed with suspicion her comings and goings inside the presidential palace and accused her of being a turncoat. But most of those she tried to help knew that they owed her their lives and what liberty they were allowed. She never lost sight of her protégés. She collected money for prisoners' families and sent letters of encouragement and books to the exiled. She never gave up. Grateful families spoke of her as the Saint of Berry or Our Lady of Good Help.

Ruth Jordan, *George Sand, a Biography*

FLORENCE NIGHTINGALE (1820–1910) British. Became famous during Crimean War for her radical improvements to army hospitals. Founded a nurses' training school at St Thomas's Hospital, 1861, improving status of nurses.

What the horrors of war are no one can imagine. They are not wounds and blood, and fever, spotted and low, and dysentery, chronic and acute, and cold and heat and famine. They are intoxication, drunken brutality, demoralisation, and disorder on the part of the inferior; jealousies, meanness, indifference, selfish brutality on the part of the superior.

Letter, May 1855

QUEEN VICTORIA (1819–1901) Acceded 1837. British. Talented, like so many Victorian women, as artist and writer, she published *Leaves from a Journal of our Life in the Highlands 1848–61* (1868) and *More Leaves* in 1883. Here she is visiting soldiers from the Crimean War.

Immediately after luncheon, we went down into the Hall again, just as the other day, and saw 26 of the sick & wounded of the Coldstreams. I thought they looked worse than the others – more suffering & sickly, &

less fine looking men. There were some sad cases; – one man who had lost his right arm at Inkermann, was also at the Alma, & looked deadly pale; – one or two others had lost theirs arms, others had been shot in the shoulders & legs, – several, in the hip joint, which impeded the action of the leg, rendering them unfit for further service. . . . 2 other very touching & distressing cases, 2 poor boys, the one, (P. Randle) aged 19, lost his leg by the bursting of a shell, in the trenches, the leg having had to be amputated quite high up – the other (P. Gilden), aged 20, looking particularly young, had had his arm so severely wounded, that it will wither & become useless. . . . I cannot say how touched & impressed I have been by the sight of these noble, brave, & so sadly wounded men & *how* anxious I feel to be of use to them, & try to get some employment for those who are maimed for life.

Journal

M.M.H.

The public has not forgotten the wholesale sacrifice of life in the Crimea to the requirements of an absurd and defective official routine, which no man had the heart or the courage to break through, though he saw before his eyes our gallant fellows perishing by hundreds for want of those very things known to be at hand, and only not available in the absence of a written order from the accredited officer, distant it might be miles, in the performance of one of his multifarious duties. Neither has the public forgotten the disorder which prevailed in the hospitals, when Florence Nightingale and her band of nurses and ladies started for Constantinople in the autumn of 1854.

Never was the presence of woman more needed, never did it carry with it more blessing and healing. With that union of firmness and gentleness so characteristic of women, united to skill and experience acquired in long years of study and observation, Miss Nightingale proceeded immediately to organise and arrange, stepping, it is said, more than once over those routine obstacles which had proved insurmountable to routine men, till order grew out of disorder, and gradually, cleanliness, comfort, and health, took the place of those frightful scenes which awaited her first arrival.

'We had,' says Miss Nightingale, 'in the first seven months of the Crimean campaign, a mortality among the troops at the rate of 60 per cent. per annum, from disease alone, – a rate of mortality which exceeds that of the great plague in the population of London, and a higher ratio than the mortality in cholera to the attacks; that is to say, that there died out of the army in the Crimea an annual rate greater than ordinarily die in time of pestilence out of sick. We had, during the last six months of the war, a mortality among our *sick* not much more than that among our *healthy* Guards at home, *and a mortality among our troops in the last five months two-thirds only of what it is among our troops at home.*'

'Florence Nightingale and the English Soldier'

HARRIET GROTE (1792–1878) British. Diarist, biographer, letter writer, versifier and essayist. Married George Grote, the historian in 1820. Leading intermediary between France and England through friendship with public men. Accomplished musician.

Englishmen really talk about the 'designs of the Czar' [Nicholas I] as something which it would be vain to gainsay, – as though we, and every one else, would be easily beaten out of every possession which he might think fit to attack! No more talk of England's magnificent ships or floating batteries, of her gallant soldiers, of her admirable artillery, from the instant Russia is named as a possible assailant. Yet the *Times* is perpetually putting forward the superiority of the Western armies in open conflict, and adducing the victories over Russian troops by even Turkish arms, as evidence how little she is to be dreaded as an *attacking* foe . . . the real objects of this ruinous war seem to me as disproportionate to the sacrifices it involves, and as little calculated to realise tangible benefits to Great Britain, as any war which could in these times be undertaken. The avowed purposes* are a sham; the real motives are the offspring of a timorous panic and delusion, reflecting small honour upon English dignity and self-reliance.

* *Id est*, the desire to uphold 'civilisation and the independence of nations.'

'The War from an Unpopular Point of View'

DINAH CRAIK (1826–87) British. Wrote seven novels for adults, of which *John Halifax, Gentleman* (1857) is the most famous, and one for children, *The Little Lame Prince* (1874), as well as a volume of poetry.

Guns of Peace (*Sunday Night, March 30th, 1856*)

Ghosts of dead soldiers in the battle slain,
Ghosts of dead heroes dying nobler far,
In the long patience of inglorious war,
Of famine, cold, heat, pestilence, and pain,
All ye whose loss makes our victorious gain –
This quiet night, as sounds the cannon's tongue,
Do ye look down the trembling stars among
Viewing our peace and war with like disdain?
Or wiser grown since reaching your new spheres,
Smile ye on those poor bones ye sowed as seed
For this our harvest, nor regret the deed? –
Yet lift one cry with us to Heavenly ears –
'Strike with Thy bolt the next red flag unfurled,
And make all wars to cease throughout the world.'

MARY ELIZABETH BRADDON (1837–1915) British. Famous after the publication, in 1862, of *Lady Audley's Secret*, which sold nearly one million copies, Mrs Braddon went on to edit magazines and write more than 70 other novels, poetry, and several plays.

Prince Louis Napoleon became the emperor Napoleon III in 1852. In these lines she is referring to Parisians welcoming him back after the war France and Piedmont waged against Austria, brought to an end by a Franco–Austrian armistice at Villafranca in 1859.

from *After the Armistice 1859*

Let us throw up our caps in the sunlight,
    Let us welcome the Prince we adore;
But let us remember there's one light,
    Our Emperor cannot restore:–

The light of young lives just departed
The light of love lost in the grave,
Past joys to the now broken-hearted,
The light of the souls of the brave . . .

EMILY DICKINSON (1830–86) American. Born in Amherst, Massachusetts. Became recluse after unhappy love affair, and began writing poetry. Only two pieces were published in her lifetime, but over 1,000 were published in series after her death.

[Letter to Louise Norcross during the American Civil War]
Mrs Adams had news of the death of her boy to-day, from a wound at Annapolis. Telegram signed by Frazer Stearns. You remember him. Another one died in October – from fever caught in the camp. Mrs Adams herself has not risen from her bed since then. 'Happy new year' step softly over such doors as these! 'Dead! Both her boys! One of them shot by the sea in the East, and one of them shot in the West by the sea.' . . . Christ be merciful! Frazer Stearns is just leaving Annapolis. His father has gone to see him to-day. I hope that ruddy face won't be brought home frozen. Poor little widow's boy, riding to-night in the mad wind, back to the village burying-ground where he never dreamed of sleeping! Ah! the dreamless sleep!

The Letters of Emily Dickinson

ELIZABETH GASKELL (1810–65) British. Wrote series of novels about conditions of the working classes in industrial cities of the North of England. Her work popular, though criticised in some quarters for being anti-authoritarian. Wrote a life of her friend, Charlotte Brontë.

Monday, June 10th 1861.
Dining-room in Plymouth Grove, breakfast things not as yet removed, your letter came *at* breakfast.
My dear Mr Norton,
. . . From what we read of the attack on Fort Sumter, 'no one killed', it sounds like a piece of bravadoing Child's play, – insolent enough, but

of a piece with the sort of bullying character one always heard attributed to the South. Now comes my great puzzle. What are you going to
do when you have conquered the South, as no one doubts that you
will? Mr Channing [a *Times* journalist] says 're-assert the right of letting
the U.S. flag float over the fortresses of the South, throwing out liberty
to the breeze' or something like this, which just tells me nothing of
what I really, & with deep interest want to know. *Conquering* the South
won't turn them into friends, or pre-dispose them to listen to reason or
argument, or to yield to influence instead of to force. You must *compel*
them then to what you want them to do. (And what *do* you want them
to do? – abolish slavery? return to their allegiance to the Union?)
Compelling them implies the means of compulsion. You will have to
hold them in subjection by force, – i.e. by military occupation. At
present your army is composed of volunteers, – but can they ever leave
their business &c for years & years of military occupation of a country
peopled by those adverse to them? Shall you not have henceforward to
keep a standing army? – If you were here I could go on multiplying
questions of this kind, but I dare say you are already tired & think me
very stupid . . .

your ever affectionate friend,
E. C. Gaskell

The Letters of Mrs Gaskell

MARY CHESNUT (1823–86) American. Married in 1846 and lived for a time
on her in-laws' plantation in the South. After helping her husband's political
career, she began nursing and writing a critical diary about the Confederacy.
Main corpus of work begun at 50: almost all unpublished in her lifetime.

August 29, 1861
Women who come before the public are in a bad box now. False hair is
taken off and searched for papers. Pistols are sought for [under]
'cotillons renversés' [lit. 'petticoats turned upside-down']. Bustles are
'suspect'. All manner of things, they say, come over the border under
the huge hoops now worn. So they are ruthlessly torn off. Not legs but
arms are looked for under hoops. And sad to say, found. Then women
are used as detectives and searchers to see that no men come over in
petticoats.

So the poor creatures coming this way are humilated to the deepest degree. (I think *these* times make all women feel their humiliation in the affairs of the world. . . . Women can only stay at home, and every paper reminds us that women are to be violated, ravished, and all manner of humiliation.)

To men – glory, honor, praise, and power – if they are patriots.

To women – daughters of Eve – punishment comes still in some shape, do what they will.

Mary Chesnut's Civil War, ed. by C. Vann Woodward, Yale University Press, © 1981 by C. Vann Woodward, Sally Bland Metts, Barbara G. Carpenter, Sally Bland Johnson, and Katherine W. Herbert.

JULIA WARD HOWE (1819–1910) American. Writer of verse, travel books and a play, she married in 1843 Samuel Gridley Howe, an anti-slavery reformer. Sharing his support for the Union cause, Julia Ward Howe wrote in 1862 'The Battle Hymn of the Republic'. The second extract reveals her later development into a committed pacifist.

The Battle Hymn of the Republic

Mine eyes have seen the glory of the coming of the Lord,
He is trampling out the vintage where the grapes of wrath are stored,
He hath loosed the fateful lightning of His terrible swift sword,
His truth is marching on.
  Glory, glory, Hallelujah! Glory, glory, Hallelujah!
  Glory, glory, Hallelujah! His truth is marching on.

Arise, all women who have hearts, whether your baptism be that of water or of tears! Say firmly: 'We will not have great questions decided by irrelevant agencies. Our husbands shall not come to us, reeking with carnage, for caresses and applause. Our sons shall not be taken from us to unlearn all that we have been able to teach them of charity, mercy, and patience. We, women of one country, will be too tender of those of another country, to allow our sons to be trained to injure theirs'. From the bosom of the devastated earth a voice goes up with our own. It says, 'Disarm, disarm! The sword of murder is not the balance of justice.' Blood does not wipe out dishonour; nor violence indicate possession. As men have often forsaken the plough and the anvil at the summons of war, let women now leave all that may be left of home for a greater and earnest day of counsel.

'Peace Appeal', September 1870

LADY JEBB, née CAROLINE LANE REYNOLDS (1840–1930) American. Married a soldier in 1856. Diarist. Described the retreat from Barrancas Barracks in the Civil War for *Harper's Weekly*. Husband died in 1868. Remarried in England, 1874, Greek scholar, Sir Richard Jebb and wrote a memoir of his life.

Jan. 11th, 1863 . . . Left New York on Sunday evening with my mind full of anxiety about my husband who was reported wounded, and arrived at Louisville on Wednesday morning, where I received the information that Addy was doing very well, and would recover without any inconvenience, and be a *whole* man, in every sense, quite a consideration in these times of sharp Surgical practice.

Journal, quoted in *With Dearest Love to All*, by Mary Reed Bobbitt

REBECCA HARDING DAVIS (1831–1910) American. Novelist. Educated at home and began writing early. First success came in 1861. Associate editor of the New York *Tribune* from 1869 to the mid-1870s.

There was one curious fact which I do not remember ever to have seen noticed in histories of the war, and that was its effect upon the nation as individuals. Men and women thought and did noble and mean things that would have been impossible to them before or after. A man cannot drink old Bourbon long and remain in his normal condition. We did not drink Bourbon, but blood. No matter how gentle or womanly we might be, we read, we talked, we thought perforce of nothing but slaughter. So many hundreds dead here, so many thousands there, were our last thoughts at night and the first in the morning. The effect was very like that produced upon a household in which there has been a long illness. There was great religious exaltation and much peevish ill temper. Under the long, nervous strain the softest women became fierce partisans, deaf to arguments or pleas for mercy. Nothing would convince some of the most intellectual women in New England that their southern sisters were not all Hecates, habitually employed in flogging their slaves; while Virginia girls believed that the wives of the men who invaded their homes were all remorseless, bloodthirsty harpies.

We no longer gave our old values to the conditions of life. Our former ideas of right and wrong were shaken to the base. The ten commandments, we began to suspect, were too old-fashioned to suit this present emergency.

I knew, for instance, of a company made up of the sons and grandsons of old Scotch Covenanters. They were educated, gallant young fellows. They fought bravely, and in the field or in hospital were kind and humane to their foes. But they came home, when disbanded, with their pockets full of spoons and jewelry which they had found in farmhouses looted and burned on Sherman's march to the sea; and they gayly gave them around to their sweethearts as souvenirs of the war.

'The Civil War'

ELIZABETH CADY STANTON (1815–1902) American. Reformer. In 1840 advocated Married Woman's Property Bill and campaigned until passed in 1848. Same year, called first Women's Rights Convention at Seneca Falls and carried first demand for woman suffrage. Co-edited, with Matilda Joslyn Gage and Susan B. Anthony, *History of Woman Suffrage*, and wrote several key books on women's rights.

MATILDA JOSLYN GAGE (1826–98) American. Suffragist. Advocated women's rights at Syracuse National Women's Rights Convention in 1852. President of New York State and National Women's Suffrage Associations. Edited magazine on the vote issue, 1878–81, and wrote *Women, Church and State* (1893).

SUSAN BROWNELL ANTHONY (1820–1906) American. Reformer and teacher. Active in temperance societies, anti-slavery and women's rights work. After the Civil War, founded *The Revolution*, a women's rights paper. Arrested and tried for voting under the Fourteenth Amendment, 1872. Campaigned in many states, contributed to periodicals and lectured in USA and UK.

Despite their campaigning for freedom for slaves, the racism in this piece is blatant, reflecting the prejudices of the time. We include the extract for its historical importance, without condoning the argument used. On 12 April 1861, the first gun was fired on Fort Sumter, and on the 14th it surrendered. The American Civil War had begun. . . .

Think of the busy hands from the Atlantic to the Pacific, making garments, canning fruits and vegetables, packing boxes, preparing lint and bandages for soldiers at the front; think of the mothers, wives and daughters on the far-off prairies, gathering in the harvests, that their fathers, husbands, brothers and sons might fight the battles of freedom. . . .

How much easier it is to march forth with gay companions and marshal music; with the excitement of the battle, the camp, the ever-shifting scenes of war, sustained by the hope of victory; the promise of reward; the ambition for distinction; the fire of patriotism kindling every thought, and stimulating every nerve and muscle to action! How much easier is all this, than to wait and watch alone with nothing to stimulate hope or ambition.

The evils of bad government fall ever most heavily on the mothers of the race, who, however wise and far-seeing, have no voice in its administration, no power to protect themselves and their children against a male dynasty of violence and force. . . .

The question naturally suggests itself, how was it possible that when peace was restored [women] received no individual rewards nor general recognition for their services, which, though acknowledged in private, have been concealed from the people and ignored by the Government.

Gen. Grant has the credit for the success of plans which were the outgrowth of the military genius of a woman; Gen. Howard received a liberal salary as the head of the Freedman's Bureau, while the woman who inspired and organized that department and carried its burdens on her shoulders to the day of her death, raised most of the funds by personal appeal for that herculean work.

Dr Bellows enjoyed the distinction as President of the Sanitary Bureau, which originated in the mind of a woman, who, when the machinery was perfected and in good working order, was forced to resign her position as official head through the bigotry of the medical profession.

Though to Anna Dickinson was due the triumph of the Republican party in several of the doubtful States at a most critical period of the war, yet that party, twenty years in power, has refused to secure her in the same civil and political rights enjoyed by the most ignorant foreigner or slave from the plantations of the South.

The lessons of the war were not lost on the women of this nation; through varied forms of suffering and humiliation, they learned that they had an equal interest with man in the administration of the Government, enjoying or suffering alike its blessings or its miseries. When in the enfranchisement of the black man they saw another ignorant class of voters placed above their heads, and with anointed eyes beheld the danger of a distinctively 'male' government, forever involving the nations of the earth in war and violence; a lesson taught on every page of history, alike in every century of human experience; and demanded for the protection of themselves and children, that woman's voice should be heard, and her opinions in public affairs be expressed by the ballot, they were coolly told that the black man had earned the right to vote, that he had fought and bled and died for his country!

Did the negro's rough services in camp and battle outweigh the humanitarian labors of woman in all departments of government? Did his loyalty in the army count for more than her educational work in teaching the people sound principles of government? Can it be that statesmen in the nineteenth century believe that they who sacrifice human lives in bloody wars do more for the sum of human happiness and development than they who try to save the multitude and teach them how to live? But if on the battle-field woman must prove her right to justice and equality, history abundantly sets forth her claims; the records of her brave deeds mark every page of fact and fiction, of poetry and prose.

In all the great battles of the past woman as warrior in disguise has verified her right to fight and die for her country by the side of man. In camp and hospital as surgeon, physician, nurse, ministering to the sick and dying, she has shown equal skill and capacity with him. There is no position woman has not filled, no danger she has not encountered, no emergency in all life's tangled trials and temptations she has not shared with man, and with him conquered. If moral power has any value in the balance with physical force surely the women of this republic, by their self-sacrifice and patriotism, their courage 'mid danger, their endurance 'mid suffering, have rightly earned a voice in the laws they are compelled to obey, in the Government they are taxed to support; some personal consideration as citizens as well as the black man in the 'Union blue.'

History of Woman Suffrage

SARAH BERNHARDT (1844–1923) French. Famous actress. Set up and ran hospital in besieged Paris during Franco–Prussian war of 1870. Acted at Front during First World War.

Oh, war! What infamy, shame, and sorrow! War! What theft and crime, abetted, forgiven and glorified!

Recently I visited a large steel works. I will not say in what country, for all countries have been hospitable to me, and I am neither a spy nor a traitress. I only set forth things as I see them. Well, I visited one of these frightful manufactories, in which the most deadly weapons are made. The owner of it all, a multi-millionaire, was introduced to me. He was pleasant, but no good at conversation, and he had a dreamy, dissatisfied look. My cicerone informed me that this man had just lost a huge sum of money, nearly sixty million francs.

'Good Heavens!' I exclaimed; 'how has he lost it?'

'Oh well, he has not exactly lost the money, but has just missed making the sum, so it amounts to the same thing.'

I looked perplexed, and he added, 'Yes; you remember that there was a great deal of talk about war between France and Germany with regard to the Morocco affair?'

'Yes.'

'Well, this prince of the steel trade expected to sell cannon for it, and for a month his men were very busy in the factory working day and night. He gave enormous bribes to influential members of the Government and paid some of the papers in France and Germany to stir up the people. Everything has fallen through, thanks to the intervention of men who are wise and humanitarian. The consequence is that this millionaire is in despair. He has lost sixty or perhaps a hundred million francs.'

I looked at the wretched man with contempt, and I wished heartily that he could be suffocated with his millions, as remorse was no doubt utterly unknown to him.

And how many others merit our contempt just as this man does! Nearly all those who are known as 'suppliers to the army,' in every country in the world, are the most desperate propagators of war.

My Double Life; Memoirs of Sarah Bernhardt

DROITS DES FEMMES [WOMEN'S RIGHTS] A weekly French suffragist journal. Here are extracts from two issues of the paper, one just before the outbreak of the Franco–Prussian war and one just after. They were translated and printed by *The Englishwoman's Review*, another suffragist journal.

13 July 1870

While I write news is being brought in every hour. The most disquieting rumours follow quickly upon assurance of peace. For my part I believe in war. If you ask me why, I reply – 'Because the government chooses to have it so'. . . . If Prussia were to give full satisfaction to the French Government on the Spanish question, it would not suffice. The object is to humiliate the King of Prussia. . . . These questions of 'amour propre' do not concern us. The two nations are friendly at bottom, and questions of dynastic interest ought to be postponed to national interests. War may be agreeable to kings; it is not agreeable to the peoples. Mothers of families write to us from all sides to ask what is to be done. . . . Let voices be raised everywhere against the war. If anything can ward off war it will be a general cry from all France. Let us protest in the name of humanity against this pastime of princes, which causes the blood of the people to flow. . . . And here women have not only the right to interfere, it is their duty to do so. Let them protest. This is what they can do. Who will dare to say now that politics do not concern wives and mothers?

When politics bring such consequences they concern everybody. The protest of women ought to be placed by the side of the protest of working men. Let it come. We will publish it.

20 July 1870

Our appeal has been heard. Numerous and energetic protests against the war have been sent us. All are written and signed by women. . . . We acknowledge their receipt, but do not publish them, for events have passed so quickly that it is no longer time. It is too late! . . .

Money and gifts in kind will be received at the office and transmitted by the editor, but this is not all. It is not enough to give one's mite or to pick lint; what is wanted are hands. There are the wounded to attend, the sick to nurse, the dying to comfort, not only in the hospitals, but on the field of battle. They tell you, oh women! that you bear none of the burdens of war. It is one of the great arguments brought against you when you ask for equal rights with men. Show now that you know how to take your share of dangerous duties!

It is no question of approving of the war, but of mitigating the evils of war.

You will have to save even those who are now called 'the enemies of France.'

Forward, then, women! Forward, volunteers of charity! Remember the mothers whose sons will be dying. On whichever side they fall, the wounded are your brothers.

Droits des Femmes (Women's Rights)

MONSTROUS REGIMENT British theatre group. This extract comes from a modern play, *Scum*.
The play was written collectively; this particular extract was written by Mary McCusker. It shows the poverty of besieged Paris.

DRUMS.
NIGHT: A SMALL AREA OF STAGE IS LIT.
ENTER MARCEL SHAKING A COLLECTING TIN MUG.

MARCEL: Guns for Paris! Guns for Paris! Give what you can, brothers and sisters. Guns for Paris! Guns for the people! Give what you can for guns for the people.
VOICE OFF: Slut! You filthy little whore! Fornicating on my doorstep like an animal. I'll throw a bucket of cold water over you if I catch you

here again. You whore! You're scum. Get back to the gutter where you belong. Scum.

ENTER LUCIE: MARCEL RECOGNISES HER.

LUCIE: Don't touch me, don't. I'm so sick of being hungry. That was the first time. You've no idea, men. You go off, leave us, leave your children. All you can think about is beating the Prussians, tactics, manoeuvres, the excitement. You don't have to listen to your child crying for its father. I used to give her pebbles to suck. We pretended they were sweets. I made a game of it. But it wasn't a game. She's dead because I couldn't feed her, house her, give her medicine. That's real. And it's real when I stand in an alley and lift my skirts for a bit of bread.

MARCEL: I didn't know.

LUCIE: Well you know now.

MARCEL: I'm collecting for guns to defend Paris. So far I've got a hundred and fifty-three francs, and a tin button.

Scum

MRS AUCKLAND. This extract comes from a speech she made to a London Peace Society Meeting.

Mrs Auckland observed that. . . . The work of women particularly must be with the young. Mothers ruled as queens in their own households over their children and she wished to recommend to them that there should not be the military drum and other military toys in the nursery. That was one means from which the little ones learned the attractions of the military march, and became imbued with the military spirit, and with the idea that 'when I am old enough I will be a soldier and carry the gun.' . . . Another point which should be seriously considered was the military drill of the schools. Sometime ago a vigorous effort was made to fire [with enthusiasm] the boys of the metropolis, and there was an extraordinary demonstration in one of the parks. This was regarded as the thin edge of the wedge which was to proceed the foreign idea of military conscription. The ladies of the

London School Board set their faces strongly against this, and it was exceedingly unlikely that it would happen again.

'Address to a Peace Society Meeting'

HELEN HUNT JACKSON (1830–85) American. Campaigned and wrote on behalf of the American Indians. Appointed Commissioner for Indian Affairs in 1883.

When the English first entered Pennsylvania messengers from the Conestoga Indians met them, bidding them welcome, and bringing gifts of corn and venison and skins. The whole tribe entered into a treaty of friendship with William Penn, which was to last 'as long as the sun should shine or the water run into the rivers'. . . .

[In 1795] Thomas Chalkley, a famous Quaker preacher . . . set off . . . to make the journey [to the Conestoga]. He says 'We . . . went on cheerfully and with good-will and much love to the poor Indians. And when we came they received us kindly, treating us civilly in their way. We treated about having a meeting with them in a religious way; upon which they called a council, in which they were very grave, and spoke, one after another, without any heat or jarring. Some of the most esteemed of their women speak in their councils.'

When asked why they suffered the women to speak, they replied that 'some women were wiser than some men.' It was said that they had not for many years done anything without the advice of a certain aged and grave woman, who was always present at their councils. The interpreter said that she was an empress, and that they gave much heed to what she said. This wise queen of Conestoga looked with great favor on the Quakers, the interpreter said, because they 'did not come to buy or sell, or get gain;' but came 'in love and respect' to them, and desired their well-doing, both 'here and hereafter.' . . .

The next year the governor himself, anxious to preserve their inalienable good-will, and to prevent their being seduced by emissaries from the French, went himself to visit them. On this occasion one of the chiefs made a speech, still preserved in the old records, which contains this passage: 'Father, we love quiet; we suffer the mouse to play; when the woods are rustled by the wind, we fear not; when the leaves are disturbed in ambush, we are uneasy; when a cloud obscures your brilliant sun, our eyes feel dim; but when the rays appear, they give great heat to the body and joy to the heart. Treachery darkens the chain of friendship; but truth makes it brighter than ever. This is the peace we desire.' . . .

There is not among these three hundred bands of Indians one which has not suffered cruelly at the hands either of the Government or of white settlers. The poorer, the more insignificant, the more helpless the band, the more certain the cruelty and outrage to which they have been subjected . . . the United States Government breaks promises now as deftly as then, and with an added ingenuity from long practice.

A Century of Dishonour

MARIA DERAISME, LOUISE DAVID and V. GRIES TRAUT of the Society for the Amelioration of Women in France.

To the President and Members of the Council of Ministers.
GENTLEMEN. – Permit us to express to you the sentiment of profound sorrow by which we are animated in view of the warlike attitude of our Government.

We regard with terror, the prospect of a war in the Far East – a war which might not improbably be the presage of a general and terrible conflagration quite out of proportion to the advantages which you think may accrue to our country. Engines of destruction, which modern science (perverted from its proper and benevolent mission) renders daily more and more murderous, now threaten absolutely to decimate the nations.

War is not a foreordained and inevitable thing; it is caused by the will of men. . . .

The women of France, who have no political voice – whom the law thus deprives of a sacred right – the women of France demand that their strong aspirations in favour of Peace, and in favour of the masses being allowed to enjoy the fruits of their labour peaceably – be heard by the Government. They demand the insertion of the principle of International Arbitration in our Treaties of Commerce, so that henceforth all

(cont'd p.68)

JOURNAL POUR LA REVENDICATION DES

DROITS DE LA FEMME

DIRECTRICE

HUBERTINE AUCLERT

La Citoyenne, by Hubertine Auclert

This cartoon comes from the cover of a women's rights journal. Under a banner saying 'Universal Suffrage', a man and a woman place their votes into an electoral urn. The man votes for war, the woman for peace. On the urn is written 'World peace, social harmony and well-being of humanity will only exist when women get the vote and are able to help men make the laws.' Beneath the picture it says, 'Woman will only really become a female citizen when she has her full rights.'

67

differences between our Government and those of other nations may
be pacifically and amicably arranged . . .

Trusting that you will accept the assurance of our profound devotion
to our country,

We have the honour of subscribing ourselves,

Maria Deraisme,   President

Louise David   ⎫
V. Gries Traut   ⎬ Vice-Presidents,

of the Society for the Amelioration of the Position of Women

Paris, November, 1883

Address to the President of France

BERTHA VON SUTTNER (1843–1914) Austrian. Influential writer and
campaigner for disarmament and international arbitration. First woman to
win the Nobel Peace Prize. This piece is taken from her best selling anti-war
novel, *Lay Down Your Arms.*

Since out of every scholar a defender of his country has to be formed,
therefore the enthusiasm even of the child must be aroused for this its
first duty as a citizen; his spirit must be hardened against the natural
horror which the terrors of war might awaken, by passing over as
quickly as possible the story of the most fearful massacres and butch-
eries as of something quite common and necessary, and laying meanwhile all possible stress on the ideal side of this ancient national
custom; and it is in this way they have succeeded in forming a race
eager for battle and delighting in war.

The girls – who indeed are not to take the field – are educated out of
the same books as are prepared for the military training of the boys,
and so in the female youth arises the same conception which exhausts
itself in envy that they have nothing to do with war and in admiration
for the military class. What pictures of horror out of all the battles on
earth, from the Biblical and Macedonian and Punic Wars down to the
Thirty Years' War and the wars of Napoleon, were brought before us
tender maidens, who in all other things were formed to be gentle and
mild; how we saw there cities burnt and the inhabitants put to the

sword and the conquered trodden down – and all this was a real enjoyment; and of course through this heaping up and repetition of the horrors the perception that they were horrors becomes blunted, everything which belongs to the category of war comes no longer to be regarded from the point of view of humanity, and receives a perfectly peculiar mystico-historico-political consecration. War must be – it is the source of the highest dignities and honours – *that* the girls see very well, and they have had also to learn by heart the poems and tirades in which war is magnified. And thus originate the Spartan mothers, and the 'mothers of the colours.'

Lay Down Your Arms

MISS ROBINSON British. She was a member of the Peace and Arbitration Society. This extract comes from a lecture reprinted in the *Women's Penny Paper* which was, in its own words, 'the only paper conducted, written and published by women.'

Since the years 1872–74, the speaker said, the armaments of Europe had nearly doubled. . . . She wished all taxation was direct taxation, so that the people might really know what they were paying towards the European armaments, for the general working people were not at all aware of how the resources of the country were being drained away for these military purposes. There was another great evil on the Continent, and that was the forced servitude, the conscription, every man being obliged to be ready when called upon to take away the life of his fellow men. . . . Great armaments were pronounced by the greater men of the country to be one of the standing dangers of Europe. She had come to the conclusion that nations kept these great armaments because they were afraid of each other. There was no bravery in it. In fact, it seemed to her that there was something cowardly, and it was because everybody was afraid of everybody else. (Applause) She thought that all war was essentially unjust, because it involved the principle that might was right, that the strongest had the right to force his will on the weakest. The crying necessity of the times was some court in which national questions could be settled, for if arbitration did not put off war for ever, nevertheless the fact of delaying war for a long time would be a great blessing, and in all probability, when people had time to think about it, the war would never come to pass.

War in the Nineteenth Century

JOSEPHINE BUTLER (1828–1906) British. Campaigned against the Contagious Diseases Acts which in the interests of the health of the armed forces discriminated against prostitutes. She writes here on conditions in Ireland.

It is scarcely possible that an English or Irish Protestant of the present day, who is not blinded altogether by religious bigotry, can look back to the past history of Ireland, especially in connection with its terrible Penal Code, without a feeling of grief and of shame. It is strange that there should be among any of us a reluctance to acknowledge that an inevitable day of retribution must follow this long course of selfish and heartless government. The sleepless eyes of Justice have never ceased to watch throughout the long centuries of wrongs done to Ireland. The narrow views, the selfish policy, and the sharp cries of alarm of those who oppose the present claims of Ireland are but expressions of a wretchedly inadequate appreciation of the meaning of history, and of the law which decrees the inevitable vindication, sooner or later, of outraged justice.

No doubt every individual opponent of Ireland's claims at the present moment has the right to say, 'I am not personally responsible for all that has been described in the past; these things were done before I was born; they happened long ago.' No, we are not personally responsible, but nationally we are deeply responsible.

Our Christianity Tested by the Irish Question

MARIA TSHEBRIKOVA Russian. Wrote many books on women and education and helped set up university courses for women. When Alexander III took power he abolished the courses and introduced many repressive measures. This comes from a much publicised letter of protest she wrote to him in 1890 for which she was arrested.

The whole of your system pushes those who are dissatisfied into the camp of the revolutionists, even those who feel a strong and natural repulsion for all ideas of blood and violence. . . . I have a horror of bloodshed, no matter who may be the victim; but when for the spilling of blood, we find that on one side decorations are distributed, and on the other there is the rope and the gibbet, it is easy to understand the sympathies of young, enthusiastic and heroic youths.

Open Letter to the Czar

WARNER SNOAD British. Published two volumes of poetry.

A Woman's Creed

Not hate but love!
The love which lies like sunshine o'er the world,
Which softens sorrow, smooths out wrinkled Fate,
And, as a benison from Heaven above,
Leaves wrong and treachery beyond Earth's gate
And finds the good in every heart impearled.

Not war but peace!
The quiet homestead and the waving corn,
The strife of voices, not of blood and fire,
The angel's clarion, bidding murder cease,
And the foul scenes of death and carnage dire
Be but a dream on memory's pinions borne.

Not slaves, but free!
Not one sex shackled by a nation's laws,
Framed first by tyranny, upheld by lust;
But, in the glorious golden time to be,
Life dawn, for both, on mutual faith and trust,
And liberty uphold truth's holy cause.

71

BERTHA VON SUTTNER (For biographical details, see p.68.)

The fraternal embrace? Universal love? . . . You are right; humanity has not yet got to that point. But it does not require mutual love [*tendresse mutuelle*] to give up killing one another. What exists to-day, and what the peace leagues are combating, is the system of a destructive, organized, legitimized hatred, such as does not in the last analysis exist any longer in human hearts.

There has been talk of late of an international conference, having in view a coalition against the danger of anarchy. Never will the foolishness of the present situation have been more glaring than when these representatives of states which are living together in absolute anarchy – since they acknowledge no superior power – shall deliberate around the same table on methods of protecting themselves against five or six criminal bombs, while at the same time they will go on threatening one another with a hundred thousand legal bombs! . . .

The evolution of humanity is not a dream, it is a fact scientifically proved. Its end cannot be the premature destruction toward which it is being precipitated by the present system; its end must be the reign of law in control of force. Arms and ferocity develop in inverse ratio, – the tooth, the big stick, the sword, the musket, the explosive bomb, the electric war engine; and, on the other side, the wild beast, the savage, the warrior, the old soldier, the fighter of to-day (a so-called safeguard of peace), the humane man of the future, who, in possession of a power of boundless destructiveness, will refuse to use it.

Memoirs of Bertha von Suttner; the records of an eventful life

DOROTHY RICHARDSON (1837–1957) British. Socialist and novelist. Pioneered 'stream of consciousness' technique. This extract comes from a novel and describes an incident in London.

They were *fighting*; sending out suffocation and misery into the surrounding air . . . she stopped close to the two upright balanced threatening bodies, almost touching them. The men looked at her. 'Don't,' she said imploringly and hurried on trembling. . . . It occurred to her that she had not seen fighting since a day in her childhood when she had wondered at the swaying bodies and sickened at the thud of a first against a cheek. The feeling was the same to-day, the longing to explain somehow to the men that they *could* not fight. . . .

Pilgrimage

EMMA GOLDMAN (1869–1940) American of Russian and German origin. Anarchist and feminist. Imprisoned for advocating birth control. Opposed American entry to First World War through journal, *Mother Earth*, which she edited. Helped form No Conscription League for which she was jailed for 21 months, then deported to the Soviet Union.

America had declared war with Spain. The news was not unexpected. For several months preceding, press and pulpit were filled with the call to arms in defence of the victims of Spanish atrocities in Cuba. I was profoundly in sympathy with the Cuban and Philippine rebels who were striving to throw off the Spanish yoke. In fact, I had worked with some of the members of the Junta engaged in underground activities to secure freedom for the Philippine Islands. But I had no faith whatever in the patriotic protestations of America as a disinterested and noble agency to help the Cubans. It did not require much political wisdom to see that America's concern was a matter of sugar and had nothing to do with humanitarian feelings. Of course there were plenty of credulous people, not only in the country at large, but even in liberal ranks, who believed in America's claim. I could not join them. I was sure that no one, be it individual or government, engaged in enslaving and exploiting at home, could have the integrity or the desire to free people in other lands. Thenceforth my most important lecture, and the best-attended, was on Patriotism and War.

In San Francisco it went over without interference, but in the smaller Californian towns we had to fight our way inch by inch. The police, never loath to break up anarchist meetings, stood complacently by and thus encouraged the patriotic disturbers who sometimes made speaking impossible. The determination of our San Francisco group and my own presence of mind saved more than one critical situation. In San Jose the audience looked so threatening that I thought it best to dispense with a chairman and carry the meeting myself. As soon as I began to speak, bedlam broke loose. I turned to the trouble-makers with the request that they choose someone of their own crowd to conduct the meeting. 'Go on!' they shouted; 'you're only bluffing. You know you wouldn't let us run your show!' 'Why not?' I called back. 'What we want is to hear both sides, isn't that so?' 'Betcha life!' someone yelled. 'We must secure order for that, mustn't we?' I continued; 'I seem unable to do so. Supposing one of you boys comes up here and shows me how to keep the rest quiet until I have stated my side of the story. After that you can state yours. Now be good American sports.'

Boisterous cries, shouts of 'Hurrah,' calls of 'Smart kid, let's give her a chance!' kept the house in confusion for a few minutes. Finally an elderly man stepped up on the platform, banged his cane on the table, and in a voice that would have crumbled the walls of Jericho, bellowed: 'Silence! Let's hear what the lady has to say!' There was no further disturbance during my speech of an hour, and when I finished there was almost an ovation.

Living my Life

RADEN ADJENG KARTINI (1879–1904) Javanese. Pioneer of education for girls in Java.

Religion is intended as a blessing to mankind – a bond between all the creatures of God. They should be as brothers and sisters, not because they have the same human parents, but because they are all children of one Father, of Him who is enthroned in the heavens above. Brothers and sisters must love one another, help, strengthen and support one another. O God! Sometimes I wish that there had never been a religion, because that which should unite mankind into one common brotherhood has been through all the ages a cause of strife, of discord and of bloodshed. Members of the same family have persecuted one another because of the different manner in which they worshipped one and the same God. Those who ought to have been bound together by the tenderest love have turned with hatred from one another. Differences of Church, albeit in each the same word, God, is spoken, have built a dividing wall between two throbbing hearts. I often ask myself uneasily; is religion indeed a blessing to mankind? Religion, which is meant to save us from our sins, how many sins are committed in thy name?

Letters of a Javanese Princess: Raden Adjeng Kartini

PRISCILLA HANNAH PECKOVER (1833–1931) British. Born into one of the founding Quaker families. Energetic worker for temperance and peace. In order to communicate with workers for peace abroad she learnt 16 languages including Esperanto. She set up numerous peace organisations. Founded a journal, *Peace and Goodwill*, which she edited for over 40 years.

War, famine and pestilence, God's three great judgments are not arbitrary. They are exponents of the unchangeable law of righteousness, that the wages of sin are Death. Science tells how pestilence is the consequence of breaking sanitary laws; History, that famine is the result of the breach of economic laws; and more evidently war is man's own making by his breaches of the moral law.

'The work of righteousness' we are told 'shall be peace' and the kingdom of God is 'righteousness, peace, and joy;' wherefore it is the duty of all who love the King to work for peace, by substituting righteousness for violence, guile, or self assertion in a national sense.

This was borne in upon the heart of Christian men and women on *both sides of the Atlantic*, at the close of the Wars of Napoleon with their hecatombs of victims and their train of disease and disastrous consequences. Something must be done to work for Peace! . . .

Here we may remark that the most complete liberty of action and of thought is found consonant with unity of object. Peace on earth and good will to men should especially be the standard of the Christian Church as it is that of her Lord; but alas! so unfaithful have the national Churches, and even the free Churches in the various countries been, that a large proportion of the workers for peace are to be found outside their borders; driven to that position by finding the Churches, as they state openly, either apathetic or antagonistic.

Peace To-day

EMILY HOBHOUSE (1860–1926) British. Campaigner on behalf of the Boers. The war in South Africa between Britain and the Boers (white settlers of Dutch descent) aroused massive jingoism and anti-Boer feeling in Britain. Emily Hobhouse describes here a women's meeting which she organised in London to protest about British treatment of Boer women and children. Although radical by the standards of the time the meeting nevertheless ignored the rights of the black South Africans.

The coming Annexation was discussed and deplored and when the obstacles to a general protest were dealt with and felt to be overwhelming, I, as Honorary Secretary of the Women's Branch of the South African Concilation Committee, proposed that we, the *women*, should hold a Meeting of Protest. . . . A date, June the 13th, was fixed, and resolving to do it on a large scale as a Demonstration of real importance, the Queen's Hall was secured. From that moment my flat in Chelsea became organizing headquarters and with the devoted help of Miss Anna Griffin we began on May the 1st the arduous work of preparation. We formed, of course, branches throughout London with excellent workers, but even so, six weeks is scant time for filling the Queen's Hall with women only and all the drawbacks of an unpopular subject in time of war. There was immense opposition to contend with and the 'Conciliation' attitude to be always maintained. The great bulk of the correspondence fell on Miss Griffin and we laboured from 8am to – often – 11pm for those six weeks. The result was a magnificent assemblage of women, representative not only of London but of the entire country, for it was attended by the Delegates of the Women's Liberal Federation which happened to be holding its meetings at that time . . . Free admission to the Hall was decided on by the Committee, but only by bearers of tickets supplied by me. There was need of this caution in those days. Besides, it was to be a purely Women's Meeting, and as a matter of fact *no* men were present, except, it was said, the organ blower! . . .

Below are the resolutions passed. . . .

Resolution I

That this meeting of women brought together from all parts of the United Kingdom condemns the unhappy war now raging in South Africa, as mainly due to the bad policy of the Government:– a policy which has already cost in killed, wounded and missing over 20,000 of our bravest soldiers, and the expenditure of millions of money drawn from the savings and toil of our people, while to the two small states with whom we are at war, it is bringing utter ruin and desolation.

Resolution II

That this meeting protests against the attempt to silence, by disorder and violence, all freedom of speech about, or criticism of, the Government policy.

Resolution III

That this meeting protests against any settlement which involves the extinction by force of two Republics whose inhabitants, allied to us in blood and religion, cling as passionately to their separate nationality and flag as we in this country do to ours.

Resolution IV

That this meeting desires to express its sympathy with the women of the Transvaal and Orange Free State, and begs them to remember that thousands of English women are filled with profound sorrow at the thought of their sufferings, and with deep regret for the action of their own Government.

Ruth Fry, *Emily Hobhouse: A Memoir*

MRS KLANZINGA Dutch settler in South Africa. Here she describes her treatment by the British who systematically burnt down Boer farmhouses and forcibly removed the women and children to primitive and badly run concentration camps where thousands died. Emily Hobhouse (see previous extract), collected and published this and many similar letters. The sufferings of the black South Africans were largely unrecorded.

[Letter from Mrs Klanzinga, taken to Mafeking Camp]
Aug. 1901
. . . I will tell you all from the beginning, but solely what I personally have seen and undergone.

On the 1st of August I was made prisoner at Welverdiend, District Wolmaransstad. In the morning of that day the English under Colonel H – approached my house. The first thing they did was to capture and slaughter all the poultry (about a hundred fowls) and the pigs. They even took a small monkey which had belonged to my little boy who had died a short time before, and to which I therefore told them I was much attached. . . .

They hardly left me ten minutes to get my things together. Though I cried, and told them my husband was a Hollander and had remained neutral, and had an appointment as medical helper to the Boers, it availed nothing. I was obliged to go. . . .

The officers took all my plates and smashed all that was breakable before my eyes, and burned the very valuable books (mostly medical works, and in costly bindings) belonging to my husband. They also took away more than three hundred sheep and silk-goats, and beat them to death with sticks. They took possession of the shepherd with a couple of mules and a horse, and armed our Kaffir boy.

In the evening, as we were incamped at an hour's distance from my house, this Kaffir came to me, and said: 'Oh! my dear missis, now I must shoot my own master, or the English will shoot me down.' I asked him what he had been told to do. He answered that at night he was to be a spy with the English, and search for and capture Boers.

When we left the house they had poured paraffin oil all over it and the other houses in the place, and had set fire to them and burned them with all they contained.

They pull down the churches and burn the pastors' houses.

We were transported to Taungs through District Bloemhof, and wherever the convoy passed, the English burned, destroyed, and captured all and everything; they even took the Kaffirs and servants and burned their straw huts. The food on our road to Taungs was scarce. Sometimes we were left without food or drink for twenty-four hours. . . .

When we arrived at Taungs, our luggage, consisting of bedding and a few clothes, was simply thrown out of the waggons on to the dirty soil, and had to be left there till the afternoon, when each had to get their own things on the railway trucks.

These were exceedingly foul, some covered with coal-dust, others with manure, none of them had even been swept. . . . We had not even sufficient water for drinking!

In that way we had to spend three nights and two and a half days. On some of the trucks were more than fifty women, children and old men. There was no space for sleeping. . . . My eldest child was two years, the youngest two months old; you can understand the state I was in. Happily I nursed the baby, or it would have died from privation. . . .

A few of the English pitied us heartily, and gave us as much help as they could, as for instance getting us some boiling water from the engine to make coffee, but most of them enjoyed the sight of us, and laughed all the time. When we reached Mafeking . . . our things were again thrown out of the trucks, and we were forced to sit and wait till we should be taken to the camp. At last a donkey-cart came for us, and I was conveyed to the camp at 2 o'clock a.m. . . .

Those women in the camp who had been there for some time, and were acquainted with all the horrors, brought us bread and coffee now and again. Some of them had been treated in the same way, and some even more inhumanly.

As for the camp life, it is, in a word, 'slow starvation and defilement.' I cannot thank God enough for having been enabled to leave it so soon, and come out alive with my two children.

The Brunt of the War

CH'IU CHIN (1879–1907) Chinese. Revolutionary leader. Founded newspaper for women in Shanghai. Arrested and beheaded by the Manchu Government.

Untitled Poem

How many wise men and heroes
Have survived the dust and dirt of the world?
How many beautiful women have been heroines?
There were the noble and famous women generals
Ch'in Liang-yu and Shen Yǔ-yin.
Though tears stained their dresses
Their hearts were full of blood.
The wild strokes of their swords
Whistled like dragons and sobbed with pain.

The perfume of freedom burns my mind
With grief for my country.
When will we ever be cleansed?
Comrades, I say to you,
Spare no effort, struggle unceasingly,
That at last peace may come to our people.
And jewelled dresses and deformed feet
Will be abandoned.
And one day, all under heaven
Will see beautiful free women,
Blooming like fields of flowers,
And bearing brilliant and noble human beings.

Reclining Mother and Child, 1906, by Paula Modersohn-Becker

OLIVE SCHREINER (1855–1920) South African. Influential writer and campaigner for transformation of the position of women.

There is, perhaps, no woman . . . who could look down upon a battlefield covered with slain, but the thought would rise in her, 'So many mothers' sons. . . . So many months of weariness and pain while bones and muscles were shaped within; so many hours of anguish and struggle that breath might be; so many baby mouths drawing life at woman's breasts; all this, that men might lie with glazed eyeballs, and swollen bodies, and fixed, blue, unclosed mouths, and great limbs tossed – this, that an acre of ground might be manured with human flesh. . . .' No woman who is a woman says of a human body, 'It is nothing!'

On that day, when the woman takes her place beside the man in the governance and arrangement of external affairs of her race will also be that day that heralds the death of war as a means of arranging human differences. . . .

It is not because of woman's cowardice, incapacity nor, above all, because of her general superior virtue, that she will end war when her voice is finally, fully and clearly heard . . . it is because, on this one point, and on this point almost alone, the knowledge of woman, simply as woman, is superior to that of man; she knows the history of human flesh; she knows its cost; he does not. . . .

It is especially in the domain of war that we, the bearers of men's bodies who supply its most valuable munition, who, not amid the clamour and ardour of battle, but singly, and alone with a three-in-the-morning courage, shed our blood and face death that the battle-field may have its food, a food more precious to us than our heart's blood; it is we especially, who in the domain of war have our word to say, a word no man can say for us. It is our intention to enter into the domain of war, and to labour there till in the course of generations we have extinguished it.

Woman and Labour

BERTHA VON SUTTNER (For biographical details, see p.68.)

It is child's play to destroy enemy fleets in a few minutes by means of pulses of radium radiation transmitted from cloud height. And both sides can do this. Forty eight hours after the so-called 'outbreak of hostilities' each of the warring nations can have defeated the other, leaving no one alive and not a single building standing in enemy territory. . . .

It is up to your will to decide whether or not to take the side of destruction.

Man's Noblest Thought

CARRIE CHAPMAN CATT (1859–1947) American. From 1915 President of National American Woman Suffrage. Supporter of peace and disarmament campaigns. Worked for appointment of women to UN commissions in her eighties. With other members of the International Woman Suffrage Alliance she drew up a manifesto to governments of Europe presented to Lord Grey in July 1914.

In this dread hour when the fate of Europe depends on decisions which women have no power to shape, we, realising our responsibility as mothers of the race, cannot stand passively by. Powerless though we be politically, we call upon the governments of our several countries to avert the threatened and unparalleled disaster. Women see all they most reverence and treasure, the home, the family, the race, subjected to certain damage which they are powerless to avert or assuage. Whatever its result, the conflict will leave mankind the poorer, will set back civilisation, check the amelioration in the condition of the masses on which the welfare of nations depends. We, women of 26 countries in the International Woman Suffrage Alliance, appeal to you to leave untried no method of conciliation or arbitration which may avert deluging half the civilised world in blood.

Quoted in *Carrie Chapman Catt: a Biography*, by Mary Grey Peck

EMMELINE PANKHURST (1857–1928) British. From 1903 leading figure with daughter Christabel in Women's Social and Political Union. Imprisoned for direct violent action in cause of women's suffrage. Although later very active in military enrolment campaigns, she responded at first to calls to support war effort with reserve, seeing the crisis as an opportunity for WSPU workers to rest and renew strength.

Dear Friend,

Even the outbreak of war could not affect the action of the WSPU, so long as our comrades were in prison and under torture.

Since their release, it has been possible to consider what should be the course adopted by the WSPU, in view of the war crisis.

It is obvious that even the most vigorous militancy of the WSPU, is for the time being rendered less effective by contrast with the infinitely greater violence done in the present war, not to mere property and economic prosperity alone, but to human life.

As for work for the vote on the lines of peaceful argument, such work is we know, futile even under ordinary conditions, to secure votes for women in Great Britain. How much less, therefore, will it avail at this time of international warfare.

Under all circumstances, it has been decided to economize the Union's energies and financial resources by a temporary suspension of activities. The resumption of active work and the reappearance of the *Suffragette*, whose next publication will be also temporarily suspended, will be announced when the right time comes.

As a result of the decision announced in this letter, not only shall we save much energy and a very large sum of money, but an opportunity will be given to the Union as a whole, and above all to those individual members who have been in the fighting line to recuperate after the tremendous strain and suffering of the past two years.

As regards the war, the view the WSPU expresses is this:–

We believe that under the joint rule of enfranchised women and men, the nations of the world will, owing to women's influence and authority, find a way of reconciling the claims of peace and honour, and of regulating international relations without bloodshed. We nonetheless believe also that matters having come to the present pass it was inevitable that Great Britain should take part in the war and with that patriotism which has nerved women to endure torture in prison cells for the national good, we ardently desire that our Country shall be victorious – this because we hold that the existence of small nationalities is at stake, and that the status of France and Great Britain is involved.

It will be the future task of women, and only they can perform it, to ensure that the present world tragedy and the peril in which it places civilization, shall not be repeated and therefore, the wspu will at the first possible moment step forward into the political arena in order to compel the enactment of a measure giving votes to women on the same terms as men.

WSPU Circular Letter, 1914

SYLVIA PANKHURST (1882–1960) British. Suffragist, socialist and artist. Unlike her mother and elder sister, Emmeline and Christabel, she opposed the First World War, establishing and editing an anti-war newspaper *The Woman's Dreadnought* (later *The Worker's Dreadnought*).

Prices rose in the first week to famine height; factories were shut down in panic; men and women thrown out of employment. Reservists were called up. Separation allowances were slow in coming, and when they came how meagre! Despairing mothers came to us with their wasted infants. I appealed through the Press for money to buy milk, but the babies were ill from waiting; doctors, nurses and invalid requirements were added, of necessity. Soon we had five Mother and Infant Welfare Centres in East End districts, and a toy and garment factory for unemployed women and girls. Before August, 1914, was out we had opened our Cost Price Restaurants, where twopenny meals to adults and penny meals to children were served to all comers, with free meal tickets for the destitute. The Gunmakers' Arms, a disused public-house, we turned into a clinic, day nursery and Montessori school. . . .

We regarded our relief work as a lever for securing similar institutions from public funds, and were amongst the first to organize such work. We agitated by meetings, processions and deputations to Government departments to protect the people from exploitation by profiteers, to secure that wages should rise with the cost of living, to gain for the women soon flocking from all quarters into what had hitherto been masculine occupations, a rate of pay equal to that of men. We set up a League of Rights for Soldiers' and Sailors' Wives and Relatives to strive for better naval and military pensions and allowances. We opposed attempts to revive the Contagious Diseases Regulations, against which Josephine Butler fought her historic fight. We toiled for the preservation of Civil Liberties, always so gravely attacked in war time. Votes for Women we never permitted to fall into the background. We worked continuously for peace, in face of the bitterest opposition from old enemies, and sometimes, unhappily, from old friends. To us came many tried militant stalwarts of the W.S.P.U. We were giving the lead to a substantial share of the Labour, Socialist and Suffrage organizations. 'We are always two years ahead of the others,' Norah Smyth used to say. Much of this activity hung on me. I had often a stiff fight to keep going with the broken health left to me from the hunger strike.

The Suffragette Movement: an Intimate Account of Persons and Ideals

MRS C. S. PEEL, OBE (died 1934) British. On editorial board of several women's magazines. Director of Women's Service, Ministry of Food 1917–18. Served on various committees in Ministry of Reconstruction. Wrote novels as well as social history.

Amongst the very first results of war psychology was the birth of the spy mania. Even before war was actually declared this burst out and gave rise to absurd and some cruel occurrences. In some cases the lives of foreign governesses and maids who had grown old in the service of British families were made a burden to them. It became necessary to obtain a permit for an alien member of any household. A child, on hearing some discussion on the subject, asked anxiously, 'Oh Mummie, must we kill poor Fräulein?'

How We Lived Then, 1914–18

A. MAUDE ROYDEN (b. 1876) British. Writer, strong supporter of women's suffrage. Edited suffrage newspaper *The Common Cause*, 1912–14. Became the first woman to hold a regular Anglican pulpit.

There is only one way to kill a wrong idea. It is to set forth a right idea. You cannot kill hatred and violence by violence and hatred. You cannot make men out of love with war by making more effective war. Satan will not cast out Satan, though he will certainly seek to persuade us that he will, since of all his devices this has been throughout the ages the most successful. To make war in order to make peace! How beguiling an idea! To make Germans peaceable by killing them with torpedoes and machine-guns – that does not sound quite so well. Yet this is what we set out to do when we 'fight German militarism' with the weapons of militarism.

The Great Adventure: the Way to Peace

JANE ADDAMS (1860–1935) American. Established Hull House (pioneering half-way house for immigrants in Chicago). President of Women's International League for Peace and Freedom from 1915. Expelled from Daughters of the American Revolution for her radicalism in 1917. Awarded Nobel Peace Prize 1931. This is from a speech at Carnegie Hall, New York, 9 July 1915.

Let me say just a word about the women in the various countries. The belief that a woman is against war simply and only because she is a woman and not a man, does not, of course, hold. In every country there are many, many women who believe that the War is inevitable and righteous, and that the highest possible service is being performed by their sons who go into the Army; just as there are thousands of men believing that in every country; the majority of women and men doubtless believe that.

But the women do have a sort of pang about it. Let us take the case of an artist, an artist who is in an artillery corps, let us say, and is commanded to fire upon a wonderful thing, say St Mark's at Venice, or the Duomo at Florence, or any other great architectural and beautiful thing. I am sure he would have just a little more compunction than the man who had never given himself to creating beauty and did not know the cost of it. There is certainly that deterrent on the part of the women, who have nurtured these soldiers from the time they were little things, who brought them into the world and brought them up to the age of fighting, and now see them destroyed. That curious revolt comes out again and again, even in the women who are most patriotic and who say: 'I have five sons and a son-in-law in the trenches. I wish I had more sons to give.' Even those women, when they are taken off their guard, give a certain protest, a certain plaint against the whole situation which very few men I think are able to formulate.

Now, what is it that these women do in the hospitals? They nurse the men back to health and send them to the trenches, and the soldiers say to them: 'You are so good to us when we are wounded, you do everything in the world to make life possible and to restore us; why do you not have a little pity for us when we are in the trenches? Why do you not put forth a little of this same effort and this same tenderness to see what might be done to pull us out of those miserable places?'

That testimony came to us, not from the nurses of one country, and not from the nurses who were taking care of the soldiers on one side, but from those who were taking care of them upon every side.

And it seems to make it quite clear that whether we are able to recognize it or not, there has grown up a generation in Europe, as there has doubtless grown up a generation in America, who have revolted against war. It is a god they know not of, that they are not willing to serve; because all of their sensibilities and their training upon which their highest ideals depend, revolt against the whole situation.

Account of her Interview with the Foreign Ministers of Europe

CRYSTAL EASTMAN (1881–1928) American. Feminist, socialist, labour lawyer and pioneer of industrial safety. Was one of founders of Women's Peace Party and of American Civil Liberties Union, set up to defend conscientious objectors. Was executive secretary of American Union against Militarism. In 1916 she and others *succeeded* in preventing what had seemed an inevitable war between the USA and Mexico. She privately lobbied the US Government, publicly campaigned through American Union against Militarism and organised unofficial meetings between Mexican and American anti-militarists.

. . . we must make the most of our Mexican experience. We must make it known to everybody that the *people* acting directly – not through their governments or diplomats or armies – stopped that war, and can stop all wars if enough of them will act together and act quickly. . . .

Then let us seriously and patiently construct the machinery for instant mobilization of the people for the prevention of any future war that might threaten this country. A war of simple wanton aggression against the United States is unthinkable. There would always be misunderstanding, false national pride, secret diplomacy, financial interests, something crooked at the bottom of it. And our plan for getting the people of the two countries into instant actual contact with and understanding of each other would always prevent it.

This would seem to be the way to begin: first, build up our own organization so that it is a real power in the land and known among liberals *all over the world.* Then educate our membership in what is expected of them if war threatens – so that we can have almost instant mobilization for service. Then get in touch with organizations like ours in other countries – especially those countries expected to be our enemies. Get them to select likely 'Joint Commissioners' who would start to meet ours on an hour's notice. (Our Mexican–American Commissioners have all pledged to start for the border on an hour's notice if war threatens again and their services are needed.) *Have the names and addresses ready.* (We wasted twenty-four hours in the Mexican crisis because we didn't know the name of a single Mexican who would act with us. There's provincialism for you. Let our plan be the beginning of a *practical* internationalism.) Also get these leaders in foreign countries to send us their membership lists. We could then distribute the names among our active members and pledge them to cable at least one 'enemy' a message of good-will to stave off war, if we send out the word. Imagine it! a thousand cables from 'enemy' to 'enemy' stating the firm friendliness of the people and their determination not to fight – all in 48 hours; and meanwhile the heads and subheads of org- anisations busy cabling stories to foreign papers, and a joint conference on its way to meet and *hold the peace.* There never could be a war if our peace forces could mobilize like that in 48 hours.

And there is no step of that program more quixotic or impossible than the El Paso Conference seemed at first.

Suggestions to the American Union against Militarism for 1916–17

EMMA GOLDMAN (For biographical details, see p.73.)

Always on the side of the under dog, I resented my sex's placing every evil at the door of the male. I pointed out that if he were really as great a sinner as he was being painted by the ladies, woman shared the responsibility with him. The mother is the first influence in his life, the first to cultivate his conceit and self-importance. Sisters and wives follow in the mother's footsteps, not to mention mistresses, who complete the work begun by the mother. Woman is naturally perverse, I argued; from the very birth of her male child until he reaches a ripe age, the mother leaves nothing undone to keep him tied to her. Yet she hates to see him weak and she craves the manly man. She idolizes in him the very traits that help to enslave her – his strength, his egotism, and his exaggerated vanity. The inconsistencies of my sex keep the poor male dangling between the idol and the brute, the darling and the beast, the helpless child and the conqueror of worlds. It is really woman's inhumanity to man that makes him what he is. When she has learned to be as self-centred and as determined as he, when she gains the courage to delve into life as he does and pay the price for it, she will achieve her liberation, and incidentally also help him become free. Whereupon my women hearers would rise up against me and cry: 'You're a man's woman and not one of us.'

Living my Life

LELLA SECOR FLORENCE American. Journalist and peace campaigner.
Helped set up Emergency Peace Federation which campaigned against First
World War.

Then came the bombshell. Diplomatic relations with Germany broke
off. . . .

Meanwhile the militarists redoubled their efforts to whip up the war
spirit. Roosevelt (the fire-eating Teddy) was the star actor in a tumul-
tuous meeting in Madison Square Garden. Thousands who couldn't
get in surged round the building and listened to impromptu speeches.
But there was not the undivided enthusiasm for war that the organisers
had expected. There was so much opposition in every part of the vast
throng that the meeting became a riot. Every interrupter was tackled in
approved Fascist style and before long almost every ambulance in the
city was busy carrying the wounded off to hospital. Hundreds were
beaten up, and many of them seriously injured. It wasn't an easy job to
get the Americans to accept war.

We decided that we must hold a counter meeting in Madison Square
Garden as soon as it could be organised. The only date available was in
four days. We booked the Garden, and on the advertising we could do
at that short notice the place was packed, with thousands unable to get
in. We resolved that it would, in fact, be a peace meeting. A large band
of young Irishmen, all of them over six feet high, offered themselves as
chuckers-out. I met them in an ante-room just before the meeting
began. They surrounded me like a small forest of trees, and I wondered
whether they could really restrain themselves, with the light of battle
shining in every eye. I made an eloquent plea. I told them that we had
refused to employ a single additional policeman, that we didn't want a
single person in the audience injured, whatever his views. They
agreed to be as gentle as lambs, and not even to tackle an interrupter
unless he became a thorough nuisance. Then they were just to lift him
out as gently as they could, and put him outside. Well, our meeting
was a thousand times more united than the war meeting had been. But
we had our hecklers. Occasionally, from the platform, I saw two of the
Irish giants lifting a persistent interrupter over the heads of his
neighbours, passing him from one group to another until he was
outside. Not a blow was struck – not a person injured.

We did not Fight 1914–1918. Experiences of War Resisters

MARY WARD (1851–1920) British. Born in Tasmania. As well as writing novels, as Mrs Humphry Ward, she was active in social and educational reform. Founded the Mary Ward Settlement in London. She describes here a visit to an armaments factory where the works superintendent comments on the attitudes of women munitions workers.

'They're saving the country. They don't mind what they do. Hours? They work ten and a half, or with overtime, twelve hours a day, seven days a week. At least that's what they'd like to do. The Government are insisting on one Sunday – or two Sundays – a month off. I don't say they're not right. But the women resent it. "*We*'re not tired!" . . .'

First of all we visit the 'danger buildings' in the Fuse Factory, where mostly women are employed. About 500 women are at work here, on different processes connected with the delicate mechanism and filling of the fuse and gaine, some of which are dangerous. Detonator work, for instance. The Lady Superintendent selects for it specially steady and careful women or girls, who are paid at time and a quarter rate. Only about eight girls are allowed in each room. The girls here all wear – for protection – green muslin veils and gloves. It gives them a curious ghastly look, that fits the occupation. For they are making small pellets for the charging of shells, out of a high explosive powder. Each girl uses a small copper ladle to take the powder out of a box before her and puts it into a press which stamps it into a tiny block, looking like ivory. She holds her hand over a little tray of water lest any of the powder should escape. What the explosive and death-dealing strength of it is, it does not do to think about. In another room a fresh group of girls are handling a black powder for another part of the detonator, and because of the irritant nature of the powder, are wearing white bandages round the nose and mouth. There is great competition for these rooms, the Superintendent says! The girls in them work on two shifts of 10½ hours each, and would resent a change to a shorter shift. They have one hour for dinner, half an hour for tea, a cup of tea in the middle of the morning – and the whole of Saturdays free. To the eye of the ordinary visitor, at least, they show few signs of fatigue.

England's Effort: Six Letters to an American Friend

Why we oppose votes for men

1.
Because man's place is in the army.

2.
Because no really manly man wants to settle any question otherwise than by fighting about it.

3.
Because if men should adopt peaceable methods women will no longer look up to them.

4.
Because men will lose their charm if they step out of their natural sphere and interest themselves in other matters than feats of arms, uniforms and drums.

5.
Because men are too emotional to vote. Their conduct at baseball games and political conventions shows this, while their innate tendency to appeal to force renders them particularly unfit for the task of government.

Alice Duer Miller, 1915

Alice Duer Miller, the American novelist and poet, lived from 1874 to 1942.

Why We Oppose Votes for Men, 1915, by Alice Duer Miller

MAY WRIGHT SEWALL (1844–1920) American. Educated North Western University. Teacher and writer. Established school for girls with second husband. Campaigned for women's suffrage in US.

Now, people say, 'Why a "Women's Peace Party" and why a women's peace movement?' Well, there are some very good reasons why. In the first place, women stand a little outside, quite outside of politics and of commercialism, which are really the causes of war; and women have been able in this terrible time to get a perspective on the situation which men have not been able to acquire; and American women knew that the women of Europe were looking to them to start something which would be an universal protest on the part of women against war. Now, it is a very remarkable thing that while women have been really the great sufferers from war, there has never before in the history of the

world been a women's protest against war. Women have been traditional sort of creatures; they have taken the values, to a large extent,
which men have developed, and they have accepted their lot in life as
one of suffering; but today women are beginning to see life in a
different way and they have decided that they do not have to accept
suffering of this sort. For this reason, the women have gathered
together to make for the first time an organized protest against war. On
Thursday evening, you will see the representation of the 'Trojan
Women.' That is a most poetic and most exquisite representation of the
sufferings of women in war, but it was made by a man and, after all, the
lesson from it is one of submission. Now, women do not want lessons
of submission in connection with war and they have decided to throw
away the old books from which these lessons were learned and to write
anew the opinion, the verdict of the women of today in connection
with this problem of war.

Women, World War and Permanent Peace

MAY SINCLAIR (1865–1946) Served with British Red Cross in Belgium with
a Field Ambulance Corps. Wrote a number of novels as well as a study on the
Brontës. Fellow of the Royal Society of Literature (1916).

There are four thousand of them lying on straw in the outer hall, in a
space larger than Olympia. They are laid out in rows all round the four
walls, and on every foot of ground between; men, women and children
together, packed so tight that there is barely standing-room between
any two of them. Here and there a family huddles up close, trying to
put a few inches between it and the rest; some have hollowed out a
place in the straw or piled a barrier of straw between themselves and
their neighbours, in a piteous attempt at privacy; some have dragged
their own bedding with them and are lodged in comparative comfort.
But these are the very few. The most part are utterly destitute, and
utterly abandoned to their destitution. They are broken with fatigue.
They have stumbled and dropped no matter where, no matter beside
whom. None turns from his neighbour; none scorns or hates or loathes
his fellow. The rigidly righteous *bourgeoise* lies in the straw breast to
breast with the harlot of the village slum, and her innocent daughter

back to back with the parish drunkard. Nothing matters. Nothing will ever matter any more.

They tell you that when darkness comes down on all this there is hell. But you do not believe it. You can see nothing sordid and nothing ugly here. The scale is too vast. Your mind refuses this coupling of infamy with transcendent sorrow. It rejects all images but the one image of desolation which is final and supreme. It is as if these forms had no stability and no significance of their own; as if they were locked together in one immense body and stirred or slept as one.

Two or three figures mount guard over this litter of prostrate forms. They are old men and old women seated on chairs. They sit upright and immobile, with their hands folded on their knees. Some of them have fallen asleep where they sit. They are all rigid in an attitude of resignation. They have the dignity of figures that will endure, like that, for ever. They are Flamands.

This place is terribly still. There is hardly any rustling of the straw. Only here and there the cry of a child fretting for sleep or for its mother's breast. These people do not speak to each other. Half of them are sound asleep, fixed in the posture they took when they dropped into the straw. The others are drowsed with weariness, stupefied with sorrow. On all these thousands of faces there is a mortal apathy. Their ruin is complete. They have been stripped bare of the means of life and of all likeness to living things. They do not speak. They do not think. They do not, for the moment, feel. In all the four thousand – except for the child crying yonder – there is not one tear.

A Journal of Impressions in Belgium

BARBARA FRANCES WOOTTON, BARONESS WOOTTON OF ABINGER (b. 1897) British. Economist and educator. Professor of Social Studies, University of London, 1948–52.

Then the blow fell. On the afternoon of September 4th – too late to get married that day – a further telegram arrived ordering Jack to leave Victoria for service overseas early on the 7th. There was nothing to be done, but to cancel the honeymoon plans, while one of Jack's friends discovered a farm which would be willing to take us after the wedding next day. This was near Haslingfield, a village about six miles from Cambridge, where in my school days I had often sat reading by a stream on solitary bicycle rides.

So, after our marriage on the 5th, to Haslingfield we went in the autumn sunshine, with the last of the corn stooks standing in the fields. Jack was twenty-six and I was twenty, and both of us were, I think, very young for our ages. In the tense emotional climate of the time, we had little conception of what we were doing and little idea of what we might be committing ourselves to. We were indeed strangers and afraid in a world we never made.

The next afternoon we took the train to London, staying overnight at the Rubens Hotel so as to be near the station for Jack's departure next day. Early the following morning, a day and a half after our marriage, I saw him off from Victoria along with a train-load of other cannon fodder.

Five weeks later the War Office 'regretted to inform me' that Capt. J. W. Wootton of the 11th Battalion Suffolk Regiment had died of wounds. He had been shot through the eye and died forty-eight hours later on an ambulance train; and in due course his blood-stained kit was punctiliously returned to me.

In a World I Never Made

DOROTHY MACKENZIE British. Like her fiancé, whose death in the First World War occasioned her temporary blindness, she was admirer of Bertrand Russell and corresponded with him on peace issues, as in this letter.

I assure you Mr Russel [*sic*] that we women want to build, and we unhappily do survive. . . .

It is very difficult to know what to do. I am an elementary teacher, and every class in the school but mine is disciplined by a military method. I have to work as it were by stealth, disguising my ideas as much as possible.. . . It is most sad to teach in these days; underpaid, overworked, the man I loved most killed for a cause in which he no longer believed!

Quoted in *Autobiography of Bertrand Russell*

AVERY GAUL (1886–?) American. Writer, b. Harriet Avery, married composer Harvey Bartlett Gaul. Author of *Five Nights at the Five Pines* (1922), *Vamp till Ready, a Comedy of the Depression* (1932), and, with Ruby Eiseman, *John Alfred Brashear, Scientist and Humanitarian, 1840–1920* (1940).

The War Wife (a song)

You left me lad with a heart of stone.
Where are you boy?
You march with flags while I stumble alone,
Where, where are you boy?

Will you ne'er come back through the long dead years.
Where are you boy?
The song of war is the sound of tears, where, where are you boy?
Where are you boy?

My life grows dark with the redd'ning sun,
My day is nigh and my travail done.
Will you hear our child when the fight is won.
Where are you boy?

GRACE FOAKES (b. 1901) British. Extract is from her account of her London childhood in an East End tenement flat.

There were no ration books and no organised rationing. You just got what you could. We would queue up for an hour for a pound of potatoes, seed potatoes so small they had to be cooked in their jackets. There was no butter or meat for us but sometimes we would get half a pound of margarine which Mother would melt and to which she would then add a meat cube in an attempt to give it a little flavour.

One year at Christmas, there being nothing else to eat, Mother made a large plain boiled pudding which she served to us with some golden syrup (saved for an emergency). I thought it quite funny to be having such a dinner on Christmas Day, but Mother sat and cried as she watched us eat it. We lived on meatless stews, which somehow she made quite tasty.

Between High Walls – A London Childhood

SYLVIA PANKHURST (For biographical details, see p. 84.)

In the side street the other day a little lad, stealing a ride on the tailboard of a motor lorry, fell, in trying to jump off, as the lorry went at full speed. Blood streamed down his face. He shrieked with pain. The children of the street flocked round him with sympathetic cries. Brought by some instinct his father rushed from the baker's shop his face blanched and distorted. He seized the little one in his arms and, stumbling with haste and terror, ran with him towards the nearest doctor's. The crowd of children kept pace with him. The mothers in the neighbouring houses hurried to their doors, grief-stricken, raising their voices in lamentation, overwhelmed by their love and pity for this distracted father and his injured child.

Yet the windows of the baker's shop are broken; they were broken after the last great air raid by angry people who believed, because they were told it by the Press, that they had cause to quarrel with these poor bakers for having been born in Russia and of the Jewish race. When the child was hurt, the natural human instinct of all these children and mothers triumphed over the evil teaching of jealousy and hate, and they saw that this was just one of their little brothers. If only the natural human instinct were given freedom to grow, undistorted by the harsh and unjust social organisation which divides the interest of human kind, we should have no anti foreign riots, no reprisals, no War, and none of the grinding competition which produces degrading poverty even in time of peace.

The Worker's Dreadnought

ROSA LUXEMBURG (1871–1919) German. Revolutionary. Imprisoned for anti-war activities, she organised the Spartacist League (Socialists opposed to the war) with Clara Zetkin and Karl Liebknecht, to whose wife, Sophie, she writes here. Murdered in 1919.

This is my *third* Christmas under lock and key, but you needn't take it to heart. I am as tranquil and cheerful as ever. Last night I lay awake for a long time. I have to go to bed at ten, but can never get to sleep before one in the morning, so I lie in the dark, pondering many things. Last night my thoughts ran thiswise: 'How strange it is that I am always in a sort of joyful intoxication, though without sufficient cause. Here I am lying in a dark cell upon a mattress hard as stone; the building has its usual churchyard quiet, so that one might as well be already entombed; through the window there falls across the bed a glint of light from the lamp which burns all night in front of the prison. At intervals I can hear faintly in the distance the noise of a passing train or close at hand the dry cough of the prison guard as in his heavy boots, he takes a few slow strides to stretch his limbs. The gride of the gravel beneath his feet has so hopeless a sound that all the weariness and futility of existence seems to be radiated thereby into the damp and gloomy night. I lie here alone and in silence, enveloped in the manifold black wrappings of darkness, tedium, unfreedom, and winter – and yet my heart beats with an immeasurable and incomprehensible inner joy, just as if I were moving in the brilliant sunshine across a flowery mead. And in the darkness I smile at life, as if I were the possessor of charm which would enable me to transform all that is evil and tragical into serenity and happiness. But when I search my mind for the cause of this joy, I find there is no cause, and can only laugh at myself.' – I believe that the key to the riddle is simply life itself, this deep darkness of night is soft and beautiful as velvet, if only one looks at it in the right way. The gride of the damp gravel beneath the slow and heavy tread of the prison guard is likewise a lovely little song of life – for one who has ears to hear.

Prison letter to Sophie Liebknecht

SIMONE de BEAUVOIR (b. 1908) French. Prominent writer whose major works include *The Second Sex* and *Memoirs of a Dutiful Daughter*. Close friend of J.-P. Sartre. Here, she describes her feelings as a young girl living in Paris during the First World War.

It was my gradually developing powers of imagination that made the world a darker place. Through books, communiqués, and the conversations I heard, the full horror of the war was becoming clear to me: the cold, the mud, the terror, the blood, the pain, the agonies of death. We had lost friends and cousins at the front. Despite the promises of heaven, I used to choke with dread whenever I thought of mortal death which separates for ever all those who love one another. People said sometimes in front of my sister and myself: 'They are lucky to be children! They don't realize. . . .' But deep inside I would be shouting: 'Grown-ups don't understand anything at all about us!' Sometimes I would feel overwhelmed by something so bitter and so very definite that no one, I was sure, could ever have known distress worse than mine. Why should there be so much suffering? I would ask myself. At La Grillière, German prisoners and a young Belgian refugee who had been excused army service on the grounds of obesity supped their broth in the kitchen side by side with French farm labourers: they all got on very well together. After all, the Germans were human beings; they, too, could be wounded and bleed to death. Why should things be like this? I began praying desperately for an end to our misfortunes. Peace was to me more important than victory. I was going upstairs with Mama one day, and talking to her: she was telling me that the war would probably be over soon. 'Oh, yes!' I cried, 'let it be over soon! No matter how it ends as long as it's over soon!' Mama stopped and gave me a startled look: 'Don't you say things like that! France must be victorious!' I felt ashamed, not just of having allowed such an enormity to escape my lips, but even of having thought of it.

Memoirs of a Dutiful Daughter

ENID BAGNOLD (1889–1981) British. Writer. Art student until she began working as a nurse. Her *Diary without Dates* (1917) about her experiences as a VAD (Voluntary Aid Detachment) caused offence to hospital authorities and she left to join a French transport unit.

O visitors, who come into the ward in the calm of the long afternoon, when the beds are neat and clean and the flowers out on the tables and the VADs sit sewing at splints and sandbags, when the men look like men again and smoke and talk and read . . . if you could see what lies beneath the dressings! When one shoots at a wooden figure it makes a hole. When one shoots at a man it makes a hole, and the doctor must make seven others.

A Diary Without Dates

ADELA PANKHURST (1885–1961) British. Socialist and pacifist. Third daughter of Emmeline Pankhurst. Emigrated to Australia. Adela Pankhurst and Cecilia John sang at anti-war meetings.

I Didn't Raise my Son to be a Soldier

I didn't raise my son to be a soldier
I brought him up to be my pride and joy,
Who dares to put a musket on his shoulder,
To kill some other mother's darling boy?

EMMA GOLDMAN (For biographical details, see p. 73.)

Streams of callers besieged our office from morning till late at night; young men, mostly, seeking advice on whether they should register. We knew, of course, that among them were also decoys sent to trick us into saying that they should not. The majority, however, were frightened youths, fearfully wrought up and at sea as to what to do. They were helpless creatures about to be sacrified to Moloch. Our sympathies were with them, but we felt that we had no right to decide the vital issue for them. There were also distracted mothers, imploring us to save their boys. By the hundreds they came, wrote, or telephoned. All day long our telephone rang; our offices were filled with people, and stacks of mail arrived from every part of the country asking for information about the No-Conscription League, pledging support and urging us to go on with the work. In this bedlam we had to prepare copy for the current issues of *Mother Earth* and the *Blast*, write our manifesto, and send out circulars announcing our forthcoming meeting. At night, when trying to get some sleep, we would be rung out of bed by reporters wanting to know our next step.

Living my Life

Women of England's Active Service League

HELEN HAMILTON British. Schoolteacher.

The Jingo-woman

Jingo-woman
(How I dislike you!)
Dealer in white feathers,
Insulter, self-appointed,
Of all the men you meet,
Not dressed in uniform,
When to your mind,
   (A sorry mind),
   They should be,
   The test?

101

The judgment of your eye,
That wild, infuriate eye,
Whose glance, so you declare,
    Reveals unerringly,
Who's good for military service.
Oh! exasperating woman,
I'd like to wring your neck,
    I really would!
    You make all women seem such duffers!
    Besides exemptions,
    Enforced and held reluctantly,
    – Not that you'll believe it –
    You *must* know surely
Men there are, and young men too,
Physically not fit to serve,
Who look in their civilian garb
    Quite stout and hearty.
And most of whom, I'll wager,
Have been rejected several times.
How keen, though, your delight,
    Keen and malignant,
Should one offer you his seat,
    In crowded bus or train,
Thus giving you the chance to say,
In cold, incisive tones of scorn:
    'No, I much prefer to stand
    As you, young man, are not in khaki!'
Heavens! I wonder you're alive!
    Oh, these men,
These twice-insulted men,
    What iron self-control they show.
    What wonderful forbearance!
But still the day may come
For you to prove yourself
As sacrificial as upbraiding.
So far they are not taking us

But if the war goes on much longer
   They might,
   Nay more,
   They must,
When the last man has gone.
And if and when the dark day dawns,
You'll join up first, of course,
Without waiting to be fetched.
But in the meantime,
Do hold your tongue!
You shame us women.
Can't you see it isn't decent,
To flout and goad men into doing,
   What is not asked of you?

ALEXANDRA KOLLONTAI (1872–1952) Russian. Writer, diplomat, Marxist agitator. Left husband and child, making work her central commitment. Member of Lenin's government until disputes when she became a diplomat abroad.

This extract comes from a novel.

Vasilisa was a communist, and had joined the Bolsheviks when war had broken out. She loathed the war, and while everyone else was busily making up garments to send to the front, frantically working overtime for Russia's victory, Vasilisa obstinately argued with them. War was a bloody business, she said – who needed it? It was nothing but a burden to people. And for all those young soldiers going off like lambs to the slaughter it was an outright tragedy!

Whenever she came across groups of soldiers in the street, marching in military formation, she'd turn her back on them. How *could* they march along so jauntily, singing and yelling at the top of their voices, going off to their deaths as though off on holiday! It wasn't as if they *had* to go, they could easily have refused. If they'd just said we're not going off to be killed or to kill other people like us there wouldn't have been a war at all. . . .

She was the only pacifist in the workshop, and would have lost her job if they hadn't needed workers so badly. As it was, the foreman just gave her a good talking to. Everyone soon knew about her pacifist views, and she was nicknamed the 'Tolstoyan'. All the other women at work tended to keep their distance from her, for hadn't she renounced her country and betrayed Russia? 'A lost cause!' they sighed whenever her name was mentioned.

Love of Worker Bees

MARGARET HOBHOUSE British. Had four sons, of whom three fought in the trenches, one killed. A fourth son, Stephen, referred to here, was imprisoned for refusing to fight. Though she thought war a necessary evil she campaigned fiercely for the rights of conscientious objectors.

To Jack

1 AIRLIE GARDENS, W. 8.
December 8th, 1917.

What a time you must be having! horrible and, I fear, disappointing. Naturally we are frightfully anxious lest you and your guns should be among the lost ones. But we will keep up our spirits, as I am sure you will, whatever may happen. I won't say anything on the situation, it is too involved and difficult, but I can't help thinking that the Lansdowne letter may have paved the way for peace, though perhaps after more fighting of a desperate kind. Paul writes airily of leave for Christmas and rabbit shooting, though perhaps he will be in the trenches, I gather at Ypres or thereabouts.

I wonder where you are? Yesterday I sent . . . a hamper to you and one to Arthur. . . . Eat it with memories of all your happy Christmases with us, literally every one of the twenty-three – a good record. We have decided not to have a tenants' dinner. There is too much sorrow about and anxiety, to meet on festive occasions. Try, dearest Jacko, to get a leave soon, unless indeed things are too grave to think of such a thing. Anyhow you seem to have killed a lot of Germans, which is a desideratum. . . . It is now twelve days since we got a letter. Field postcards would be thankfully received, if no time for writing.

Now for my news. My six months' labours are crowned with success. To-day Stephen has been released! I have made superhuman efforts, written simply hundreds of letters and published several. I sent you one in a really excellent copy of the *Herald*. Stephen and Rosa have gone off to the seaside together, and I hope may live happily ever afterwards and that he may for the future fall in with the Law of the Land, until he can get it altered. His protest has no doubt had its effect and he is at present a very well-known character. I hope he may live to preach the Gospel of Love to a better world.

In the meantime, my dearest boy, my heart is with you in your great struggle and effort. God bless you and keep you!

Quoted in *Margaret Hobhouse and her Family*, by Stephen Hobhouse

IRISH WOMEN'S INTERNATIONAL LEAGUE

In helping to prevent the enforcement of Military Service in Ireland we are helping to prevent the growth of an evil thing. That evil thing is MILITARISM.

Militarism means that the power to fight is given first place in the life of the Nation.

Where militarism prevails, men are valued for their strength in fighting, or their ability to make weapons for killing people. Women are valued for the children they can rear to serve in the armies. Children are taught that battles and fighting and killing of enemies is fine work and are trained to take part in it.

Militarism is tyranny of the worst sort, for it makes men slaves in body and mind. It robs them of freedom to think for themselves and to follow their own conscience. It compels them to sacrifice life without any thought or scruple.

We Irishwomen are not indifferent to the agonies and cruelties of the battlefields of Europe. We love liberty and justice as ardently as any people, and would fight for them as faithfully; but we do not believe that liberty can be won or justice secured through hatred or violence.

In the past four years we have seen men fight and die in thousands for freedom; and yet tyranny grows up in our midst; militarism flourishes in once free countries; all that is beautiful and desirable and useful in life is daily sacrified and set aside. Therefore we appeal to the men of Ireland to help the friends of liberty with other weapons than those of steel, by other methods than those of bloodshed. We appeal to them to carry on the fight for freedom with faith in the powers of reason, justice and the united will of an unconquerable nation.

If we stand out in such a spirit against Conscription and against every form of militarism, we may not only save our own national cause most effectively, but we may win a triumph for the world-cause of Human Liberty.

A New Way

CRYSTAL EASTMAN (For biographical details, see p. 88.)

Why a *Woman's* Peace Party?, I am often asked. Is peace any more a concern of women than of men? Is it not of universal human concern? For a feminist – one who believes in breaking down sex barriers so that women and men can work and play and build the world together – it is not an easy question to answer. Yet the answer, when I finally worked it out in my own mind, convinced me that we should be proud and glad, even as feminists, to work for the Woman's Peace Party.

To begin with, there is a great and unique tradition behind our movement which would be lost if we merged our Woman's Peace Party in the general revolutionary international movement of the time. Do not forget that it was women who gathered at The Hague, a thousand strong, in the early months of the war, women from all the great belligerent and neutral countries, who conferred there together in friendship and sorrow and sanity while the mad war raged around them. Their great conference, despite its soundness and constructive statesmanship, failed of its purpose, failed of its hope. But from the beginning of the war down to the Russo–German armistice there was no world step of such daring and directness, nor of such honest, unfaltering international spirit and purpose, as the organization of the International Committee of Women for Permanent Peace at The Hague in April, 1915. This Committee has branches in twenty-two countries. The Woman's Peace Party is the American section of the Committee, and our party, organized February 1 and 2, is the New York State Branch.

When the great peace conference comes, a Congress of Women made up of groups from these twenty-two countries will meet in the same city to demand that the deliberate intelligent organization of the world for lasting peace shall be the outcome of that conference.

These established international connections make it important to keep this a woman's movement.

But there is an added reason. We women of New York State, politically speaking, have just been born. We have been born into a world at war, and this fact cannot fail to color greatly the whole field of our political thinking and to determine largely the emphasis of our political action. What we hope, then, to accomplish by keeping our movement distinct is to bring thousands upon thousands of women – women of the international mind – to dedicate their new political power, not to local reforms or personal ambitions, not to discovering the difference between the Democratic and Republican parties, but to *ridding the world of war.*

'A Program for Voting Women'

KÄTHE KOLLWITZ (1867–1945) German. Artist and sculptor. Political and social content of her work led to the Kaiser vetoing gold medal awarded for her prints and in 1930s Hitler ordered her works to be removed from public display. A son was killed in the First World War and her grandson in the Second World War.

To Richard Dehmel. Reply by Käthe Kollwitz.
In the *Vorwaerts* of October 22 Richard Dehmel published a manifesto entitled *Sole Salvation.* He appeals to all fit men to volunteer. If the highest defense authorities issued a call, he thinks, after the elimination of the 'poltroons' a small and therefore more select band of men ready for death would volunteer, and this band could save Germany's honor.

I herewith wish to take issue with Richard Dehmel's statement. I agree with his assumption that such an appeal to honor would probably rally together a select band. And once more, as in the fall of 1914, it would consist mainly of Germany's youth – what is left of them. The result would most probably be that these young men who are ready for sacrifice would in fact be sacrificed. We have had four years of daily blood-letting – all that is needed is for one more group to offer itself up, and Germany will be bled to death. All the country would have left would be, by Dehmel's own admission, men who are no longer the flower of Germany. For the best men would lie dead on the battlefields. In my opinion such a loss would be worse and more irreplaceable for Germany than the loss of whole provinces. . . .

I respect the act of Richard Dehmel in once more volunteering for the front, just as I respect his having volunteered in the fall of 1914. But it must not be forgotten that Dehmel has already lived the best part of his

Wounded Men on Duppas Hill, Croydon, by Dorothy Coke

A VAD Convey at Night, a Puncture by the Roadside, by Olive Mudie-Cook

life. What he had to give – things of great beauty and worth – he has given. A world war did not drain his blood when he was twenty.

But what about the countless thousands who also had much to give – other things beside their bare young lives? That these young men whose lives were just beginning should be thrown into the war to die by legions – can this really be justified?

There has been enough of dying! Let not another man fall! Against Richard Dehmel I ask that the words of an even greater poet be remembered: 'Seed for the planting must not be ground.'

KAETHE KOLLWITZ

The Diary and Letters of Kaethe Kollwitz

LADY CYNTHIA ASQUITH (1887–1960) British. Married to Herbert Asquith, son of Prime Minister. Friend of D. H. Lawrence and secretary to J. M. Barrie.

7 Oct. 1918

I am beginning to rub my eyes at the prospect of peace. I think it will require more courage than anything that has gone before. It isn't until one leaves off spinning round that one realises how giddy one is. One will have to look at long vistas again, instead of short ones, and one will at last fully recognise that the dead are not only dead for the duration of the war.

Diaries 1915–1918

SARA TEASDALE (1884–1933) American. Poet. Work much influenced by poetry of Christina Rossetti. Died after an overdose.

There Will Come Soft Rains

There will come soft rains and the smell of the ground,
And swallows calling with their shimmering sound;

And frogs in the pools singing at night,
And wild-plum trees in tremulous white;

Robins will wear their feathery fire
Whistling their whims on a low fence-wire;

And not one will know of the war, not one
Will care at last when it is done.

Not one would mind, neither bird nor tree,
If mankind perished utterly;

And Spring herself, when she woke at dawn,
Would scarcely know that we were gone.

KATHERINE MANSFIELD (1888–1923) New Zealander. Settled in Britain where her short stories received literary acclaim. Married to John Middleton Murry. Died in France of TB. Younger brother was killed in First World War.

London, [November 1918]

. . . These preparations for Festivity are too odious. In addition to my money complex I have a food complex. When I read of the preparations that are being made in all the workhouses throughout the land – when I think of all those toothless old jaws guzzling for the day – and then of all that beautiful youth feeding the fields of France – Life is almost too ignoble to be borne. Truly one must hate humankind in the mass, hate them as passionately as one loves the few, the very few. Ticklers, squirts, portraits eight times as large as life of Lloyd George and Beatty blazing against the sky – and drunkenness and brawling and destruction. I keep seeing all these horrors, bathing in them again and again (God knows I don't want to) and then my mind fills with the wretched little picture I have of my brother's grave. What is the meaning of it all?

The Letters and Journals of Katherine Mansfield

FLORA THOMPSON (1876–1947) British. Worked in postal service and published *Lark Rise to Candleford*, her autobiography about rural life from the turn of the century. One of her brothers, Edmund, was killed in the First World War.

And all the time boys were being born or growing up in the parish, expecting to follow the plough all their lives, or, at most, to do a little mild soldiering or go to work in a town. Gallipoli? Kut? Vimy Ridge?

Ypres? What did they know of such places? But they were to know them, and when the time came they did not flinch. Eleven out of that tiny community never came back again. A brass plate on the wall of the church immediately over the old end house seat is engraved with their names. A double column, five names long, then, last and alone, the name of Edmund.

Lark Rise to Candleford

MRS C. S. PEEL (For biographical details, see p. 85.)

Men were expected to do their duty as a matter of course, but women were first scolded for wanting to work, then gibed at as idlers and slackers and required to become 'Saviours of their country'. Yet during the debate in the House of Lords prior to the granting of the suffrage to women over 30, those on whom it appeared that the safety of the country depended were constantly referred to as 'irresponsible persons'. The vote was 'given' to them in 1918 rather as a biscuit is given to a performing dog which has just done its tricks particularly well.

How We Lived Then, 1914–18

EMMELINE PETHICK-LAWRENCE (1867–1954) British. Suffragist, socialist, pacifist. Co-founder of Women's Social and Political Union but disagreed with latter's militancy and moved towards Women's Freedom League (opposed to violent direct action).

The Armistice was declared on November 11th, 1918, and the nation went wild with joy. On November 25th writs were issued for a general election. The Labour Party of the Rusholme division of Manchester invited me to stand as candidate for Parliament. The sole reason that I accepted this invitation was that an opportunity was offered to explain publicly the reasons why I believed that the only chance of permanent peace in Europe lay in a just settlement after the war. The mood of the country, excited by press propaganda or by the election slogans, 'Hang the Kaiser!' 'Make Germany Pay!' was for vengeance. The idea was fostered that Germany could pay for the entire cost of the war, and dreams of wealth for the country in which all would share seized the imagination of the people.

In Rusholme I found war fever at its height while there was next to no Labour organization to deal with the situation. My thoughts turned to Max Plowman. If anybody could help me to carry out the big task that I had undertaken, he was the one to do it. He came at once at my urgent request. We had little more than a fortnight to convert the mass of electors, who were ready to foam at the mouth with fury at the bare mention of Germany. There was no trouble in getting people to attend meetings, for a woman candidate was a novelty. I realized at once that my supporters were not the women – this election was their chance of 'doing their bit' and they were all for 'going over the top' to avenge their husbands and their sons. My supporters were the soldiers themselves. They spoke from my platform, they canvassed the constituency, and those who were abroad sent letters to be read at my meetings.

Polling took place on December 14th in Rusholme and the rest of the country, but the result was not declared until the men, who were not yet demobilized, sent in their votes from the field. It was these votes which saved my deposit and placed me above the Liberal candidate. It was a strange experience for one who had given eight years of life as I had, in the endeavour to win votes for women, to watch working-class mothers, with their babies and small children, eagerly going to the poll to record their votes against me. But not more strange after all than that soldiers should vote for a pacifist. What really mattered was that the electors on that day voted, although they did not know it, for another world war. The 'khaki election' or 'the coupon election', as it was called, added the sanction of the people of the whole country to the many other inducements afforded to the victors to make the Treaty of Versailles an instrument of vengeance.

My Part in a Changing World

ANGELA BRAZIL (1869–1947) British. Art school education. Travelled widely with mother on death of father. Began writing fiction about girls' public school life at age of 36.

This is our first term since peace was signed. I can remember our first term after war was declared. I was only in IIIa then – quite a youngster! Hetty Hughes, who was head girl, made a speech, and told us what we ought to do to try to help our country. I think some of us here have never forgotten that. We nearly hurrahed the roof off, and we formed a Knitting Club and a Soldier's Parcel Society on the spot. Well, today the Empire is at peace, but our country needs help as much as ever, or even more. It's making a fresh start, and we want the new world to be a better place than the old. Hundreds of thousands of gallant young lives have been gladly given to establish this new world – in this school alone we know to our cost – and we owe it to our heroic dead not to let their sacrifice be in vain. We want a better and a purer England to rise up and make a clean sweep of the bad things that disgraced her before. . . . Of course you'll ask me: 'Well, and how are we going to help?' That's just what I want to talk about. We pride ourselves on being practical at the College. Some of us thought we might start a new society, to be called, 'The Rainbow League'. It's a sort of 'Guild of Helpers', and we want to do all kinds of jolly things to help in the town, something like our old 'Knitting Club' and 'Soldier's Parcel Society', only of course different. We could give concerts and make clothes for war orphans, and toys for the hospitals, and scrapbooks for crippled children. There are heaps of nice things that you'll just love doing. It's called 'The Rainbow League', because a rainbow was set in the sky after the Flood, to help people to remember, and we want, in our small way, not to let the Great War be forgotten, but to do our bit to help the future of the race.

A Popular Schoolgirl

MRS WRIGLEY (b. 1858) British. Worked all her life from the age of eight in a series of manual jobs. One of her earlier employers paid for night classes in reading and writing.

I joined the Suffrage, because having had such a hard and difficult life myself, I thought I would do all I could to relieve the sufferings of others. I took great interest in all women's organisations. When the war broke out, I helped on the Relief Committees all through the war. . . . When investigating cases for relief we came across many pitiful homes where father had gone to the war, and four or five children had to be fed. I don't think we should have had war if the women could have had the vote before, and a voice in it. There's no mother or wife in England nor Germany that would give their loved one to be killed. Now we are working for peace.

Life As We Have Known It, by Co-operative Working Women

HARRIOT STANTON BLATCH (1856–1940) American. Leader in woman suffrage movement. From 1907 to 1915 President Women's Political Union. From 1917 headed speaker's bureau of the US Food Administration.

Women can save civilisation only by the broadest cooperative action, by daring to think, by daring to be themselves.

Mobilising Woman-Power

CARRIE CHAPMAN CATT (For biographical details, see p.82.)

At the American Peace Commission 1918 she demanded a place for women –
   'In every treaty at the close of previous wars, the seeds of new wars have lain dormant. If women are not heard at the peace conference now to be held, this war will not have been a war to end wars!'

Quoted in *Carrie Chapman Catt: a Biography*, by Mary Grey Peck

MARGARET SANGER (1883–1966) American. Arrested in 1915 for violating laws against birth control literature. Established birth control clinic in Brooklyn in 1916.

[Woman] must and will see past the call of pretended patriotism and of glory of empire and perceive what is true and what is false. . . .

She will discover what base uses the militarist and the exploiter make of the idealism of people. Under the clamor of the press, permeating the ravings of the jingoes, she will hear the voice of Napoleon, the archetype of the militarists of all nations, calling for 'fodder for cannon.'

'Woman is given to us that she may bear children,' said he. 'Woman is our property, we are not hers, because she produces children for us – we do not yield any to her. She is, therefore, our possession as the fruit tree is that of the gardener.'

That is what the imperialist is thinking when he speaks of the glory of the empire and the prestige of the nation. . . . Behind the boast of old-age pensions, material benefits and wage negotiations, behind the bombast concerning liberty in this country and tyranny in that, behind all the slogans and shibboleths coined out of the ideals of the peoples for the uses of imperialism, woman must and will see the iron hand of that same imperialism, condemning women to breed and men to die for the will of the rulers.

Upon woman the burden and the horrors of war are heaviest. Her heart is the hardest wrung when the husband or the son comes home to be buried or to live a shattered wreck. Upon her devolve the extra tasks of filling out the ranks of workers in the war industries, in addition to caring for the children and replenishing the war-diminished population. Hers is the crushing weight and the sickening of soul. And it is out of her womb that those things proceed. When she sees what lies behind the glory and the horror, the boasting and the burden, and gets the vision, the human perspective, she will end war. She will kill war by the simple process of starving it to death. For she will refuse longer to produce the human food upon which the monster feeds.

Woman and the New Race

GERTRUDE BUSSEY (d. 1961) American. Professor of Philosophy, Goncher College, USA. Vice President WILPF at time of her death.
MARGARET TIMS (contemporary) British. Author of biographies on Jane Addams and Mary Wollstonecraft. Former Secretary of British Section of WILPF.
WILPF grew from the International Woman Suffrage Alliance whose planned conference in Berlin 1915 was cancelled. From the subsequent Hague International Congress of Women developed twelve committees forming the International Committee of Women for Permanent Peace. At the end of the war its name was changed to the Women's International League for Peace and Freedom, working for the removal of the causes of war. The League is still at work today.

Spontaneously Lida Gustava Heymann rose from the platform and embraced [a French delegate], crying:

'A German woman gives her hand to a French woman, and says in the name of the German delegation that we hope we women can build a bridge from Germany to France and from France to Germany, and that in the future we may be able to make good the wrongdoing of men.'

Mlle Melin replied in an impassioned speech, repudiating the statesmen of Versailles and urging the women of the world to unite their forces internationally. Emily Green Balch rose too and raised her hand in a solemn pledge to work with all her power for the abolition of war. Every woman present at the Congress stood with raised hand and joined her in this pledge. . . .

The whole Congress, indeed, was an occasion of powerful emotion. The marks of war were visible for all to see in the faces of the delegates from the defeated countries. Some had been present four years earlier at the Hague, and the change in them was pitiful. Scarred and shrivelled by hunger and privation, they were scarcely recognisable. The American delegates, especially, were deeply shocked. 'Food is a subject that has never never left my mind for a day since I came here,' wrote Dr Alice Hamilton to a friend at home. The continuation of the Allied food blockade for months after the Armistice, seemed almost a worse crime against humanity than the war itself.

Pioneers for Peace – Women's International League for Peace and Freedom 1915–1965

HUDA SH'ARAWI (1882–1947) Egyptian. Founder member of Egyptian women's movement. Campaigning to reform girls' education, opened own school in 1910. Divorced by husband after her vow to abandon veil in 1923. Attended conference in 1946 calling for abolition of all atomic weapons.

Played a part in nationalist demonstrations against the British in 1919 when League of Nations proceedings revealed Allied promises to the Arab world would not be honoured. Along with over 350 other women she presented this petition to the British High Commissioner.

Your Excellency

We, the women of Egypt, mothers, sisters, and wives of those who have been the victims of British greed and exploitation, present the following petition to Your Excellency. We deplore the brutal, barbarous actions that have fallen upon the quiet Egyptian nation. Egypt has committed no crime, except to express her desire for freedom and independence, according to the principles enunciated by Woodrow Wilson at the Paris peace conference [of 1918] and accepted by all nations, those neutral as well as those involved in the World War.

We present this petition to Your Excellency in the hope that you will convey it to your government, for she has taken upon her shoulders the fulfillment and implementation of the promises made to Egypt [at the League of Nations].

We ask and beseech you further to inform your government of the barbarous actions which have been taking place in Egypt, when your soldiers have been firing on civilians, children, and unarmed men. Why? Because these people have objected, in peaceful demonstration, to your forbidding of Egyptians to leave the country and present their own case at the peace conference, as other nations have done. They were also objecting, in peaceful demonstration, to the British arrest and deportation of some of our Egyptian men to the island of Malta.

We hope, Your Excellency, that our petition, a petition from Egyptian women, will gain your acceptance and approval so that you will then return to the support of the principles of liberty and peace.

Middle Eastern Muslim Women Speak

CORNELIA SORABJI (1866–1954) Born at Nasik in India. Studied at Deccan College, Poona and later read law at Oxford. Returned to India to practise law. First woman to be called to the Bar there in 1919.

The extract is from a speech delivered in Britain at a conference in 1924 to discuss 'The prevention of the causes of war'.

There is a saying, the saying of the people who stand for disunion, whose business in life is to set one person or one nation against another. – 'Do not get too near your enemy; he may be a good fellow after all.' As a matter of fact, your enemy is very often 'a good fellow,' and the people who stand for union are going to try and get near him, are going to get to know him. Moreover, they are going to get nearer and to know better, not only their enemy or some-time enemy, but also those whom at present they call friends and allies, that they may 'understand,' may acquire the understanding heart, which will teach them to realise that there are differences of personality, differences of expression, differences of circumstance, and that all these differences are nevertheless one, and can together be made to yield a reason for union and not for disunion.

I have spoken of the person who unites and of the person who separates. If you think about that, it is not a bad division of people, – the unifiers and the disintegrators. We recognise them in society. Those who are sensitive to atmosphere feel at once when a disintegrator comes into the room. Unifiers are, as it were, the affirmative, and disintegrators the negative side of personality. And the thing which some of us have to remember is to turn away from recognition: for recognition of a disintegrator weakens the affirmative side of our own personality.

'The International Mind in Individuals'

Nie Wieder Krieg! (No More War), 1924, by Käthe Kollwitz

NADEZHDA MANDELSTAM (1899–1980) Russian. Trained as painter, writer. Fluent linguist. Married to poet Osip Mandelstam who was imprisoned in Stalinist times and died in 1938. Wrote two books of memoirs, *Hope against Hope* and *Hope Abandoned*. First name means 'hope'. She comments on the atmosphere of terror during Stalin's era.

When I used to read about the French Revolution as a child, I often wondered whether it was possible to survive during a reign of terror. I now know beyond doubt that it is impossible. Anybody who breathes the air of terror is doomed, even if nominally he manages to save his life. Everybody is a victim – not only those who die, but also all the killers, ideologists, accomplices and sycophants who close their eyes or wash their hands – even if they are secretly consumed with remorse at night. Every section of the population has been through the terrible sickness caused by terror, and none has so far recovered, or become fit again for normal civic life. It is an illness that is passed on to the next generation, so that the sons pay for the sins of the fathers and perhaps only the grandchildren begin to get over it – or at least it takes on a different form with them.

Hope Against Hope: A Memoir

DORA RUSSELL (b. 1894) British. Indefatigable campaigner on many issues, including peace, women and education. Campaigning against nuclear weapons and power in the 1980s.

Hedonism demands a certain degree of security, but not more than we can give to all mankind if we so desire. Away with hypocrisies, timidities, doubts. Away with the darkness of ignorance. Let those men and women who know, who enjoy, and who are unafraid, open the prison gates for the rest of mankind. Let them teach and live, conquer public opinion, show that they can do better than those that traffic in the old wares of superstition and hate. These feed upon destruction and despair, but they shall flourish on security and peace. Let such men and women build a human society in the image of human beings vivid, warm, and quick with animal life, intricate and lovely in thought and emotion. Let this society have the natural grace and agility of an uncorseted body whose form springs from the play of living muscles, whose deftness and sure purpose arise from thought and action closely intertwined. Such a society, by virtue of its inner resilience, would have no need to meet danger, disease, and death with the eternal makeshifts of war, remedial artifice, and trumpery fables. Such a society, like the human beings that composed it, would be at home in the world, not fearing change but perpetually developing in suppleness and wisdom, perpetually devising new forms and new sources of delight.

Men and women, you have not only a right to such happiness, but the means to this happiness lies ready to your hand. Are they so simple that you must forever pass them by?

The Right to be Happy

STORM JAMESON (b. 1891) British. Novelist, playwright and literary critic. An active peace campaigner especially on behalf of exiled writers. Travelled widely in Europe for this work.

Let us not say: 'Will you choose war or peace?' Let us say: 'Will you choose the sovereign independence of your country, armed to enforce its rights, or will you choose peace?' Let us say: 'Our enemies are not the men and women of another country. They are ourselves.' They are elderly professors to whom war is a theme; they are newspaper proprietors who have so few wits or so withered a conscience that they persist in bawling that we should abandon the hope of advancing beyond international anarchy and save ourselves by building more aeroplanes than all the other nations who are building more aeroplanes than all the other nations; they are the interested persons who make instruments of war and sell them, with a happy impartiality, to every country which can pay for them; they are the 'realists' who accept a disorder which exists; they are the romantically-minded who imagine that war is still, after the invention of poison gas and the rest, what they call 'practical'; they are writers in whom it induces a flow of pseudo-mysticism; they are women who commit the indecency of assenting to wars which others will fight; they are all of us in those moments when, losing faith, we think of a war as something other than it is – the blasphemous betrayal of the future of man.

Challenge to Death

HELENA M. SWANWICK (b. 1864) Born in Bavaria; moved to Britain in 1868. Studied Moral Sciences at Cambridge. Wrote for the *Manchester Guardian* and woman's suffrage paper *The Common Cause*. Awarded Order of Companion of Honour for peace and woman's suffrage work.

Women do, I believe, hate war more fervently than men and this is not because they are better than men, or wiser, but because war hits them much harder and has very little to offer them in return. That little would be even less than it is if it were not the sorry truth that, as substitutes for men in wartime, women are given opportunities for training, variety of work, emolument, honours and services which are

(cont'd p. 126)

Women's International Boycott
to Prevent War.

A new effort is being made by women to take action against the tradition that nothing can be done to prevent war.

It is with despair that they see each government taking cover in the face of a deadlock in disarmament, or the negotiations between nations resolving themselves into the final use of armed force.

Women in all nations hate war—they don't want to see their husbands and sons mangled, gassed, or torn to pieces, and they have learnt that many of those who return in safety are nervous wrecks or embittered for life. Women in all nations regard air-raids with dread.

Women know that war means poverty and unemployment, both to those that win and those that lose. Warfare does not settle disagreement.

Women must do something at once, independently of nations, governments, leagues, political parties or the man in the home.

Here is a suggestion—perhaps a world solution. It is so simple that it only needs loyal co-operation from women in all nations to make it effective :—

(1). WOMEN ARE THE WORLD-SHOPPERS.

(2). THEY CAN REFUSE QUIETLY TO BUY ANY IMPORTS FROM A NATION ENGAGED IN OR THREATENING WAR.

(3). IT IS DIFFICULT TO DECIDE IN A WAR WHICH IS THE GUILTY PARTY.

(4). WOMEN CAN ACCEPT THE RULING OF THE LEAGUE OF NATIONS AS TO WHICH COUNTRY IS THE OFFENDER.

Women's International Boycott to Prevent War,

(5). INDIVIDUALLY, THEY ARE FREE TO DECIDE TO BOYCOTT THE AGGRESSOR, OR BOTH WARRING NATIONS, AS A PROTEST AGAINST WAR.

(6). This is direct and passive resistance. It would have a tremendous effect if it came from a body of women in all nations.

(7). No country, party or man would be endangered by this personal refusal.

This idea has been circulated by means of a "snowball" letter, to which, already, there has been an international response.

A notice will be sent from their central committee of the imports which should be boycotted.

Will every woman who agrees and is willing to join in the Boycott of War keep the snowball rolling by—

(a). Sending copies of this leaflet to her friends or writing to them.

(b). Enrolling herself as a member by sending her name to our temporary headquarters :—

The Women's International Boycott of War,

57, Petersham Road, Richmond,

Surrey, England.

Any member can buy a small badge in the shape of a brooch for 8d.

Some Imports to Britain.

ITALY.	ABYSSINIA.	JAPAN.		CHINA.
Almonds.	Hides & Skins.	Cotton.	Silk.	Beans.
Lemons.	Coffee.	Matches.	Toys.	Ground Nuts.
Cheese.	Beeswax.	Copper.	Camphor.	Oils.
Tinned Vegetables.	Ivory.	Ironware.		Cotton.
Fruit.	Civet.	Pottery.		Wool.
Wine.		Porcelain.		Silk.
Stockings.		Straw Plaiting.		Hides.
Silk, Raw.		Knitted Goods.		Metals.
Manufactured.		Matting.		Minerals.
Rayon, Artificial.		Paper.	Peas.	Tea.
Oil.		Tea.	Rice.	
		Refined Sugar.		

Cole & Co. (Westminster) Ltd., Printers, S.W. 1.

by a group of the same name

denied to them in peace time. Even the married woman becomes a person in war and may teach in the schools that are allotted in peace to celibate women only. Old suffragists cannot forget the curious standard of values which resulted in British women being told that they were given the vote in 1918, not on account of their patient toil for ages as workers and mothers, nor in virtue of their common humanity, nor because they had a peculiar contribution to make to political life, but because they had helped to carry on the war. Sometimes, in a nightmare of what might be the logical outcome of this sort of thing, I see women in the near future turning themselves into bombers, as they turned themselves into munitions workers. Why not? They can fly as well as men, they are as brave as men, and it would not take them long to learn the art of releasing bombs. That would release them from the hideous passivity of waiting until men had decided that enough 'women and children and homes' had been destroyed to warrant calling off the devil of war. They would at least have their share in this very peculiar sort of exhilaration; in the sport of kings. . . .

Wars have always taken a heavier toll of citizens, especially of the very young, of the old and of women, than they have of soldiers. In the world war it has been estimated that, while the deaths of soldiers in all countries may have reached ten millions, those of civilians, by pestilence, famine and homelessness, in addition to direct deaths by bombardment and massacre, reached between two and three times that number. . . . The losses of women whose children were maimed and killed or slowly starved have a quality of lonely desolation unmatched even by the sufferings of men in battle.

The Roots of Peace

CLARA ZETKIN (1857–1933) German. Marxist law reformer, pacifist and political anarchist. Jailed in 1914 for anti-war activities.

. . . far too many do not shrink from demanding from the workers once more new sacrifices of blood and property for imperialist wars. 'We went through the World War with its terrible demands and horrors, let the young men now bear what we had to bear,' so declaim, in heroic pose, men who in their time in the trenches piteously complained of being cannon fodder for capitalist profits, and after the conclusion of peace swore, 'no more war.' The meanness of their attitude is self-evident. The progressive workers have always felt it to be their elementary duty that the fight of the 'old generation' should spare oncoming youth the pain that they suffered, in order that the youth might reap where their fathers sowed, in order that they might grow beyond them, promoting the rise of mankind to higher life in freedom and culture. With our glances firmly fixed on the fate, the rights and the tasks of the youth, we say: 'The workers are against imperialist wars.'

In the misery-laden atmosphere, with unemployment totalling thirty-five millions, not a few are led astray by the imperialist war provocateurs and war makers, through the illusion that massacres of the peoples will provide bread. Men and women who for years have suffered bitter want, who have often hungered and frozen for months together without bread or shelter, find employment in war industries. Their propertyless, exploited slave existence compels them to hard servile labour there. The boom in the armament industry allows its controlling, profit-swallowing 'magnates' to pay to individual working men and women and clerks, and to small groups of them, higher wages for overtime and premiums for special output. Such expenditure is tainted with the corruption of bribery for the purpose of splitting the workers and crippling their power of resistance to imperialist wars; they are insurance premiums paid for carrying through the latter. The growth of the armament madness of the bourgeois states increases their military budgets and their need for revenue. For what those employed in the armament industry take home as wages, the masses of the workers must pay in taxes and through tariffs.

The Toilers against War

MAUREEN DUFFY (contemporary) British. Writer and biographer. With others, founded the Writers' Action Group and has worked for establishment of writers' trade union. This piece comes from a novel written in 1975.

Old man Moloch picked up another soldier and bit his head off before stuffing the still wriggling limbs into his maw. A leg twitched over his chin and tickled him until his red tongue lolled and sucked it in. He could never decide whether Tommies or Gerries tasted better, or the rank sauciness of half a dozen poilus. Some days he fancied one, some days another. Austrians he took in a string of sausages, a mess of Alpini bolognesi, a flock of Turkeys. But best of all he decided was a sauerkraut of Russians and Germans. Nearly two million each of them he reached down for and smacked his chops over as he plucked them from their barbed wire pens of the deepfreeze of the snowfields.

He

sat behind his machine gun and waited for Moloch to get him too, tit for rat-a-tat-tat. But when the great hand lifted him up to the rank mouth it opened in a belch and the hand dropped him back, blinded, seared, gasping for air; still kicking.

She

looked up and saw the air which was now Moloch's blood bathtub darken with his new playthings that dropped their load on the streets, and sometimes themselves in a slowly descending inferno, smashing houses and people and nearly a thousand years of the city's invulnerability. The queues stretched for hours while the profiteers and black marketeers got rich quick. Now there was margarine, guns and no butter.

Moloch laughed and pissed all over Europe turning the trenches to mud so men slithered and rotted, became his sewer rats, and between the lines he set his land, Noman'sland where nothing lived or stirred among the craters he had stamped or blasted with his barrage of farts.

So they fed him year after year in the hope that one day he would be satiated and fall asleep. Then the rats who were left could creep out of their holes, run a stake through his heart and bury him forever. But when they tried they found he had no heart and all they could do was lock him up with treaties and leagues until he grew strong enough to break them or one of the rats grew bold enough to let him loose again.

Capital

GERTRUDE STEIN (1874–1946) American. Writer. Studied psychology and medicine. Went to live in France where she became a leading literary figure. Drove ambulances at the Front with her life-long lover Alice B. Toklas.

There is too much fathering going on just now and there is no doubt about it fathers are depressing. Everybody now-a-days is a father, there is father Mussolini and father Hitler and father Roosevelt and father Stalin and father Trotsky and father Blum and father Franco is just commencing now and there are ever so many ready to be one. Fathers are depressing. . . .

Everybody's Autobiography

KATHARINE TREVELYAN British. Writer and broadcaster. Married to Georg Götsch, a music teacher with whom she lived in Nazi Germany. She writes here of her lover Andreas.

One time to our shame we, who were so one, were not in agreement. I felt that every live German who loved his country from his heart should cast himself before this terrible Juggernaut of Nazidom and either help to deflect it to its destruction, or die failing to do so. Andreas was not in agreement, finding some virtue in being alive when the evil storm abated; so at one of our very rare meetings there was silence and tension between us; we had no words – no way to get over our mutual wrath. It was as though our two countries strove within us and could not be at one. We sat silent and aloof. There was no bridge. Then Andreas got up, took off my shoes and stockings, got a basin of warm water and a towel, and kneeling down, washed my feet. I was ashamed – perhaps quite as ashamed as Peter was – but the bridge was built and the traffic and commerce could start again from the one shore to the other.

Fool in Love

VIRGINIA WOOLF (1882–1941) British. Educated at home. Married Leonard Woolf 1912 and started Hogarth Press. Member of the 'Bloomsbury Group'. Wrote novels and feminist texts. Drowned herself during the Second World War in one of her recurrent depressions.

'Therefore if you insist upon fighting to protect me, or "our" country, let it be understood, soberly and rationally between us, that you are fighting to gratify a sex instinct which I cannot share; to procure benefits which I have not shared and probably will not share; but not to gratify my instincts, or to protect either myself or my country. For,' the outsider will say, 'in fact, as a woman, I have no country. As a woman I want no country. As a woman my country is the whole world.' And if, when reason has said its say, still some obstinate emotion remains, some love of England dropped into a child's ears by the cawing of rooks in an elm tree, by the splash of waves on a beach, or by English voices murmuring nursery rhymes, this drop of pure, if irrational, emotion she will make serve her to give to England first what she desires of peace and freedom for the whole world.

Three Guineas

HELENA M. SWANWICK (For biographical details, see p.123.)

There are peculiarities in the lives of women which tend to make them more interested in personality than men, who are too fond of turning human beings into things, so that they may use them; of drilling them to be soldiers, robots, tools, members of a gang; of undermining personality and responsibility, so that no one, in the end, can even say who makes that ghastly thing called war. Blind men of science provide the engines wherewith gallant youths, equally blind, will, at the command of helpless politicians, blindest of all, destroy alike men, women and children. Men have taken that most personal of all motives, religion, have institutionalised it, have locked it up . . . have given the key to priests, and then declared women unfit to be priests. I do not know if they are, but I wish they may be. Men have made of religion an instrument of domination; therefore a cause of war. They have made of government an instrument of domination; therefore a cause of war. Even trade and industry, the arts of speech and of writing they have used to dominate their fellows, to make history and poetry and music the weapons of war. It is time to redress the balance, now that men have devised means wherewith to destroy humanity itself.

The Roots of Peace

STORM JAMESON (For biographical details, see p.123.)

The war began on a day of unusual beauty, clear hot sun, dazzlingly white clouds below a blue zenith, a high soft wind. An old man's dry croaking voice, full of bitterness – more, it seemed, because he had been duped than for any other reason – reached us in the garden.

'Consequently we are at war with Germany . . .'

Journey from the North

EVAN ZIMROTH (b. 1943) American. Dancer, then poet and teacher of English. Published poems include *Giselle Considers her Future* (1978).

Planting Children: 1939

Oh quick, garner the children.
Stash them in baskets, egg crates,
dresser drawers, anywhere;
kiss their thin necks in the hollow
where the blood pulses,
kiss their warm ears. The train already
is raising dust,
the lists are drawn up, the cows
no longer look up from pasture.
It is the iron hinge, the parting.
Now, quick, shove the babies underground
like spuds: let them root there
for forty years, let them
come up story-tellers, all eyes.

Seed Corn must not be Ground, 1942, by Käthe Kollwitz

GERTRUDE BUSSEY and MARGARET TIMS (For biographical details, see p. 117.)

We declare the doctrine that war is inevitable to be both a denial of the sovereignty of reason and a betrayal of the deepest instincts of the human heart. With a sense of our share in the failure to prevent the wars of the past and the present, and in sorrow for the suffering, the desolate and the oppressed, we, the members of this congress, urge the women of all nations to work for their own enfranchisement and unceasingly to strive for a just and lasting peace.

Pioneers for Peace

MARGARET MEAD (1901–78) American. Anthropologist. Studied
cross-cultural comparisons between the lives of women and men. In her
autobiography (1972) she recalls tearing up every page of an almost
completed book on hearing of the bombing of Hiroshima, because 'every
sentence was out of date'.

The tie-up between proving oneself a man and proving this by a
success in organized killing is due to a definition which many societies
have made of manliness. And often, even in those societies which
counted success in warfare a proof of human worth, strange turns were
given to the idea, as when the plains Indians gave their highest awards
to the man who touched a live enemy rather than to the man who
brought ih a scalp – from a dead enemy – because the latter was less
risky. Warfare is just an invention known to the majority of human
societies by which they permit their young men either to accumulate
prestige or avenge their honor or acquire loot or wives or slaves or sago
lands or cattle or appease the blood lust of their gods or the restless
souls of the recently dead. It is just an invention, older and more
widespread than the jury system, but none the less an invention.

But, once we have said this, have we said anything at all? Despite a
few instances, dear to the hearts of controversialists, of the loss of the
useful arts, once an invention is made which proves congruent with
human needs or social forms, it tends to persist. Grant that war is an
invention, that it is not a biological necessity nor the outcome of certain
special types of social forms, still, once the invention is made, what are
we to do about it? The Indian who had been subsisting on the buffalo
for generations because with his primitive weapons he could slaughter
only a limited number of buffalo did not return to his primitive
weapons when he saw that the white man's more efficient weapons
were exterminating the buffalo. A desire for the white man's cloth may
mortgage the South Sea Islander to the white man's plantation, but he
does not return to making bark cloth, which would have left him free.
Once an invention is known and accepted, men do not easily relin-
quish it. The skilled workers may smash the first steam looms which
they feel are to be their undoing, but they accept them in the end, and
no movement which has insisted upon the mere abandonment of
usable inventions has ever had much success. Warfare is here, as part
of our thought; the deeds of warriors are immortalized in the words of
our poets, the toys of our children are modeled upon the weapons of

the soldier, the frame of reference within which our statesmen and our diplomats work always contains war. If we know that it is not inevitable, that it is due to historical accident that warfare is one of the ways in which we think of behaving, are we given any hope by that? What hope is there of persuading nations to abandon war, nations so thoroughly imbued with the idea that resort to war is, if not actually desirable and noble, at least inevitable whenever certain defined circumstances arise?

In answer to this question I think we might turn to the history of other social inventions, and inventions which must once have seemed as firmly entrenched as warfare. Take the methods of trial which preceded the jury system: ordeal and trial by combat. Unfair, capricious, alien as they are to our feeling today, they were once the only methods open to individuals accused of some offense. The invention of trial by jury gradually replaced these methods until only witches, and finally not even witches, had to resort to the ordeal. And for a long time the jury system seemed the one best and finest method of settling legal disputes, but today new inventions, trial before judges only or before commissions, are replacing the jury system. In each case the old method was replaced by a new social invention. The ordeal did not go out because people thought it unjust or wrong; it went out because a method more congruent with the institutions and feelings of the period was invented. And, if we despair over the way in which war seems such an ingrained habit of most of the human race, we can take comfort from the fact that a poor invention will usually give place to a better invention.

For this, two conditions, at least, are necessary. The people must recognize the defects of the old invention, and someone must make a new one. Propaganda against warfare, documentation of its terrible cost in human suffering and social waste, these prepare the ground by teaching people to feel that warfare is a defective social institution. There is further needed a belief that social invention is possible and the invention of new methods which will render warfare as out of date as the tractor is making the plow, or the motor car the horse and buggy. A form of behavior becomes out of date only when something else takes its place, and, in order to invent forms of behavior which will make war obsolete, it is a first requirement to believe that an invention is possible.

'Warfare is only an Invention – not a Biological Necessity'

INGEBORG BACHMANN (1926–73) Austrian. Poet and short story writer. Wrote doctoral thesis on philosophy of Heidegger. Awarded Büchner Prize 1964.

Every Day

War is no longer declared
but continued. The unheard-of thing
is the every-day. The hero
keeps away from the fighters. The weak man
has moved up to the battle zones.
The uniform of the day is patience,
its decoration the humble star
of hope worn over the heart.

It is awarded
when nothing goes on,
when the drumbeat subsides,
when the enemy has grown invisible
and the shadow of everlasting arms
covers the sky.

It is awarded
for desertion of the flag,
for courage in the face of the friend,
for the betrayal of unworthy secrets
and for the non-observance
of every order.

STEVIE SMITH (1902–71) British. Poet, novelist and illustrator. Worked as a publisher's secretary. This piece is a complete short story.

In the Beginning of the War

The British Nation is biological, said the refugee professor to the girl, who was attending some political parties. This party was left-wing political-literary.

135

There was a young refugee doctor of science who had been speaking about underground movements in Germany before the war, messages handed round on cigarette wrappings, it was very exciting, like *I was a Spy*, it had all that appeal.

She spoke to the young doctor afterwards and said he must not think this party was representative of England, the people at this party, she said, were vociferous but had little influence. A shrewd expression came over the doctor's face as she said this and he glanced apprehensively around. I have often wondered, he said, where are the right-wing intellectual persons? Place hunting, said the girl, they are in office perhaps or hope to be. These people . . .? They are writers to-night, their emotions are conditioned by christian ideas, although they would not admit it, a lot of the younger ones are against Christianity they say, but for all that their thoughts have a christian impetus, politically they are immature and vanity is evident in their speeches. (She had been saying this to the professor when he, wishing to dispel her depression, said the British nation was biological.) The girl sighed. I suppose, she said, the groups and societies that these people form have a high nuisance value, but now that the war has started it is I think only a matter of time before Government takes steps against them. That the Government has not already done so, said the Professor, is I suppose a measure of the Government's contempt for them. Yes, sighed the girl, these people are good but they are not wise.

The next day she and the doctor and the professor went to a meeting in a committee room at the House of Commons. It was held by the Inter-University Peace Aims Group. On the platform sat brilliant Sir Sefton Choate, MP for North Devon, flanked by three undergraduates on either side, looking pretty serious. Sir Sefton spoke in detail about a book he had written. The girl had read his book and was interested in his ideas, but, she thought, to put them into action would necessitate a complete upheaval, both social and political, was war the time? She became sunk in gloom and the professor and the doctor too looked grey with sadness. They had so recently come from Halle an der Sale and Vienna. They knew how strong Germany was in the strength of a lie, and how a lie is strong because it can be so much simpler than the truth. Truth, thought the girl, is so many-sided, how long indeed it may take for truth to prevail.

The meeting was now open to discussion. Many people who had

been holding their breath for this moment sprang to their feet, but the Chairman decided who was the first. This one was a clergyman and after coughing a little he said he noticed with something akin he might almost say to consternation that he alone of his cloth had seen fit to come forward in public witness to the ideals for which we were, were we not, fighting, fighting, he would add, a battle not on the Flanders fields but in the hearts of our own people, there must be there, he said, a rebirth, a resurrection, a regeneration . . . he felt . . . After five minutes he sat down although there was a three-minute limit. Three members of the CP then rose simultaneously but after talking it over one stayed standing. He spoke about the unrighteousness of war, the bogey of nazi-ism, the bogey of atrocity stories, the bogey of war sacrifices. Almost before he had finished the Peace Union person was on his feet. All right, the Chairman let him stand. It was much the same. The girl and the professor and the doctor came out during this speech and went to a coffee bar just along the passage. The girl was sorry for the doctor he was so sad. Never mind, said the girl, they have little influence. The bogey of nazi-ism, screamed the doctor. Never mind, said the girl again, for them you must know there is only one bogey, Chamberlain. They also have no experience of war, they will forgive the Germans for the pain they have given to other people. It is not so good to be stoical about other people's sufferings. The Germans have inflicted little pain on England because England is so strong. The conversation went on over the terrible coffee and the sandwiches. In the street, said the girl, the common people are saying: The Germans are asking for it, now they will get it. That is a greater truth than they realize. But perhaps they do realize it. After coming from the committee room I feel humble about the common people because the others are such fools. The girl thought she would write a jingo poem about it, 'For every blow they inflict on Jewry, And other victims of their fury, They ask for death on bended knee, And we will give them death and we, Will give them death to three times three.'

From the cosy House of Commons they looked out on to the bleak plains of war. It will take England a long time to warm up, said the girl, feeling more wretched and like Sam Hoare than ever. Oh, said the professor, certainly England is biological but oh if she would only come to it more quickly and in the end I would say, though it may sound not right with less cumulative strength, there will be very little left when she has finished. They are asking for death, kept on the girl, Freud said the German race had a stronger death wish than any other people. They ask for death, only on death can a new Europe be built. They hold out their hands and ask for death, when we do not give it to them they behave more and more extremely, they cry at last 'Have we not yet earned death?' It is not suffering they ask or I would give, it is death; their peace is the peace of the grave.

After the professor had left them the girl hooked her arm affectionately into the doctor's. As a matter of fact, she said, I feel even more grey with sadness than he. My thoughts go in a dance round my head but the music is sad. They walked in silence by the river. Then she said: I remember before the war none was more fertile and emphatic in atrocity stories than the political person with left-wing inclinations. Then there was indeed revelations. But now because Government sings the sad song at once it becomes for them not true. For they no more than Government care for absolute truth but only for party expediency. The atrocity stories are always true, there is nothing that has been written that has not been done over again many times. The Government book about the atrocities is keyed down, it is not half the truth; the scatological and sexual nature of nazi cruelty Government will not present to the British people because of the law about obscene publication and because of la pudeur anglaise that is so famous.

The doctor now began to weep and silently the tears fell down, he did not sob. He was thinking of the cruelties and that the time was set to death. There is a time in history when death is petitioned, no one shall say the people nay, death they will have. 'From the manure of our corruption . . .' cried the doctor. Yes, said the girl, interrupting, that is the food of our vanity, an age flatters itself on its evil and in a bath of abasement looks to the future for a grand and different birth, we are impatient and death is the scope of our immediacy, pat-come upon command.

ELENA SKRJABINA (b. 1906) Russian. Kept a diary of her wartime experience. Became a refugee after the evacuation from the Siege of Leningrad when one and a half million people died.

November 26 [1941]

The death rate grows. They say that as many as 3,000 people die daily. I don't think this is an exaggeration. The city is literally flooded with corpses. Relatives or friends take them to be buried, tied on by twos and threes to small sleds. Sometimes you come across larger sleighs on which the corpses are piled high like firewood and covered over by a canvas. Bare, blue legs protrude from beneath the canvas. You can be certain this is *not* firewood.

You observe death so closely every day that you stop reacting to it. The feeling of pity has vanished. No one cares. The worst thing is the harsh realization that it is scarcely likely that we will escape the common fate. Sooner or later they will carry us out and throw us into a common grave. It is impossible to bury each corpse separately. There aren't enough coffins. If relatives want to have a proper funeral, they must wait until a coffin is freed, that is, until the preceding corpse is driven to the gravesite, taken out of his coffin, buried, and the coffin handed down to those next in line.

November 29

My former maid, Marusa, appeared unexpectedly, unexplainedly. She brought a loaf of bread and a voluminous sack of cereal. Marusa is unrecognizable. She is not the same barefoot, unkempt girl I knew. She wore a squirrel jacket, an attractive silk dress, and an expensive scarf. Added to all this, a blooming appearance . . . just as if she had come from a vacation. She is not at all a citizen of a hungry, embattled city. I asked why. It turns out that the reason is very simple. She works in a food warehouse. The director of the warehouse is in love with her. Whenever the workers are searched before they leave, Marusa is searched just for the sake of appearance. She carries out several kilos of butter, sacks of cereal, rice, and canned goods – all hidden under her fur jacket. Sometimes, she says, she has even managed to take out several chickens. She takes everything home, and in the evenings the director comes to eat and relax. At first Marusa lived in a dormitory. Then her brigade leader made her aware of the advantages of joint living and invited Marusa to live with her. Now this woman makes use of Marusa's rich harvest to feed her own relatives and friends. Obviously, she is a very clever person. She has completely taken charge of foolish and good-hearted Marusa and under the guise of a kindly person exchanges Marusa's food products for various things. Thus, Marusa's wardrobe has improved. She is delighted over these trades and little interests herself with where her precious booty goes. Marusa told me all this naïvely, adding that now she will try to see to it that my children did not go hungry.

Writing this, I have to think about what is happening in our unfortunate, besieged city. Thousands of people die daily, but some people have the richest comforts even under these conditions. True, during Marusa's visit I did not consider these things. Moreover, I begged her not to forget us and offered her anything which might interest her.

Siege and Survival

STEVIE SMITH (For biographical details, see p.135.)

The Poets are Silent

There's no new spirit abroad,
As I looked, I saw;
And I say that it is to the poets' merit
To be silent about the war.

DIANA ATHILL (b. 1917) British. Worked for the BBC during the Second World War and afterwards as a publisher. The following extract is from her autobiography.

I was no longer a pacifist in any formal sense. To make gestures against the war once it had come seemed as absurd as to make gestures against

(cont'd p. 142)

Centerville, California, May 9th, 1942, by Dorothea Lange

In Spring, 1942, the US government ordered 110,000 residents (⅔ native-born Americans) of Japanese ancestry to be defined as aliens and moved to a number of large internment camps. This was a response to the Japanese attack on the US naval base at Pearl Harbor, Hawaii, in 1941.

an earthquake or a hurricane. The horror had materialized and it must be endured, but to *participate* in it any further than I was compelled to do by *force majeure* did not occur to me. A mute, mulish loathing of the whole monstrous lunacy was what I felt; almost an indifference to how it ended, for no matter who won the war, it had happened; human beings – and I did not recognize much difference between German human beings and English ones – had proved capable of making it happen, and that fact could never be undone.

This refusal to take any part not forced on me seems to me now an unmistakable measure of smallness of spirit. To remain detached from the history of one's time, however insane its course, is fruitless even on the private level, since only by living what is happening (whether by joining it or by actively opposing it) can the individual apprehend its truth. Detestable as the 'white feather' mood of the First World War certainly must have been, an expression of all that was most ridiculous in 'patriotism' and most hysterical in suffering ('My man is going to be killed so why shouldn't you be killed too?'), it had in it a grain of truth: there can be no separateness from the guilt of belonging to the human species – not unless the individual withdraws into a complete vacuum and disclaims participation in the glories as well. There are two honest courses when war strikes: either to make some futile but positive gesture against it and suffer the consequences, or to live it – not in acceptance of its values, but in acceptance of the realities of the human condition. I did neither, and I have no doubt that I was wrong. . . .

It follows, naturally, that one should be to some extent 'engaged' at all times, not only in times of crisis: that I am no less wrong now than I was then, since I still take no part in any sort of political or social activity; I have never marched against the hydrogen bomb, I have never distributed leaflets urging the boycotting of South African goods. Whether, believing this, I shall some day turn to action, I do not know: given my record, it seems unlikely. Both by conditioning and by instinct I continue to cling to the wrappings of self-indulgence which keep safe my privacy and my female sense of another kind of truth running beside the social one: the body's truth of birth, coupling, death that can only be touched in personal relationships, and in contemplation.

Instead of a Letter

LOUISE YIM (b. *c.* 1900) Korean. Her efforts to free Korea from foreign domination and to improve the position of women in that country are recorded in her book.

On the heels of my refusal to co-operate, I received an order from the Japanese Army to vacate the school building. Friends came to me in last-minute efforts to make me change my mind. I refused. I began to suspect some of these friends. I wondered how many of them were compromisers who were fulfilling their obligations to the Japanese by trying to influence me.

When military officials came to take over the school, I told them, 'You will have to kill me before any soldier steps inside my school building. I have traveled thousands of miles and worked day and night for ten long years to establish this school. As long as my soul remains on earth, I will not let you enter. The school cannot be used for any other purpose but educating Koreans.'

The Japanese threatened and pleaded and tried 'logic.'

'The Army has the right to use any building it wants. If all school buildings in Japan and Korea are being used for the Army, you must give up your building too.'

I would not compromise.

One morning, I looked out of my window and saw a company of Japanese troops dismounting from trucks. They formed ranks and marched toward the school. I rushed to the door and stood in front. The Japanese officer ordered me away.

'You will have to run a bayonet through me if you want to enter.'

He shouted commands. His men fixed bayonets. He ordered me to leave for the last time. I did not move. And then he marched his men back to the trucks and they drove away. I had expected to die. I did not know why they withdrew.

The story spread throughout Seoul and into the provinces. I had been the first Korean to defy the Japanese to their face without suffering arrest, torture, or death.

My Forty Year Fight for Korea

AUSTRALIAN WOMEN'S WEEKLY

Women's part in the war is to be steadfast. The King's message is clear. . . . Women have their own battleground in this war. They are the second line of defence. The majority serve best by keeping the family cheerful and happy, in keeping the doors of the home bolted against uncertainty, panic or nerves. Men must fight and women work so that peace may come again. Mouths must be fed, beds made, socks darned. The cycle of women's work must go on, and in these simple everyday tasks women find a reservoir of courage which is an inspiration to their children . . . they must try to make their home a sanctuary – somewhere where can be forgotten for a little time the madness of this world. . . . Homemaking is our greatest key industry and the women running our homes have a tremendous task and a responsibility. Particularly is this so in wartime.

Editorial, 7 October 1939

PEARL S. BUCK (1892–1973) American. Missionary and writer. Childhood in China with missionary parents. Won Pulitzer Prize in 1932 and Nobel Prize for Literature in 1938. Based permanently in USA from 1934.

. . . incredible as it may seem to the rational mind, many women do really believe that merely because they are women they are more moral than men – 'nicer', if you like, more fastidious and purer and more spiritual. I cannot pronounce that word 'spiritual' aloud. I have not done so for years. It arouses such feelings of repulsion and ferocity in me that I feel my tranquillity menaced. For, content with their so-called spiritual superiority, women have let their souls rot into pettiness and idleness and vacuity and general indifference in a world crying and dying for want of real superiority of spirit and moral worth, so that the spectacle does not bear contemplation. If women were really superior to men in righteousness or spirituality, could they sit blind and deaf and dumb, knitting their interminable knitting, crocheting and talking and going to teas and bridge parties and knitting again, and filling the theatres day in and day out, and rolling bandages and knitting again, and exchanging recipes and knitting, and re-arranging their furniture and curling their hair and painting their nails and going to fashion shows and knitting, knitting, knitting, while the world goes down to darkness and dismay through lack of bold goodness and moral integrity and real unselfishness? Where is this moral superiority that will do nothing but knit while heads roll off in revolutions and war crashes upon our great cities so that ruins are all that we shall have left if the world goes on as it now is?

Of Men and Women

NELLA LAST (b. *c.* **1890)** British. As a volunteer observer for Mass-Observation, an organisation set up in 1937 to 'record the voice of the people', she kept a diary of her life in Barrow, Lancashire, during the Second World War.

Friday 4 December 1942

We all came out from the canteen early, as the evening squad turned up well on time, and there was a good number of them. As I was getting my coat, a quiet tired voice asked for the one in charge, and when I went back I saw a haggard man in civvies, who had a suit-case. He wanted to sell Christmas decorations – folded paper-chains, awful-looking roses etc. He said he was a discharged soldier, and would have shown his papers. A cold chill seemed to blow on me – like when you see the first falling leaves, which tell of bitter winter only round the corner. The phrase, 'discharged soldier', brought such visions of the last war's aftermath. We *must* have plans, water-tight plans, to avoid it after this war. *Surely,* if the countries of the world spent the same money on peace, for one year, as they do for war, it would be a help. I don't understand about 'markets' and 'economics' – I'm very dumb – but I know how I plan ahead and work in my own little sphere, so that things go fairly smoothly, or as well as it is in my power to make them. . . .

Thursday, 19 August 1943

Two women have sat side by side for years at the Centre, sewing at bandages. One has lost two sons at sea – and now learns her airman

Ruby Loftus Screwing a Breech-ring, by Laura Knight

Commissioned by the Ministry of Munitions as testimony to the accuracy and precision of women workers in manufacturing armaments.

son has to be 'presumed dead'. Her daughter had to join the W.A.A.F. The other one's three sons work in the Yard – have good jobs – and the daughter of twenty-eight is 'reserved', since she is considered necessary as a secretary to a boss in the Yard. I look round the big room at faces I've known and loved for over four years. My heart aches and, even in that small circle, the bravery and courage, the 'going on' when only sons have been killed, when letters don't come, when their boys are taught to fight like savages if they are commandoes – when they are trained and trained and *trained*, for bodies to endure, and to go and kill other women's lads, to wipe all the light from other mother's faces.

Nella Last's War

YOKO MATSUOKA (b. 1916) Japanese. Educated in USA, including some years at Swarthmore, a Quaker college. Returned to Tokyo in 1939. Her autobiography describes her attachment to two cultures.

About this time, all unmarried girls who were not working outside of their homes were recruited to work in factories. It was no longer patriotic to marry young and bear many children. The old slogans disappeared from sight, and women were exhorted now to produce 'more airplanes.' Kwoko [my sister] commented cynically, 'It would take twenty years before a human being could be useful as a soldier. Apparently the Government decided they couldn't wait that long. And pregnant women are not very useful in factories.'

Daughter of the Pacific

ANNE FRANK (1929–45) Dutch. Daughter of German Jews. Family hid from Gestapo from 1942 until discovered in 1944. Anne died in Bergen-Belsen concentration camp 1945. Her diary was found by neighbours in the hide-out. These extracts were written when Anne was 14.

Wednesday, 19th April, 1944

My darling,
Is there anything more beautiful in the world than to sit before an open window and enjoy nature, to listen to the birds singing, feel the sun on your cheeks and have a darling boy in your arms? It is so soothing and peaceful to feel his arms around me, to know that he is close by and yet to remain silent, it can't be bad, for this tranquillity is good. Oh, never to be disturbed again, not even by Boche.

Yours, ANNE.

As you can easily imagine we often ask ourselves here despairingly: 'What, oh what is the use of the war? Why can't people live peacefully together? Why all this destruction?'

The question is very understandable, but no one has found a satisfactory answer to it so far. Yes, why do they make still more gigantic 'planes, still heavier bombs and, at the same time, prefabricated houses for reconstruction? Why should millions be spent daily on the war and yet there's not a penny available for medical services, artists, or for poor people?

Why do some people have to starve, while there are surpluses rotting in other parts of the world? Oh, why are people so crazy?

I don't believe that the big men, the politicians and the capitalists alone are guilty of the war. Oh, no, the little man is just as keen, otherwise the people of the world would have risen in revolt long ago! There is an urge and rage in people to destroy, to kill, to murder, and until all mankind, without exception, undergoes a great change, wars will be waged, everything that has been built up, cultivated and grown, will be destroyed and disfigured, after which mankind will have to begin all over again.

I have often been downcast, but never in despair; I regard our hiding as a dangerous adventure, romantic and interesting at the same time. In my diary I treat all the privations as amusing. I have made up my mind now to lead a different life from other girls and, later on, different from ordinary housewives. My start has been so very full of interest, and that is the sole reason why I have to laugh at the humorous side of the most dangerous moments.

I am young and I possess many buried qualities; I am young and strong and am living a great adventure; I am still in the midst of it and can't grumble the whole day long. I have been given a lot, a happy nature, a great deal of cheerfulness and strength. Every day I feel that I am developing inwardly, that the liberation is drawing nearer and how beautiful nature is, how good the people are about me, how interesting this adventure is! Why, then, should I be in despair?

Yours, ANNE.

The Diary of a Young Girl

Girl with Baggage for Transport, by Ruth Heinova

Ruth Heinova: born 19 February 1934, in Prague. Deported to
Theresienstadt 30 July 1942. Died 23 October 1944 in Auschwitz.

ALENA SYNKOVA (b. 1929) Czechoslovakian. Born in Prague. Deported to
Theresienstadt concentration camp, July 1942, where she wrote this poem.
Returned home after the liberation.

I'd Like to Go Alone

I'd like to go away alone
Where there are other, nicer people,
Somewhere into the far unknown,
There, where no one kills another.

Maybe more of us,
A thousand strong,
Will reach this goal
Before too long.

Starvation Winter, 1944, by Emmy Andriesse
Taken during the German Occupation of Holland.

FANIA FENELON (b. 1918) French. Singer. Member of French Resistance.
Here, she is writing of her imprisonment in Auschwitz, 1943–5. This extract
describes a rare occasion when a group of women were allowed to go for a
walk outside the prison.

We set off on foot. Well-shod, warmly dressed, we emerged from the
camp like smartly turned-out princesses, or so we thought. It was good
to walk along a road. Under a stiff layer of snow, I saw a bit of yellowed
grass: 'Look, Clara, grass! It still exists.'

I was about to stop, but the sight of our guard prevented me. He was
so young that he shouldn't have been hardened yet, unless of course
he was all the more fanatical because of it, but his eyes, which had a
fine golden look to them, glinted coldly when they came to rest on us,
as empty as the gaze of the others, all the others.

What was marvellous was that, as we moved away from Birkenau,
the frightful smell of burnt flesh which always filled our nostrils faded,
giving way to smells of life. It was an easy two miles to Auschwitz,
which seemed to be a peaceful little town. Its Polish roofs, rather flat
and snow-covered, stood out clearly against the cold, pale winter sky.

'Fania! Houses – chimneys with smoke.'

It was true. This smoke was that of people who were alive, warming
themselves, preparing food; it was light, blue and yellow, so different
from that which, black as soot and thick as tar, billowed from our
crematoria.

People were going quietly about their business; the shops had
windows even if there was not much in them. We passed a few people,
women, little old ladies trotting along, elderly men. Not a single young
person of either sex. Where were they? At the war? It was a silent town;
the snow we sank into muffled all noise. As we passed, no one turned
round, no one vouchsafed us a look. There was neither curiosity nor
hostility; we didn't exist. When would we cease to be nothing?

These people, doing normal things, going in and out of their houses,
these women doing their shopping, holding young children with
apple-red cheeks, did they know that they were happy? Did they know
that it was marvellous to see them, that for us they represented life?
Why did they begrudge us a look? They couldn't fail to notice us, to
know where we came from; our striped garb, the scarfs hiding our
shaven heads, our thinness betrayed our origins. When they went out

walking, they were not forbidden to pass by the camp of Birkenau, whose sinister appearance hardly concealed its function. Did they think that those five chimneys, with their sickening smoke, were for the central heating? What exactly was I asking for? That that little town of five or six thousand inhabitants should revolt, that its Germanic population, resettled there since the German victory, should rise up and liberate the camp? Why should they have felt responsible for us? A sudden surge of violence sent the blood into my head: they were all responsible! All men were. The indifference of a single one was our death sentence.

I stared at them intensely. I didn't want to forget their ratlike faces. They didn't see us. How convenient! They didn't see our striped clothes any more than they saw the detachments of 'moslems' who wandered haggard through their peaceful little town, surrounded by SS and dogs. I was sure that later, after the war, those people would say that they 'didn't know', and they would be believed.

The Musicians of Auschwitz

GERTRUDE ELIAS (contemporary) Austrian. Graphic artist and journalist. Has campaigned for third world, peace movement and women's rights, organising many exhibitions and editing Movement for Colonial Freedom's journal *Liberation*.

Psychoanalysts and psychologists in war-worn poverty stricken Vienna did not dare attack the establishment – the system, which was responsible for war and unemployment. Instead they coined such terms as 'inferiority complex' and 'the death wish' which they pretended were 'deeply ingrained in human nature'. This political escapism and pessimism of the psychologists had a dismal and demoralizing effect on a generation faced with the rise of fascism in Central Europe. It conditioned them to accept 'failure' as a personal calamity and 'guilt-feelings' drove thousands to take their own lives instead of fighting those who were really guilty.

A medical profession which literally has its finger on the pulse of the population will be compelled to side with the progressive forces and demand radical changes of a social system which breeds misery, alienation and disease.

'Poverty, Politics and Mental Health'

JILL TWEEDIE (b. 1936) British. Writer, particularly on women's issues. Regular contributor to *The Guardian* newspaper.

Fritz Stangl was an ordinary Austrian cop when he met and married Teresa, his wife. He loved her and she loved him and they continued to love each other for thirty-five years until they were parted by his death. A-a-h. How romantic. Mind you, Teresa Stangl admits she was terribly angry when her husband volunteered to join the Austrian Nazi Party:

> I just knew that day that he wasn't telling me the truth. And the thought that he had lied to me all this time, he whom I had believed incapable of lying, was terrible for me. And to think – oh, it was a terrible blow, just a terrible blow. My man . . . a Nazi . . . It was our first real conflict – more than a fight. It went deep. I couldn't . . . you know . . . be near him, for weeks, and we had always been so close; this had always been so important between us. Life became very difficult.

But not, of course, *too* difficult – love surmounts such obstacles, that is what love is for. Frau Stangl, a devout Catholic herself, managed to surmount the next obstacle, too, though with misgivings. Fritz signed the Party's form renouncing his allegiance to the Catholic church. 'That was the second awful blow for me: finally we couldn't talk about it any more.'

To test her love further, Fritz Stangl was sent as police superintendent to a pleasant, well-to-do suburb of Berlin, to the General Foundation for Institutional Care. There he was told his future duties. He reported to Schloss Hartheim, pleased still to be in Austria and close to his beloved wife. His duties were to supervise the gassing of 'patients' – the first stage of Hitler's euthanasia programme. For years, while countless thousands of 'patients' were killed at Hartheim, Fritz Stangl saw his wife frequently. She asked what he was doing but only casually, since she was used to her Fritz being unable to discuss service matters. Frau Stangl was, on her own admission, aware of the existence of the euthanasia programme, but says she did not know Schloss Hartheim 'was one of those places' till after the war.

Fritz Stangl's second promotion made him Kommandant of Sobibor. 'I can't describe to you what it was like,' said Stangl to Gitta Sereny who interviewed him in prison after the war:

> The smell. Oh God, the smell. It was everywhere. Wirth wasn't in his office. I remember, they took me to him . . . he was standing on a hill, next to the pits . . . the pits . . . they were full . . . full . . . I can't tell you; not hundreds, thousands, thousands of corpses . . . oh God. That's where Wirth told me – he said that was what Sobibor was for. And that he was putting me officially in charge. . . .

Now Frau Stangl was married to a man whose work was supervising the mass murder of a race, a promotion from merely gassing those considered 'unworthy to live', the criminally insane, the mentally deficient, the tubercular and, of course, the odd gipsy, homosexual and political hostage. Under Stangl, about 100,000 men, women and children were gassed. Herr Stangl ordered specially tailored riding-boots and white jodhpurs and jacket. Staying at a nearby house on one of her visits to her husband, Frau Stangl was told by a drunken officer exactly what was happening at Sobibor. She was horrified.

> When he rode up and saw me from afar, his face lit up – I could see it. It always did – his face always showed his joy the moment he saw me. He jumped off his horse and stepped over – I suppose to put his arm round me. But then he saw at once how distraught I was. 'What's happened?' he asked. 'The children?' I said, 'I know what you are doing in Sobibor. My God how can they? What are *you* doing in this? What is your part in it?'

Fritz Stangl eventually calmed his wife, telling her he was only in charge of construction work. She says she cried and sobbed and couldn't bear him to touch her.

> He just kept stroking me softly and trying to calm me. Even so, it was several days before I . . . let him again. I can't quite remember the sequence of events, but I know I wouldn't have parted from him in anger.

Not long afterwards came the final promotion. Herr Stangl was made Kommandant of Treblinka, the largest of the five death camps in a two-hundred-mile circle around Warsaw. . . . The official figure given for the deaths Stangl supervised is 900,000. . . .

And what of the loving wife during this time, the wife married to the man named in an official commendation as 'the best camp commander in Poland'? Why, she was busy with women's work. On one of his brief visits to her 'we started our youngest, Isolde'.

Can we excuse Frau Stangl, say she was a victim of events she never understood, believe she was bewildered and confused, afraid for her children, caught up in the general chaos of the holocaust? Surely we can say, at the very least, what could she have done? How could she, a mere woman and loving wife, possibly have attempted to change the inevitable?

Gitta Sereny put a question to her after her husband's death in 1971:

> Would you tell me what you think would have happened if at any time you had faced your husband with an absolute choice; if you had said to him: 'Here it is; I know it's terribly dangerous, but either you get out of this terrible thing, or else the children and I will leave you.' If you had confronted him with these alternatives, which do you think he would have chosen?

Frau Stangl took more than an hour to answer that question. She lay on her bed and she cried and then she composed herself and answered:

> I have thought very hard. I know what you want to know. I know what I am doing when I answer your question. I am answering it because I think I owe it to you, to others, to myself; I believe that if I had ever confronted Paul [her pet name for Stangl] with the alternatives: Treblinka or me; he would – yes, he would, in the final analysis, have chosen me.

Teresa Stangl, a small pretty woman from Linz, could have persuaded one of the nine camp commandants of Nazi Germany to leave his post and flee. It is impossible to tell what repercussions this might have had, how many others might have been given a flash of humanity, a burgeoning resistance, through this event. But though she loved her husband deeply – *because* she loved her husband deeply – she did nothing. No one had ever suggested to her that love has some morality, that to be 'in love' did not excuse horror outside the cosy family circle, that responsibility to the outer world must intrude. Blinkered, devoted, worried but faithful, whenever she had the opportunity she received her man into her bed, fresh from the naked shit-stained Jews, clutching their babies, whipped into the chambers. And in so doing, she lived out to the extreme the article of our faith: love conquers all.

The view that women are the natural guardians of morality is not my view. In essence, women have the same proclivities as men towards good or evil. Nevertheless a large part of the female sex has been forced into the guardian role through history, if only because the strictures of society have weighed more heavily upon them and their opportunities for action have been very much more limited. Confined, in both senses, their habitat has always been love or what passed for love, an intimacy with the personal feelings of those around them, husbands, sons and lovers. So women are the mirrors that best reflect the intrinsic amorality of love – the record of men loving or living with monsters is thin as women monsters are thin; powerless, bounded by domesticity, it is hard to wreak much havoc in the world.

In the Name of Love

ANNA PAWELCZYNSKA (b. 1922) Polish sociologist. Member of Resistance, for which she was arrested in 1942. Spent two years in Auschwitz. Later, wrote a study of relationships in concentration camp, from which this is an extract.

It is not true that 'suffering enobles.' Suffering can strengthen, but it can also totally shatter. Life can be lived within the conventions of decency without banging one's head against the wall of human misfortunes. But should there arise in a person a real need for such an understanding, should he be capable of tearing himself away from normal routine, should he manage to turn his back on socially sanctioned personal ambitions and egoisms – he will expose himself to a life considerably more painful but perhaps richer. The understanding of ultimate situations allows one to look life or death in the eye with courage; it allows one to view the affairs of men against the background of history. It also enables one to understand that the ability to inflict terror and commit crime and the capacity to resist violence have shaped the history of one generation after another. Only the psychic and historical manifestations of that resistance are different.

Introduction to *Values and Violence in Auschwitz*

CHRISTA WOLF (b. 1929) (East) German. Novelist, writer and editor. A socialist critic of the State. In this novel Christa and her family are refugees fleeing from the advancing Russian army.

In January 1945 she traveled west with the last vehicles to get away, in the small cabin of a munitions truck. Worse than actual events was the fact that not even the horror itself could surprise one now. Nothing new under this sun, only the end, as long as it lasts. And the certainty: that it had to come. That's what a village inn must look like when mankind conspires to crowd into it, everyone, because of an unknowing fear. Pale-faced women, exhausted children, and soldiers about their daily business of moving away and on. The weariness that doesn't only come from six nights without sleep; the most important thing slips through one's fingers, and one doesn't even notice it. It is crouching on the floor; lucky if you've got a bit of wall to lean against. Christa T., to ward off despair, pulls a child to her lap. Then the radio overhead begins to roar: once more, even in hell itself, this fanatical overplayed voice, loyalty, loyalty to the Führer, even unto death. But she, Christa T., even before she's understood the man, feels herself going cold. Her body, as usual, has understood before her brain has, and the brain now has the heavy task of catching up, working up the terror that's in her limbs. So that is what it was all about, and this is how it must end. There's a curse on the people sitting here and on me as well. Except that she can't stand up any more when the song comes: there it is. I'm staying here. I'll hug this child. What's your name? Anneliese, a pretty name . . . *Über alles in der Welt* . . . I'm not going to raise my arm any more. I have the child, small warm breath. I won't sing the song with them any more. How they sing, the girls sitting along the bar; and even the soldiers, who were smoking and cursing as they leaned against the wall, stand up stiffly, pulled up straight by the song. Oh, your straight backs. How shall we ever stand up straight again?

The Quest for Christa T.

NELLY SACHS (1891–1970) German. Poet. Nobel Prize for Literature 1966.
Escaped from Nazi Germany to Sweden in 1940. This poem is written in the
Jewish mystical tradition.

Chorus of the Rescued

We, the rescued,
From whose hollow bones death had begun to whittle his flutes,
And on whose sinews he had already stroked his bow –
Our bodies continue to lament
With their mutilated music.
We, the rescued,
The nooses wound for our necks still dangle
before us in the blue air –
Hourglasses still fill with our dripping blood.
We, the rescued,
The worms of fear still feed on us.
Our constellation is buried in dust.
We, the rescued,
Beg you:
Show us your sun, but gradually.
Lead us from star to star, step by step.
Be gentle when you teach us to live again.
Lest the song of a bird,
Or a pail being filled at the well,
Let our badly sealed pain burst forth again
and carry us away –
We beg you:
Do not show us an angry dog not yet –
It could be, it could be
That we will dissolve into dust.
Dissolve into dust before your eyes.
For what binds our fabric together?
We whose breath vacated us.
Whose soul fled to Him out of that midnight
Long before our bodies were rescued
Into the ark of the moment.
We, the rescued,

We press your hand
We look into your eye –
But all that binds us together now is leave-taking,
The leave-taking in the dust
Binds us together with you.

TAKAKO OKIMOTO (b. 1937) Japanese. Written when aged 15 about the A-bomb falling on Hiroshima when she was 8.

The 6th of August 1945 – which I do not forget – the things that happened this day are deeply carved in my heart. That cruel war that snatched away so many precious human lives in one second – even now I shudder when I think of it. I am all alone after losing my father and mother and all my brothers and sisters. And no one can take their place. All of them, as a result of that A-bomb, were struck down one after another. My oldest brother was never found after he left to work with the Labor Service Group. My second brother's whole body was covered with burns and he died the next day at the Koi Grammar School. We left his body there at the Koi school and Father and Mother and the rest of us returned to the country. Since there were no good doctors in the country, my mother returned to town for treatment. At night a man came saying that she had become suddenly worse and called us back to town. My father and my little sister and I took the first morning train to town. When we arrived a strange, bad odor was rising everywhere, and the sights we saw! Everything imaginable was in ruins. You could not see a trace of the former Hiroshima. When we somehow managed to reach home we found that Mother had breathed her last a few minutes before. I cried for all I was worth. We cremated Mother's corpse on the stony river bed. Here and there all along the shore people were cremating corpses. And that evening just after we arrived back at my uncle's house in the country with Mother's ashes, my big sister died. Because I was still so little I didn't know what I ought to do but I put all my energy into nursing the father and sister who were left to me. But my little sister who was so cute died the day after my big sister's funeral. Father was able to go to my big sister's funeral but he no longer had any strength to get up for my little sister's funeral. I wonder whether the priest who came for my sisters' funerals had also breathed the poison? He was no longer around at the time of Father's funeral.

As they all died like this one after another, there is no doubt that my father who lasted the longest must have lost all hope.

But even so when I asked him, 'Father, how are you this morning?' Father always answered to keep my spirits up, 'This morning I feel a little better.'

The fact was, his bodily health kept getting only worse. Full of anxiety over me because he was leaving me all alone, Father departed from this world.

Before he died Father often said, 'Father doesn't want to die. Since our house and our clothes have all been burned by the A-bomb, let's both of us go in our rags to the country and be farmers.' He said this often.

On the 15th of August Japan finally became a defeated country. Many beggars appeared in front of the station, and thieves and armed bandits have turned up one after the other, and it has become a world where you aren't safe for a minute.

What has caused this sort of thing? It is because of war. If there were no wars such miserable people would never appear and the world would always be a place of peace. In the new Constitution, renunciation of war is determined. Even if it isn't a case of war between one country and another, even inside the country of Japan, in spite of the fact that we are the same kind of people, there is always war going on. As long as this is the case we will not become a peaceful country. In order to build a peaceful country, I believe we must first be considerate of each other.

Children of the A-Bomb

CALL TO A NATIONAL DELEGATION OF AMERICAN WOMEN FOR PEACE

On August 8, 1945, ONE HUNDRED AND FORTY THOUSAND PEOPLE were killed in a fraction of a second when the Atom bomb was dropped on Hiroshima by order of the U.S. Government. Thousands of women and children were maimed for life and still others will give birth to a generation of deformed human beings.

Five years later, the threat of Atomic war hangs over us.

The present conflict in Korea, costing the lives of our husbands and sons and those of Koreans, has brought the danger of an Atomic World War even closer. Such a war would mean total destruction for us, our children, and for all mankind.

On August 8, 1950, a national delegation of women will go to Washington to see President Truman. We will demand that neither the Atom nor the Hydrogen bomb will be used by our government now – in Korea – or ever, anywhere in the world.

We will urge, as women, as mothers, who are being asked to give the lives of our sons to war, that every possible step be taken by our government to achieve a peaceful settlement of the fighting in Korea.

We believe that to admit the legal and effective government of China to the United Nations would restore the United Nations to its proper function and set the machinery in motion for the pacific settlement of all disputes between nations. We believe that Prime Minister Jawarahal Nehru's proposals for the mediation of the Korean conflict should be re-examined. We believe that such proposals would form the basis for a peaceful solution of the war in Korea.

The time for such mediation is NOW . . .
before more of our boys are sacrificed!

Already plans for total war mobilization are taking place. War taxes threaten to wipe out wage gains of millions of workers. The housing program is crippled. Profiteers, taking advantage of death in Korea, are raising the prices of food, clothing and other necessities, bringing them beyond the reach of millions.

AS MOTHERS, AS WOMEN, WE DEMAND THAT THIS BE STOPPED!

WE REFUSE TO ACCEPT A FUTURE FOR OUR CHILDREN, OUR FAMILIES, AND OUR PEOPLE, IN WHICH THE GREAT RESOURCES OF OUR NATION ARE USED FOR WAR, NOT PEACE, AT HOME AND ABROAD.

We believe that the great resources of our country now being made available for war should be used for the fulfillment of our democratic heritage.

TEN BILLIONS – which is to be allotted for war preparations – can provide jobs, decent homes, more schools, health protection and an adequate standard of living for all Americans in a land in which our children can grow up in peace and happiness.

It is because we so strongly believe in the necessity for peace, that we, AMERICAN WOMEN FOR PEACE, Negro and white, from nationality groups, civic organizations, church groups, parent-teacher associations, peace organizations, trade unions, professional groups and housewives have UNITED FOR PEACE.

THE AMERICAN WOMEN FOR PEACE invite you to join with us in this National Women's Delegation for Peace *to carry our demands to our President and to our Congressmen.*

An aroused womanhood for peace can do what statesmen, militarists, heads of governments and the United Nations have failed to do!

MOTHERS WHO FIGHT FOR THE LIVES OF THEIR CHILDREN CAN SAVE THE PEACE!

AMERICAN WOMEN WANT PEACE AND LIFE . . . NOT WAR AND DEATH!

JOIN THE AMERICAN WOMEN'S PEACE DELEGATION!

Come to Washington on August 8th!

The Fight for peace is every woman's fight!

JACQUETTA HAWKES (b. 1910) British. Archaeologist and writer. Assistant principal of post-war reconstruction secretariat. Worked for UNESCO. Active in Campaign for Nuclear Disarmament in the 1950s.

Jacquetta Hawkes wishes it to be known that she can no longer support Britain's unilateral disarmament in the changed circumstances of the 1980s.

Even a blind person entering the large Assembly Hall at Church House would have known this was an extraordinary meeting. It sounded quite unlike any other. For the voices were those of hundreds of women filing into their seats without a single manly bass to deepen the pitch. But the sound had none of the shrillness one notices in a girls' school or even in a women's college; this must, I think, have been because the audience were of all ages, from the students to elderly women, and the older voices softened the total blend.

It had been raining all day, and now was raining harder than ever.

War Business, by Gertrude Elias

163

All the tickets had been sold several days before, but quite a large queue of women hopeful of getting places was lined up in Great Smith Street. The management of Church House, whether because they disliked the meeting, or because it is how they would normally behave, were so hostile to the queuers when they asked if they might come into the ample corridors to escape the downpour, that, without the slightest provocation, they actually called in the police. A peacemaker from the Campaign arrived in time to end this one-sided war. . . .

The overall plan of the programme was to begin on a note of cool intellectual argument, with emphasis on the genetical dangers which are of such special concern to women, and to work up to a deliberate and controlled evocation of emotion. Many people have accused the leaders of the Campaign of emotionalism, and they in turn have denied it, but as the Chairman said at the beginning of the meeting, with the evident approval of the audience, there is such a thing as *right emotion* and women are more able than men to experience it without shame, and act upon it with intelligence.

The first speech came from Marghanita Laski. . . . Her closely-reasoned arguments against the claims that Britain's possession of the Bomb really made us a first-class power, strengthened our influence with the United States, or deterred Russia from attacking us, was followed by a speech by Dr Winifred de Kok, the TV Women's Doctor. . . . Dr de Kok . . . spoke with a simple appeal that would have held the least intellectual member of a Mothers' Union. Yet while she was talking of the horror for women of an increased expectation of defective children, she was also expressing the all-important moral case against the statistical view of human life. Ten thousand freak babies may be a minute percentage of the world's births, but to calculate individual suffering with decimal points is the beginning of evil.

Dr Antoinette Pirie, who followed, is probably the most effective of the scientific speakers for the Campaign. She has a sympathetic warmth about her, and while she is meticulous in her facts, she has none of that refusal to relate them to opinions and value judgements, that makes most scientists appear such wan neuters in public debate. After estimating the harm already done to all the peoples in the world by bomb tests, and the incalculable damage to our genetical inheritance that would result from nuclear war, she flung in the grimly humorous suggestion that male sperm should be banked now, and AID made compulsory for many generations of mothers after a war. Children only half of whose genes were damaged might offer a chance for the survival of the species.

After this mental harrowing, the audience were allowed a little relief by Mrs Amabel Williams-Ellis's lively exposure of the dishonest futility of preparations for Civil Defence. The opening half of the meeting ended with what might be called the first of the set pieces. The actresses Frances Rowe and Rosamund John read extracts from the press and official publications, carefully arranged in counterpoint to suit the two alternating voices. As the almost incredible expressions of stupidity, folly and madness built up by way of the expendability of Britain, to space warfare, megacorpses and city-sized craters, the audience made sounds of indignation, horror and bitter amusement, evidently following every shot in this quick-firing repartee.

The second part of the programme began with three young women speaking for two or three minutes each – as a student (Hope Edwards, secretary of the Combined Universities Committee), as a teacher of philosophy (Iris Murdoch who gave a mathematically exact analysis of relative and absolute reasons for opposing our nuclear armament), and an 'ordinary' mother of young children (Mrs Macaulay). After this arpeggio, Diana Collins struck a full chord with her fine, direct declaration of the moral issue as she saw it as a Christian. Her final moving plea for international morality in place of an utterly discredited 'realism' led to the frankly emotive part of the evening, as Mrs Edita Morris, who with her husband runs the Hiroshima Rest Centre, rose to introduce letters written to her by the wife of a young Japanese who was dying of radiation leukaemia thirteen years after his exposure.

Jill Balcon has great restraint combined with intense sensibility and as she finished the letters (so unemotionally and sometimes so naïvely written) with the death of the man and the widow left wondering if she too, with her children, must soon face the same ghastly suffering, the hush in the hall was complete. By a common understanding, no one applauded. Second after second went by of this numbed, motionless silence. It was a cruel situation for the next performer, and it is doubtful whether anyone but Peggy Ashcroft could have carried it off. To follow this tragedy of real life with anything but a great work of art, required unique powers, but she possesses them. The beauty of her voice combined with her extraordinary ability to project emotion enabled her to bring the exhortation to women to resist war, which had been written for the occasion, to a telling climax.

'Women against the Bomb'

WOMEN'S GROUP of the Campaign for Nuclear Disarmament.
The meeting referred to is the one described in the previous extract by Jacquetta Hawkes.

If tennis players wear frilly knickers, if film stars have babies or divorces, if skirt lengths go up or down, this is news.

Yesterday, through pouring rain, some 800 women filled to the doors a meeting in London on nuclear disarmament. . . .

This was a serious and profoundly moving meeting which collected the amazing sum of £700 and which could well start a women's movement against Britain's nuclear armaments at least as powerful as the movement for women's suffrage.

Unfortunately, apart from the *Daily Worker*, this meeting was virtually ignored by the Press. . . .

It seems that so long as we are trivial, we are assured of space in the Press. When we are deeply serious over a matter of life and death we are ignored.

Press Statement, *Daily Worker*, 30 June 1958

KATHLEEN LONSDALE (1903–71) British. Scientist, pacifist. Imprisoned in 1943 for refusing to register for civil defence duties. Visited Russia during the Cold War as a Quaker representative. This extract comes from the Swarthmore lecture she gave in London in 1953.

All forms of non-violent resistance are certainly much better than appeasement, which has come to mean the avoidance of violence by a surrender to injustice *at the expense of the suffering of others* and not of one's self, by the giving away of something that is not ours to give. This meaning of appeasement, the buying of peace for ourselves temporarily by pandering to international blackmail, has rightly come to be despised and to be regarded as an encouragement to aggressors and despots. It should be distinguished sharply from the admission, which personal or international integrity might sometimes demand, that we have made a mistake or have ourselves done wrong, and are ready to make open amends or to reverse our policy. No considerations of national or individual prestige should prevent the correction of error when it is realized. This is a *sine qua non* in the search for truth, and is evidence of strength and not of weakness of personal or of national character, even when it means temporary humiliation.

When, however, our own hands are clean, then oppression should be met by a truly non-violent campaign, which even though it may involve civil disobedience *under Divine compulsion*, must not involve any hatred or bitterness. The aim is to prevent oppression or despotism, by changing the heart of the oppressor; and therefore the one essential axiom involved is that in human nature there is something inherently good, that there is, as Friends put it, 'that of God in every man', to which an appeal may be made. It was this belief that constituted the power of Gandhi over his fellow-countrymen as well as over those whose actions and attitude he wished to change. It was a partial understanding of this belief that enabled more than 300,000 Indians to suffer undeserved imprisonment rather than to obey unjust laws. Not many of them, of course, realized as clearly as Gandhi did the fundamental aim of their action even when he had explained it to them, but it was nevertheless an appeal to the better nature of those who had made the laws and it succeeded to the extent that India was freed from British domination without revolution, though it took about 25 years to do it.

Friends are not naïve enough to believe that such an appeal to 'that of God' in a dictator or in a nation which for psychological or other reasons is in an aggressive mood will necessarily be successful in converting the tyrant or preventing aggression. Christ was crucified; Gandhi was assassinated. Yet they did not fail. Nor did they leave behind them the hatred, devastation and bitterness that war, successful or unsuccessful, does leave. What can be claimed, moreover, is that this method of opposing evil is one of which no person, no group, no nation need be ashamed, as we may and should be ashamed of the inhumanities of war that are perpetrated in our name and with our support.

Early Friends often referred to the element of goodness inherent in man as the 'Seed'. A seed does not grow instantaneously; it needs the constant stimulus of warmth and nourishment over a considerable period of time for effective germination. Even then it may die. But who are we to say when a seed has really died? The refusal of the Tolstoyans to perform military duties in Russia has not apparently succeeded in lessening the dependence on military might of the Soviet Union, any more than the protests of a few Quakers and others have succeeded in lessening the dependence of the western powers on atomic weapons. But Tolstoy's books are, even today, very widely read indeed in the U.S.S.R., and it may yet be that God will perform the miracle of spring in that country, with our help or without it. Meanwhile our main responsibility is with our own country and its government and policies, with those whom we may help and not with those who may harm us.

Removing the Causes of War

DORA SCARLETT British. Worked for the English Section of Radio Budapest 1953–6. Her book relates events leading up to and during the uprising in Hungary in October 1956.

The tanks squatted like great toads across Stalin Avenue, outside the railway stations, and at every bridgehead. The Soviet troops did not commit many atrocities. . . . But they were different from the troops of the first intervention [two weeks earlier], of whom so many had deserted to the Hungarians. The troops of the second intervention had been rushed in from Rumania and the Ukraine at top speed; they had been thrown into battle at once, and had had only the crudest political instruction about their task; they had been told that they were going to fight 'fascists, landlords and capitalists'. It was said that some of them thought they were in Berlin; others thought they were at the Suez Canal [because of British–French military presence there], and mistook the Danube for it; this I am convinced was only a 'Budapest joke' but, like most Hungarian jokes, it had its kernel of political truth. When things calmed down and the boys and girls who had learnt Russian at school tried out their knowledge on the Soviet troops, they found that most of them had only the vaguest notion of what had been happening in Hungary, and what justification there could be for their own part in it.

Window onto Hungary

MARTHA GELLHORN (b. 1908) American. War correspondent for *Collier's Weekly* in Spain, Finland, China, England, Italy, France, Germany and Java; and war correspondent for *The Guardian* newspaper in Vietnam and Israel.

I do not hope for a world at peace, all of it, all the time. I do not believe in the perfectibility of man, which is what would be required for universal peace; I only believe in the human race. I believe that the human race must continue. Our leaders are not wise enough, nor brave enough, nor noble enough, for their jobs. We, the led, are largely either sheep or tigers; we are all guilty of stupidity, the ruling human sin. This being so, we can expect wars; we have never been free of them. I hate this fact and accept it.

But nuclear war is unlike any other kind of war that has threatened mankind, and cannot be thought of in the old known terms. Nuclear war reaches a dimension unseen before in history. That dimension is towering, maniacal conceit.

The Face of War

SIMONE DE BEAUVOIR (For biographical details, see p. 98.)
In writing of an Algerian woman tortured by French soldiers, de Beauvoir exposes events in French colonial Algeria and calls for peace.

'I am only one among thousands of other detainees,' Djamila told her lawyer the other day, and that is no less than the truth. There are fourteen thousand Algerians confined in French camps and prisons, seventeen thousand in gaol in Algeria itself, and hundreds of thousands more filling the Algerian camps. The efforts made on Djamila's behalf would fail in their purpose if they did not create a general revulsion against the suffering inflicted on her fellow-prisoners – sufferings of which her own case furnished a by no means extreme example. But any such revulsion will lack concrete reality unless it takes the form of political action. The alternatives are simple and clear-cut. Either – despite your willing and facile grief over such past horrors as the Warsaw ghetto or the death of Anne Frank – you align yourselves with our contemporary butchers rather than their victims, and give your unprotesting assent to the martyrdom which thousands of Djamilas and Ahmeds are enduring in your name, almost, indeed, before your very eyes; or else you reject, not merely certain specific practices, but the greater aim which sanctions them, and for which they are essential. In the latter case you will refuse to countenance a war that dares not speak its true name – not to mention an Army that feeds on war, heart and soul, and a Government that knuckles under to the Army's demands; and you will raise heaven and earth to give this gesture of yours effective force. There is no alternative, and I hope this book will help to convince you of the fact. The truth confronts you on all sides. You can no longer mumble the old excuse 'We didn't know'; and now that you *do* know, can you continue to feign ignorance, or content yourselves with a mere token utterance of horrified sympathy? I hope not.

Introduction to *Djamila Boupacha*

SALLY MUGABE (contemporary) Born in Ghana. Married Robert Mugabe and worked with him for independence of Zimbabwe. Secretary of Women's Affairs in first Zimbabwean government.

In 1962 the women held their first public demonstration. It was during this demonstration that Sally along with 2,000 women was arrested. They all had decided to hold a protest demonstration at the office of the Prime Minister, Edgar Whitehead. Early that morning they converged upon the Prime Minister's office. The police came and told them to disperse. The women insisted that they wanted to see the Prime Minister in order to hand him a resolution. But the police gave them an ultimatum. When it expired the women still refused to leave; so the police arrested them all. They were subsequently charged with trespassing and obstruction.

'They put us into police jeeps and took us to prison. In a few minutes the news had spread all over the country and other women started protesting and they, too, were arrested. In Salisbury alone, over one and a half thousand women were arrested, some with babies on their backs, others with children screaming.'

They were taken to court but refused to plead guilty, arguing that they had done nothing wrong beyond protesting peacefully and legally. They were nevertheless convicted and sentenced to six weeks' imprisonment or fined six pounds each. They all decided to go to prison since some of the women were earning such low wages that they could not afford to pay the fine.

Although they suffered greatly positive things happened while they were in prison. Their plight was reported in the world media and for the first time the world heard that the women of Zimbabwe had joined the men to fight oppression.

'My life in the struggle'

PEGGY DUFF (d. 1981) British. Political campaigner. Active from the start in the Campaign for Nuclear Disarmament.

It [CND] started, or rather they started, for there were many of them, in the late fifties in response to the escalation in nuclear testing and in the quantity and quality of nuclear weapons. They were fed by crises that threatened us with nuclear annihilation, from Berlin to Cuba. The campaigns spread across the world party because fall-out does not discriminate between countries and partly because in the new small world in which we live campaigns tend to proliferate as rapidly as weapons and wars. Where are they now? Quite a lot of them are dead – in Canada, in Scandinavia, in Australia. Others have widened their aims to new concerns – in the United States, in Germany, in France. CND persists in Britain – but the CNDs no longer dominate the peace movements or the Left.

You could blame it on frustration. They won mass support for what looked like a simple, single issue and, in the absence of any real progress except in general awareness of the nuclear danger and one partial test ban treaty, most of them declined or died. That is the simple answer, but not the only answer. The trouble is and was that the simple moral issue to which the campaigns clung as the source of all evil was a symptom rather than a cause. The invention and development of nuclear weapons co-incided with and was fed by a similar escalation in the cold war. But it was the cold war which enlarged the danger and made the weapons so threatening. The two were indivisibly linked. CND in Britain partly recognised this when it extended its aims from 'Ban the British Bomb' to 'Ban the Blocs', but not wholly, for the main reason for the change was ethical. There was little political recognition that the bombs were the children of the blocs, that the blocs were the offspring of the cold war, and that the cold war was sustained and nourished by political systems, especially in the West, but also in the East. It is not surprising, therefore, that frustration erupted. There were too many people in CND who disliked and distrusted politics and too few with either the will or the capacity to transform the movement into a different and more political entity.

So they remained, especially in Britain, issue-orientated campaigns, concerned only with nuclear disarmament. CND agreed to oppose chemical and biological weapons because, like nuclear weapons, they are indiscriminate. But for anything else it did it insisted on providing a link with the issue of nuclear war. So they excused their involvement in protest against the war in Vietnam by the danger of a nuclear world war in Indo-China – as if, but for that, it would have been acceptable. . . .

Disarmament has degenerated into controlled rearmament which perpetuates the hegemonies of the two Great Powers. The Non-Proliferation Treaty did nothing to restrict their stockpiles of nuclear weapons and, more recently, faithful Britain has been assisting the United States in continuing the use of chemical weapons in Vietnam by tabling a treaty at Geneva which concerns only biological weapons and by excluding CS gas from its interpretation of the 1925 Geneva Protocol. Co-existence between the USSR and the US continues to increase. There remains the over-riding danger that such co-existence could leave one or both free to act against China, against revolution and liberation in the Third World or within their own spheres of influence.

What can the campaigns do? They can wrap themselves up in their single issues and in the purity of their pacifist concerns, ignoring the essential links between repression and arms, between imperialisms and the arms race, between liberation, revolution, and peace. If so, they will, no doubt, survive and do good work, mounting small campaigns on single issues in Ruislip, Porton or Nancecuke. But, in my view, this is a form of escapism, like peace research. If we want to be an integral part of a world movement seeking a dual liberation – of the oppressed of the Third World, and of the repressed of the developed world, we have to relate to that, for wars will cease and disarmament will become a practical possibility only in the context of these two liberations. But as long as the dual repressions continue, new movements will arise and it may be possible that radical change will come, not through orthodox organizations with carefully worked out programmes and ideologies, but from a mass refusal to conform, even by the technocrats who are the new proletariat of industrialized societies. It was, after all, a mass refusal by Vietnamese peasants to conform that eventually led more Americans than ever before to question the nature of their own society.

Such movements may be very uncomfortable to live with. Their rhetoric may offend our sensibilities, their anarchism our sense of order, and they will not always be non-violent. But while it may be sad for the CNDs to see their black and white symbol which originally meant nuclear disarmament moving out of their hands as the symbol of new protests and with other marchers, it is still concerned with the death of man and the safety of the unborn child.

When the 7,000 people arrested in Washington during the protests against the war in Vietnam stood in the RFK Stadium into which they were herded in the form of a giant CND symbol, where were the thousands who sat in Trafalgar Square ten years earlier?

When the men of the 101st Airborne Division of the US Army carved out a gigantic CND symbol on the scarred soil of Vietnam with a bulldozer, where were the hundreds of thousands who marched from Aldermaston?

'No man,' wrote John Donne, 'is an island.' That goes for CNDs too.

Left, Left, Left

CITÈKÙ NDAAYA (b. 1929) Zaire. Poet. A kàsàlà is an ancient song of lament.

Ndaaya's Kàsàlà

Ndaaya, I, am so poor
  you can hear my pestle pounding after sundown.
Already I stand at the crossing of the roads,
  why then have I come to these lamentations . . .?
This death of yours is men's affair, O Ntumba,
  were it women's affair I'd brandish my pestle.
Why I am what I am remains impenetrable:
  born a man – they would have handed me a sword –
  would I not have become a hero?
Am I not as things are vagabond with a strong gullet?
Could I not then fight as they fight . . .
Dear brothers,
  death came to me like a thief in the night,
  as I went to bed with a divided heart.
The drums of a famous musician, the intrepid one,
  today they are sounding my rhythm.
Ah, daughter of the Ngandu,
  were voice strong as drum
  it would already have reached my mother . . .
But tears will never awaken the dead,
  sooner vase will fill up . . .
War has ravaged me today, sister of Cibangu,
  but who remains to protect Ndaaya?
I must call my comrades, but who will respond?
  who dares summon the strong?
At the crossroads
  I have trapped bitter crickets
  I have grubbed for ashen cicadas
And I go to bed with a divided heart
  restless, I have counted beams
  vagabond, have counted roofs

(cont'd p. 176)

The Widow I, 1922–23, by Käthe Kollwitz

Daughter of those who bathe till their bodies gleam as with oil,
   ah, my brothers, misfortunes weigh me down:
   one part orphan
   one part sterile
But what can I say that men might give me credence?
Ah, sister of Cibangu, human things alter:
   a young woman becomes old
   she-goat turns billy-goat:
   another, having given birth,
   look – suddenly she's sterile,
   like Ndaaya.
Did I not give birth to a child with gums strong as cut-teeth?
O daughter, quickened in me by ritual,
   since you left, I've been inconsolable
   at the crossroads
Child planted in me by ritual
   see how women of my age prosper:
   third wives moved up to first place
   others demoted
At dangerous crossroads I call
   daughter, returned to my womb by ritual
   Mbombo
   Silence

LAUREL SPEAR (contemporary) American. Writer and poet.

An Event in Asia and Shaker Heights

In an isolated event
Somewhere in Asia,
A boy twenty
Steps on a mine
And is instantly killed.

This sets in motion
A chain

That ends at the door
Of an apartment
In Shaker Heights,
Where an embarrassed soldier
Dressed in green
Must tell
A tremble-chinned lady
Gray curls flattened
To her head
With the man
Half bald behind her,
That all the years
Of care
For this human being
Carried under her heart,
Through childhood
To adult
Have been obliterated.

MARGARET FLANAGAN EICHER (contemporary) American. Writer.

Personal End of a War

I think my brain stopped when I read the words
because there was nothing in my head –
nothing –
and you know my thoughts
have always been like birds in an aviary
flying all ways in color;
it had all closed down to a gray silence.
Then you took the letter from me
and touched my arm
and a Roman candle went up inside me
and I remembered from the beginning:
a fat baby
a happy boy

a young man like you young again,
a young man with a heart like a sounding guitar.

They said he was a hero.
Do you think a hero in the family
is better than a living son?

NHAT CHI MAI Vietnamese. Buddhist nun. Immolated herself in protest against the war in Vietnam.
The following letter was left by her to explain her action.

I offer my body as a torch
to dissipate the dark
to waken love among men
to give peace to Vietnam

the one who burns herself for peace

I am only an ordinary Vietnamese woman, without talent or ability. But I feel pain every time I look at the situation of my country. I want to say that the empty words you have been using, 'to defend freedom and happiness for Vietnam,' have lost all their meaning. . . .

How many tons of dollars and bombs have been dropped on our people to destroy both their souls and bodies? . . . All this is neither freedom nor happiness. Do you realize that most of us Vietnamese feel in the bottom of our hearts this hatred toward those Americans who have brought the sufferings of war to our country? . . .

I feel pain every time I think of the sufferings of my people, and I also feel sorry for the fate of American soldiers and their families. They too have been pushed into this absurd and ugly war! People have been using beautiful words to intoxicate them.

What kind of honor will the U.S. get from a 'victory' over a tiny country like Vietnam . . .?

Nhat Chi Mai,
from A Letter to the U.S. Government

One who Burns herself for Peace

ROBIN MORGAN (b. 1941) American. Poet and writer, socialist. Began working for the women's movement in 1967. This poem comes from a series inspired by the work of three Vietnamese poets.

The Vigil

As summer unfurls the snails in their shells,
the fishing boats return to women who must celebrate
their husbands' catch. Such men smell of seaweed.
Her husband hunts different prey, in the hills.

Each morning she sits by the old pagoda
and listens to the schoolbells
and presses the just-buds with the tip
of her finger, beaded with tears,
a hematic dew.
They have put her on posters, plucky, smiling,
standing beside her anti-aircraft gun.
What do they know, fools,
what do they know?

She should write him, perhaps, that she is pregnant.
What to name this child with his almost-forgotten face?
If it is a girl, Napalm.
If it is a boy, M-14 or Shrapnel.
Child she did not want.
Man she did not want.
War she did not want.
They have named her 'exemplary
revolutionary woman' – those men who sit
with their feet up on their desks,
those plump men wearing khaki or creased black
pajamas, grey business suits or tie-dyed t-shirts.
Fools, what do they know?

An abortion is not permitted 'this late.'

Each evening she waits for sleep until dawn.

(cont'd p. 181)

Help Run the US Army, by Florika

She should write him, perhaps,
but why? She can watch behind closed eyes,
seeing him joking with his comrades as they praise
the strength of his seed.
He is closer to them
than he ever was to her.
Still, when he returns, she must smile
and serve him tea.
It is reactionary to think otherwise.
It is also against tradition.

But one night she lies curled tightly in no shell,
netted like a gasping salmon that would strain against
all mesh to batter upstream through reddening rivers
toward that mountain source –
and knows who the bells have been mourning,
and knows why she has not written,
and knows that what she never had is lost,
and knows that only some jungle weed blooms, like her belly,
from his corpse,
while red ants speak through his mouth.

From 'Four Visions on Vietnam'

VERA G. RICE (contemporary) British. Edited *Call to Women* peace magazine
for many years.

Dolls for boys (so long as they have guns!) are *in* – according to the
report on the Brighton Toy Fair in *The Times* (6/2/67). In a world that is
supposed to be striving for peace the most boosted toy in the USA and
Britain is a model of the American soldier hero currently fighting in
Vietnam. If one of the purposes of toys is to enable the child to
overcome fear by identifying with the power the toy is supposed to
represent – what is the purpose of 'Action Man'? Why are the manufac-
turers so concerned to keep alive the myth that war is a glorious
adventure? Is this just a profitable business venture or are our sons
being deliberately conditioned for a future role?

A spokesman for the US 73 Airborne division quoted in *The Times* (13/2/67) has said that villages in the 'Iron Triangle' would be flattened – 'It will be a free fire area'. So, in this heroic war to defend freedom, whole villages are to be erased and a people having little but their small piece of land, their family home and the bones of their ancestors to call their own – are uprooted. Ben Suc is a pile of rubble. It was in the area designated by the United States for a policy of kill all, burn all, and destroy all. The town has been bulldozed to the ground, the surrounding forest land set alight, 176 of its people killed, and the remainder herded into 'refugee' camps.

Editorial, *Call to Women*

GILLIAN MARY LEE (contemporary) Aged 12 when she wrote this poem.

The Cow and Calf

While looking through a magazine
I saw a picture
A picture of a cow and calf
They looked so peaceful and gentle
Yet, when I looked at the article
And read a little
I found that the story wasn't so peaceful
It was a true story about a town
A little town
As small as the calf
Which is surrounded by war
The war in Vietnam
Yet the people have to go on living
Living with the war
The war, so near that bombs can be heard falling
Bringing injury, destruction and death
While men in far off countries
Safe, in their ten roomed houses

With colour televisions
Decide their fate.
The cow and calf
Gently licking each other
Are the sign of a party
A party in the local election
They were holding an election
While people were dying close by
Dying horribly
I carry on reading
Somewhere in war-torn countries
Babies are going hungry
Dying of malnutrition
While I am reading
Of a local election.

CORETTA KING (b. 1927) American. Lecturer, writer and concert singer. Actively opposed Vietnam War, member of Women Strike for Peace and Women's International League for Peace and Freedom.

Exactly a week before the murder of Dr Martin Luther King Jr, his wife, who is a member of the WILPF, went from Atlanta to Washington to support, at a large press conference, Dorothy Hutchinson's proposals for a peace settlement in Vietnam:

As long as we kill men, women and children in Vietnam, millions of poor people face unnecessary death and suffering in America. As long as we lay waste to the beautiful countryside and communities of Vietnam, we shall see destruction and chaos in the ugly ghettoes of America. As long as we are poisoned by hatred of a freedom-seeking people in Asia, the sickness of racism will exploit our own minorities and corrupt the American majority.

Let us think for a moment of what we are doing in Vietnam and what we could be doing in America. We spend a million dollars or more on a bomber to kill in the war. One million dollars could provide decent housing for 100 poor American families. We spend at least $350,000 to kill each so-called 'enemy' soldier in the war. That amount of money could provide a guaranteed income of $10,000 a year for 35 years for an impoverished family without work or income. We are destroying schools in Vietnam and neglecting schools in America. War brings disease and starvation to Vietnam while ill health and lack of food plague our American poor people.

I am here today to join my colleagues in the Women's International League for Peace and Freedom in this demand for an honourable peace in Vietnam. I am also here to relate the injustice of the present war to the injustice of poverty and racism at home. The two problems are inextricably bound together.

Statement at WILPF conference

DOROTHY HUTCHINSON (contemporary) American. Quaker.
International chairperson of WILPF and member of World Federalists (campaigners for a world parliament).

After centuries of colonialism, most colonies have become nations during the short twenty years since World War II. This very fact insures ceaseless unrest in the remaining vestiges of colonialism, such as Angola and Mozambique until they, too, are freed. Overt imperialism also sees the handwriting on the wall. The Vietnam War is demonstrating that it is impossible for even the greatest Power quietly to assume control of even the weakest as was the accepted practice in the 19th century. Revolutionary violence has also a breeding ground in the political inexperience of new nations, in the intolerable poverty with which they and many older nations are struggling and in the tug-of-war between the Status-Quo Powers and the Revolution-Promoting Powers which seek to control their destinies.

It is small wonder that, while there were only fifteen internationally significant outbreaks of violence between nation states during the past eight years, there were 149 violent revolutions of one sort or another.

The coming decades will see increasing numbers of revolutionary outbreaks unless:–

1. Vastly increased economic aid relieves intolerable conditions of two-thirds of the world's people.

2. The Status-Quo and Revolution-Promoting Powers forego unilateral political and military interference to serve their own ends in these areas.

3. Adequate international peace-keeping and peace-making machinery is devised for helping to achieve peace with justice, when internal disorders threaten world peace.

This Revolutionary Age puts WILPF in a grave dilemma. During the entire half century of our efforts for Peace and Freedom we have advocated achieving all kinds of goals solely by peaceful means. In facing the violent revolutions of this time, it is both difficult and perhaps unprofitable for us to decide, on the one hand, whether a relatively bloodless military coup is preferable to rule by a repressive government which cannot be ousted by constitutional means, or, on the other hand, whether even the most desirable political change warrants the wholesale massacre of all who stand in the way.

It behoves us rather, to face the *inevitability* of violence, when conditions conducive to revolution build up explosive pressures, even though we do not condone the violence. Our major efforts must be to remove the causes of violence rather than to pass judgment after the fact.

The dangers of this time must be made to serve as opportunities for achieving freedom from political and economic feudalism within nations and freedom from political and economic imperialistic pressures from outside.

The world's great opportunities for adequate economic development, for insuring political freedom, for co-operative coexistence of ideologies for the elimination of war are closely interrelated. None can be realised unless all of them are embraced. Only as the world takes steps toward a warless world will material and mental resources be diverted toward economic development and away from the imperialistic adventures and cut-throat competition which are integral to the Great Power struggle for security. Only as world economic development begins to relieve human misery and strengthen nationhood will revolutionary violence begin to decrease and the weaker nations begin to escape from imperialistic control by the strong.

(cont'd p. 187)

Demonstration outside the Stock Exchange, 1982, by Paula Allan

It was recognition of such intricate inter-relationships as these which caused the founders of WILPF to include both Peace and Freedom in our name and programme. These inter-relationships must still dictate the scope of our concerns.

'Opportunities Masquerade as Problems'

DOROTHY DAY (1897–1980) American. Lived in voluntary poverty as a pacifist leader involved in the workers' movement. Founder of the paper *The Catholic Worker* and of 'houses of hospitality' for the poor and unemployed.

At least we can avoid being comfortably off through the exploitation of others. And at least we can avoid physical wealth as the result of a war economy. There may be ever-improving standards of living in the US, with every worker eventually owning his own home and driving his own car; but our whole modern economy is based on preparation for war, and this is surely one of the great arguments for poverty in our time. If the comfort one achieves results in the death of millions in the future, then that comfort shall be duly paid for. Indeed, to be literal; contributing to the war (misnamed 'defence') effort is very difficult to avoid. If you work in a textile mill making cloth, or in a factory making dungarees or blankets, your work is still tied up with war. If you raise food or irrigate the land to raise food, you may be feeding troops or liberating others to serve as troops. If you ride a bus you are paying taxes. Whatever you buy is taxed, so that you are, in effect, helping to support the state's preparations for war exactly to the extent of your attachment to worldly things of whatever kind.

Loaves and Fishes

BETTY THOMAS MAYHEN (contemporary) American.

To My Black Sisters

Our sons are dying together
Not here where you and I were always divided,
but in some distant place against another colored people

Is my son dying because I denied you?
Is my son never to reach manhood because I denied your
 son his?
Am I paying the price of not accepting you as one of my
 own?
In my whiteness I looked away from your Black
 womanhood
When your children suffered and died, I said,
they are not mine they're Black
When you and yours were murdered, brutalized and
 humiliated, I turned away
When your children exploded and said BLACK was
 BEAUTIFUL did I not panic?

How many crimes and corpses must I view to rid myself
of a whiteness not human,
Before I dare reach out and touch your hand.

GLORIA EMERSON (contemporary) American. Correspondent in Vietnam
from 1970–2 for the *New York Times* newspaper.

Then came a demonstration so different from all the others that it
surprised even those people in Washington, DC, who had seen it all.
The veterans of Vietnam massed in Washington, DC – only men who
were veterans and could prove it – and threw back everything at the
white marble Capitol, the building where Congress said yes to the war.
They threw back medals for valor; they threw back stripes torn from
sleeves, their campaign ribbons and sometimes parts of dress uniforms. Some Vietnamese in Saigon were a little shocked. Their own
newspapers and magazines and radio made no mention of such a
thing, but a few of them heard of it. An ARVN lieutenant, in from the
field, was bewildered, for he had known American infantrymen for
seven years and he could not imagine any of them doing this. At first
the lieutenant thought the Americans wanted more money for having
fought so far from home. It took some doing to persuade him this was
not the reason.

 'Who do they want to win the war?' the lieutenant asked me. His
English was good.

'They think the war is a crime,' I said. 'They are ashamed of the war.'

The lieutenant looked snarled: he was so sure that the Americans, above all, wanted to win the war. . . .

The five-day demonstration, organized by Vietnam Veterans Against the War, was the first time that Americans who had fought in a foreign war demanded an end to it, were not proud of being a part of it, did not think it best that their country win, and hurled back the rewards they had been given for doing their duty, for being the men their fathers and the nation wanted. . . .

A study was conducted of the veterans encamped on the Mall. Most of the men were between twenty-one and twenty-five; few had finished college, unable to capitalize on college draft deferments. A majority had enlisted. Nearly half their fathers were blue-collar workers. Most of the veterans began to change their mind about US involvement in Vietnam during their first three months there.

On Friday, April 23, they broke camp. It was estimated that more than two thousand men had come from all over the country; half had camped on the Mall. There is no plaque there to show which tree is the one they planted, or how it is doing. The last American troops did not leave Vietnam for another twenty-three months; the war went on for another four years. Most of the veterans did not try again in the same way to stop the war, or to redeem themselves. They saw it was no use. One by one, they fell away.

Winners and Losers

MARYA MANNES (b. 1904) American. Writer and lecturer.

. . . life demands that the duality in men and women be freed to function, released from hate or guilt. All wars derive from lack of empathy: the incapacity of one to understand and accept the likeness or difference of another. Whether in nations or the encounters of race and sex, competition then replaces compassion; subjection excludes mutuality.

Only through this duality in each can a man and woman have empathy for each other. The best lovers are men who can imagine and even feel the specific pleasures of women; women who know the passions and vulnerabilities of the penis – triumphant or tender – in themselves.

Without empathy, men and women, husbands and wives, become tools of each other: competitors, rivals, master and slave, buyer and seller. In this war the aggressions of the wholly 'feminine' woman are just as destructive (mostly to the male) as the aggressions of the wholly 'masculine' man.

For centuries the need to prove this image of masculinity has lain at the root of death: the killing of self and others in the wars of competition and conquest; the perversion of humanity itself.

We need each other's qualities if we are ever to understand each other in love and life. The beautiful difference of our biological selves will not diminish through this mutual fusion. It should indeed flower, expand; blow the mind as well as the flesh. When women can cherish the vulnerability of men as much as men can exult in the strength of women, a new breed could lift a ruinous yoke from both. We could both breathe free.

Out of My Time

MONIQUE WITTIG (b. 1935) French. Writer.
From an experimental novel in which she explores her particular vision of a feminist consciousness and style.

The women address the young men in these terms, now you understand that we have been fighting as much for you as for ourselves. In this war, which was also yours, you have taken part. Today, together, let us repeat as our slogan that all trace of violence must disappear from this earth, then the sun will be honey-coloured and music good to hear. The young men applaud and shout with all their might. They have brought their arms. The women bury them at the same time as their own saying, let there be erased from human memory the longest most murderous war it has ever known, the last possible war in history. They wish the survivors, both male and female, love strength youth, so that they may form a lasting alliance that no future dispute can compromise. One of the women begins to sing, Like unto ourselves/ men who open their mouths to speak/a thousand thanks to those who

have understood our language/and not having found it excessive/have
joined with us to transform the world.

Les Guérillères

ADRIENNE RICH (b. 1929) American. Writer, poet, teacher. First book of
poems published 1951. Chose to share 1974 National Book Award with two
other women poets.

Splittings

1.

My body opens over San Francisco like the day-
light raining down   each pore crying the change of light
I am not with her   I have been waking off and on
all night to that pain   not simply absence but
the presence of the past   destructive
to living here and now   Yet if I could instruct
myself, if we could learn to learn from pain
even as it grasps us   if the mind, the mind that lives
in this body could refuse   to let itself be crushed
in that grasp   it would loosen   Pain would have to stand
off from me and listen   its dark breath still on me
but the mind could begin to speak to pain
and pain would have to answer:

We are older now
we have met before   these are my hands before your eyes
my figure blotting out   all that is not mine
I am the pain of division   creator of divisions
it is I who blot your lover from you
and not the time-zones nor the miles
It is not separation calls me forth   but I
who am separation   And remember
I have no existence   apart from you

2.

I believe I am choosing something new
not to suffer uselessly   yet still to feel
Does the infant memorize the body of the mother
and create her in absence?   or simply cry
primordial loneliness?   does the bed of the stream
once diverted   mourning   remember wetness?

But we, we live so much in these
configurations of the past   I choose
to separate her   from my past we have not shared
I choose not to suffer uselessly
to detect primordial pain as it stalks toward me
flashing its bleak torch in my eyes   blotting out
her particular being   the details of her love
I will not be divided   from her or from myself
by myths of separation
while her mind and body in Manhattan are more with me
than the smell of eucalyptus coolly burning   on these hills

3.

The world tells me I am its creature
I am raked by eyes   brushed by hands
I want to crawl into her for refuge   lay my head
in the space   between her breast and shoulder
abnegating power for love
as women have done   or hiding
from power in her love   like a man
I refuse these givens   the splitting
between love and action   I am choosing
not to suffer uselessly   and not to use her
I choose to love   this time   for once
with all my intelligence

ELAINE MORGAN (b. 1920) British. Writer.
This is an extract from her book expounding a revolutionary theory of evolution.

. . . aggression is for fighting people with.

The child with his shoelace or his quadratic equation is not more likely but less likely to solve his problem if his heart is pounding, his breath coming fast, and his bloodstream being pumped full of sugar and adrenalin; and though the man who kicked his front door in attained his objective of entry, it was not by the best or quickest method. Physical processes may be toned up during a period of aggressive arousal, but the process of reasoning is impaired.

Admittedly, other emotional responses may have the same effect. Fear is another emotion, once a valuable life preserver, which in a civilized context often leads to mindless and maladaptive behaviour.

But there is one important difference between these two reaction systems. Nobody writes paeans in praise of fear. This is because nobody enjoys experiencing it. Whether at its lower chronic level of anxiety or its high-level intensity of panic, people find it distressing. They seek to dispel it in their friends. 'Don't be afraid,' they say. 'There's nothing to worry about.'

Of aggression the opposite is true. As a popular form of arousal it rivals sex. It invigorates; it gives a sense of well-being and increased stature; it is immediately emotionally rewarding. It can be secondarily rewarding, too, because people who behave aggressively tend to get more of their own way than people who don't. For these reasons there is a strong tendency for people (both male and female) to seek out and repeat situations that arouse feelings of aggression in them, or to return to them mentally and rehearse them over and over in their minds so that the delicious shot of adrenalin will once more flow through their veins.

To put it in the simplest terms, aggression can be addictive. We have no need to visit a chemist or use a hypodermic in order to inject into our bloodstream a dose that can blow the mind. We have a do-it-yourself kit. And in dealing with our friends we do not seek to dampen down this tendency as automatically as we seek to dampen down fear. We more often feel it as an act of empathy to stoke it up: 'Yes, I don't blame you . . . it's outrageous . . . I don't know why you put up with it . . .

He ought to be shot . . .' Only after a man has had his first coronary will his doctor suddenly put this stimulant on the dangerous-drugs list, saying: 'Cut out the whisky and don't let yourself get worked up.' (The patient may be able to get help with his drink problem, but nobody's yet founded an Aggressives Anonymous.)

The Descent of Woman

BARBARA DEMING (b. 1917) American. Writer, active campaigner for non-violence and women's movement.

Dear Leah (for I am moved, as I go, to write this response more directly to you) – you write, 'It seems to me there are two possibilities at the moment: either men will learn peace from women, or women will learn violence from men.' I feel, as you do, that men had better learn to be 'more like women.' But women have changing to do, too, haven't they? I think they have to do that changing first, or men are not likely to change.

You say, 'For centuries women have quietly collaborated with the evil in men by supporting their egos and not asking where the money came from. This collaboration hopefully is about to end.' Yes. But how? You write, 'It can either end by women resigning themselves to doing their own dirty work as learned from men,' and reaping comparable rewards – the wrong ending – 'or it can be resolved by men abandoning their prerogatives and learning to be "more like women."' But can we expect men on their own to take this action? When has a privileged group – as a group – ever volunteered to abandon its prerogatives? Women will have to insist on it – won't we? And won't we have to *learn* to insist? And to do this, won't we have to learn *not* to be quite the women that we have been 'trained and expected' to be? For wouldn't you agree that we have been trained to make *too much room* for other souls, and that we now have to learn to say: 'I need my own room, too. I am not just a need of yours – for a mother, a wife, a mistress, a maid – or even a guru. I am another person, with my own legitimate needs. And speaking of legitimate needs, what you think you need in me you *don't* need and you can't have. (Neither can *I* have it – from you or from any other person.) You want me to be part of you, one of your belongings. I insist that you see me as myself. (And I'll of course try to see you in that way.)'

Spoken like a good guru, you may reply. But not the gentle, the 'womanly' guru a man is likely to seek out. These are words almost bound to be spoken in anger – and less coherently than I have written them down. If our self-assertion does not require violence (my faith is that it does not), it does, I am afraid, require anger. To burst us out of the training that tells us we need no space for ourselves – need only to help men feel *their* space.

I appreciate your fear that in the act of trying to assert ourselves we could become as inconsiderate as men, and in effect *lose* ourselves (the world then lost, too). I experience that fear myself. And yet I think there is a sense in which we have to fear that very fear. Have you read Phyllis Chesler's *Women and Madness*? She points out that women are put away in asylums either for overplaying the assigned female role – being *too* passive, too helpless, too self-destructive – or for rejecting that role and becoming the slave in revolt, the angry one. Our present society allows men (that is, white men) to be angry, but not women. Each one of us, I suspect, as she feels her anger bursting forth, sees herself as society would like her to – sees *herself* as a mad woman, and is appalled. But we have to recover from this. (I am talking to myself, now, as much as to you, *I* have to recover from this.)

I do more and more think that it will be at the very point at which we can feel at ease with our anger, experience it not as madness but as sanity, that we will be enabled to become healers – truly, that is nonpassively, nonviolent. While we still fear it – while the accusing look in the eyes of the men from whom we withdraw our collaboration can still elicit in our own souls *self*-accusation (which is unbearable), our anger will be violent, will wish to strike those men dead (those men and also women who still collaborate). But once we feel confident that our anger has a right to be – that *we* have a right to be – we will again find that we want to leave 'room for other souls, respecting the space which they inhabit,' simply making the altogether appropriate demand that these others learn to do this too.

With love to you –

We Cannot Live without our Lives

DORA RUSSELL (For biographical details, see p.122.)

I want to repeat here what, with many others, I have been saying for more than fifty years – that the cold war between communist and non-communist, like the sectarian war between Catholic and Protestant in Ulster, is a nonsense. I do not deny that very sharp religious and political differences exist, but these cannot be settled by blowing to pieces cities and human bodies. To destroy your whole world because you disagree is sheer idiocy.

But I want to add a view that I think perhaps I alone or very few have held also for fifty years. This is that the enemy of mankind is what we have made of our industrial way of life. The rivalry of ideologies is used to obscure from us the truth that it is the industrial technological system which is making an end of democracy and paralysing our creative initiatives.

It is not a question of capitalism versus communism, it is the machine itself which we have allowed to evolve in our midst into what Eisenhower called the 'military industrial complex'. This is rampant, both East and West, setting out on its computerised Juggernaut course, harnessing our wealth, our work, our best brains in the service of aggression and violence. It wastes our scarce resources and pollutes our earth; as well as destroying bodies, it murders the generous impulses of the heart.

The Vietnamese people stood up to it and paid a very heavy price. The united efforts of the peoples of the world will be needed to curb this monstrosity. Human survival and that of our planet are at stake, not only in the risks of nuclear war and armaments, but in our whole vision of the destiny and purpose of human life.

There is scarcely any part of our planet undiscovered; thus there is no refuge from the global problems that we face. Prophets of gloom abound. But we cannot afford to be pessimistic. First we must go on tirelessly trying to make the world's statesmen turn their minds to the real issues instead of the petty, involving personal careers or groups, with which they are – short-sightedly – concerned.

Next we must look for our allies – all those who still have faith in the forces of life with good purposes in every living thing. There are many born who would only seek to create, to think, to have children. The cruelty and devastation of war are forced upon them. There are now millions who are aware that we have taken a wrong direction – that the ends and values of our societies must change.

I can see no way but to hold fast to this belief and communicate it to others, in the hope that it will help to create thoughtful and tolerant democracies whose very existence must bring the arms race to an end and deliver humanity from the fatal impasse created by its own folly.

Letter to *Call to Women*

Grandmothers, 1982, by Frances Connelly

Taken at the Families against the Bomb demonstration, in London.

197

MURIEL RUKEYSER (1913–80) American. Poet and writer.

This Morning

Waking this morning,
a violent woman in the violent day
laughing.
                    Past the line of memory
along the long body of your life
in which move childhood, youth, your lifetime of touch,
eyes, lips, chest, belly, sex, legs, to the waves of the sheet.

I look past the little plant
on the city windowsill
to the tall towers bookshapes, crushed together in greed,
the river flashing flowing corroded,
the intricate harbor and the sea, the wars, the moon the planets
                    all who people space
in the sun visible invisible.
African violets in the light
breathing, in a breathing universe. I want strong peace, and delight,
the wild good.
I want to make my touch poems:
to find my morning, to find you entire
alive moving among the anti-touch people.

            I say across the waves of the air to you:
today once more
I will try to be non-violent
one more day
this morning, waking the world away
in the violent day.

ELISE BOULDING (contemporary) American. Researcher in disarmament, sociology department, Dartmouth College, New Hampshire.

Women's peace and world order roles have traditionally been of two kinds. On the one hand it has been the woman's task to rear soldiers and to fight on the battlefield herself when needed. On the other hand she has symbolized the gentler arts of peace and nurturance and has struggled to counteract the effects of militarism in ways appropriate to her situation. Women have thus always been involved in both the defense systems and the nurturance systems of every society. The image of the fifth world – the invisible continent of women – as consisting of that set of spaces in society where the capacity for love, relationship, and wholeness is undividedly fostered in children and reinforced in adults, is in one sense profoundly false. Society has hung a distorting mirror over every hearth.

Because most treatments of 'the woman as peacemaker' emphasize her nurturance roles in the family, it is necessary to point out the relationship between family life and militarism. Very rarely do women rear their sons to counteract militarism, except in deviant pacifist subcultures. A study of conscientious objectors in the United States during World War II showed that many of their mothers, particularly those outside the historic peace churches, opposed their taking the pacifist position. This means that a great deal of the nurturance practiced by women is an enabling device to make existing societal defense systems work. In one sense women prepare children and men for lifelong combat, whether in the occupational sphere, the civic arena, or the military battlefield.

The emphasis on peacemaking as inherent in the woman's familial role misleads us twice over. Not only is the role of mother two-edged, but also from one-third to one-half of women in any given historical era do not live out what we consider 'typical' familial roles.

While unpartnered women are also coopted into the general process of performing nurturance roles, they stand outside male-dominated systems to an extent that partnered women do not. They may be an important unrecognized resource for alternative approaches to peace-making.

The spontaneous capacity for sisterhood, the knowledge of the inner workings of neighborhoods and community life, the skills of the

199

scientist, the scholar, the humanist, and the politician – all these belong to women. If ever there was a time to reconceive what society is about, and to create new working models of public roles to make possible behaviors that will recreate the body social, it is now. The old roles will not disappear. Nurturers will always be needed, but women are increasingly teaching men to share these roles. In the long run, the old hearth-battlefield dichotomies are better solved by teaching men to be nurturers than by teaching women to be soldiers. The public structures of nurturance, the welfare institutions of society, are no longer women's exclusive province. Nonetheless, the historic role of protest, the Lysistrata role, cannot and must not disappear. Public demonstrations can harness anguish to new social directions, but the emphasis now needs to be on the new direction, not only on the anguish.

'Women and Peace Work'

LYSISTRATA PETITION In September 1977 feminists in Italy organised an international march from Rome to Seveso (the town where the release of a poisonous chemical has resulted in many miscarriages and the birth of malformed babies).

Lysistrata was a character in a play by Aristophanes, in which she incites the women from opposing sides in the Grecian wars to refuse their husbands all sexual favours until they desist from war-mongering. The campaign is successful.

The following is the statement from the Italian group:

When you have finished playing little soldiers then we will be able to speak of serious things.

We women of all countries seeing the undiscussable, lamentable and universal outbreak of the system of patriarchal, phallocratic power, whether capitalist, socialist or other, we demand answers and political changes which are imperative now. In fact, the function of reproduction – consensual or not – that society imposes on all women is incompatible with the ending of totalitarian violence chosen and imposed by men of all nations. We do not give life, we will not give any more life, we will refuse from this day on to give life that you will slaughter. We won't raise children so that you can teach them to kill and die. We declare the men with power incompetent, irresponsible liars, hypocrites and fools. In fact, if there is a social contract, we are part of it. In this case it is no longer acceptable that you oblige us to give life and sacrifice, as you say so graciously, *our own lives* while at the same time we are not even asked for our opinions on your little chess games in which some billions of human beings are your pawns. We refuse from this day to be part of your game.

Instead we want:–

an immediate end to all wars in all parts of the world
an immediate destruction of all nuclear energy systems even if you
    say these industries are for peaceful uses
an end to military service whether voluntary or obligatory
the irreversible destruction of all the industries for arms production
the fusion of all metal from all arms existing on the earth to create
    machinery of agriculture and peaceful toys for children
the immediate end to all propaganda that promotes any kind of
    violence between human beings, violence against women and
    children first
an immediate end to the production of all artificial foods.

We know that all of this is possible. We therefore reject all technocratic talk that you attempt to use to demonstrate that these demands are utopian. From this day on we will begin to spread among women the idea of a STRIKE AGAINST CHILDBIRTH, and if necessary, a STRIKE AGAINST SEXUAL RELATIONS WITH MEN until these demands are realised.

Not only do we hold up half the sky but also more than half the land we live on. The land we live on belongs to us, the air we breathe belongs to us; we will not concede any more rights to you until you respect them. We don't know what to do anymore with the killing mania that characterises you and which you have imposed on us for the last 5,000 years.

You are running the world on death because death is your obsession. We will not die with you so have a nice death. Bye bye.

KATE MILLETT (contemporary) American. Lecturer in literature and philosophy, sculptor and film-maker. Her publications include *Sexual Politics*.

My deepest commitment to non-violence comes from having suffered violence as a child. Where violence begins. Violence begins with how we abuse children. And growing up, these children perpetuate the violence they've known upon other children. There is a kind of panic, a terror when you're a child being beaten that can make you kill one day. Later. That can make men into soldiers. It can also make one into the psychologically violent species women are. The violence done to children is the root then, the first imprint learned that makes war or atrocity possible. I believe there's a killer in all of us. I know there's one inside me. When you know the killer in you and you know also that you do not want to kill, you have to set yourself upon a course of learning. Not to kill that killer then, but to control it. To accept the responsibility of your knowledge that killing other human beings is in fact easy. A possibility. But not what you want to do.

Take this then at the political level. Consider the current discussion on the expediency of revolutionary violence. The question of violence and the movement. The idea of armed revolutionary violence begins with a peculiar idea. That there are two kinds of human beings in the world – them and us. If they hurt one of us, it's bad. If we hurt one of them, it's good. This is essentially inhuman because it denies the humanity of the other, now an enemy. Once begun there is no logical termination to violence. After you've killed the first, why not the second? How does one decide? In a society which is racist or capitalist or sexist how much of a racist or capitalist or sexist do you have to be to get it in the head? I'm one. You're one. What is the safe percentile? How do you stop ideological crime once you've started it? How do you preserve the purity of revolution when you have already committed crimes in its name? How in the name of justice will you attain the justice you went out to get? With the first act of cruelty committed in the name of revolution, with the first murder, with the first purge and execution, we have lost the revolution.

I've been talking about politics. Where the means corrupt and prevent the end. Politics is repetition. It is not change. Change is something beyond what we call politics. Change is the essence politics is supposed to be the means to bring into being. The argument for change is an argument for the end of violence. Of all kinds. Economic, psychological, political, social, physical. We are women. We are a subject people who have inherited an alien culture. We have never taken the initiative. It will be difficult. But as outsiders we're somehow fortunate in having the opportunity to do something not only very grand but very different. To discriminate carefully and select from among the possibilities of the past. Better yet, to invent. As women we have already begun to develop a new social dynamic, challenging the traditional hierarchy of station and place in meetings, the conventional notions of leadership, authority, and talent. More than that, we are challenging the traditional separation of the public and personal, those segregated categories of life we've inherited from the past. In discovering the vital integrity of all human experience, we've reintegrated and subsumed these artificial distinctions. In all these ways we are forging a new politic. Or rather we are transcending what is usually called politics and arriving at change. And the first prerequisite is to transcend all the violence we feel towards each other and the world. I'm recommending something that I know sounds extreme, something about which I feel continual doubt and ambivalence. I'm saying that we must invent then a new method for the conduct of human life.

Flying

GRACE PALEY (b. 1922) American. Short story writer, poet and teacher. Active in War Resisters League. Co-founder of Greenwich Village Peace Center.

She was . . . one of the White House Lawn 11 who on Labor Day of 1978 stepped off a White House guided tour onto the grass, and unfurled a banner that read 'No Nuclear Weapons – No Nuclear Power – USA and USSR'. The action was planned to coincide with the work of seven other Americans who traveled to Moscow and unfurled an identical banner in Red Square. Charging both countries responsible for the 'death march inherent in their escalation of nuclear development,' the protestors in Washington were arrested for unlawful entry (the same crime as the Watergate defendants). While in jail, Grace prepared the following statement which she intended to read to the jury on behalf of the White House Lawn 11. She was not permitted to read it in court, but it stands as a clear message of the attitude and beliefs which form her work.

The reason I'm here is that I live next door to a school. Every morning the kids go in kind of solemnly and at three they come flying out. You know how nice and lively they look. But I and my friends really and truly believe they will never grow up. Certainly they'll never get to be 56 (which I happen to be this very day).

So, while the great important powers of the world are piling up arms, nuclear armaments – all the noise and terror of coming war – we did a small, quiet, simple thing. We stepped out onto the grass of our own President's public home and our friends unfurled a banner in the public place of Russian power and we said, 'Listen! Stop!'

We did this in order to be seen and heard through the media far and wide, but our short walk across the grass was, in fact, risky and it turned out to be dangerous for us.

Whatever you decide about us – guilty or not guilty – we hope you hear what we're saying. Otherwise, you'll be taking risks much greater than we've taken and the grass of the whole world will be dangerous to all children.

In fact, there won't be any grass, and there won't be any children.

The seven protestors in Moscow were also arrested but released within an hour. The White House Lawn 11 were found guilty, fined $100, given a suspended sentence of 180 days, and put on probation in Washington for three years.

'In These Times'

PAT ARROWSMITH (b. 1930) British. Poet and writer. Pacifist, socialist. Organiser for Committee of 100 (non-violent direct action group) and CND. Member of White House Lawn 11. Gaoled 10 times between 1958 and 1977 for political activities.

Greenhouse

Line upon line of cuttings,
tangle of tendrils and foliage vibrant
with sap, lit here and there by
geranium flame.

Clusters of fern absorbing the
soil's wetness,
breathing out an earthy musk into
the warmed air.

Flower pots crowded into
glowing ranks stretch
away down the staging seemingly
for ever.

The greenhouse pulsates with life.
Populated with plants it is
the world in a bubble –
all we need.

We do not strain to
look beyond the transparent walls
nor remember that glass
is brittle.

We do not notice the
sky outside start to thicken,
turn to steel, descend as though
to crush us.

Are caught unawares by
the thunder's sharp explosion shivering
the fragile structure that
surrounds us.

A hail of silver bullets
strikes the pane above us.
We look up at last
and realise

how thinly screened we are;
how soon our shelter may be shattered,
our world splintered into
smithereens.

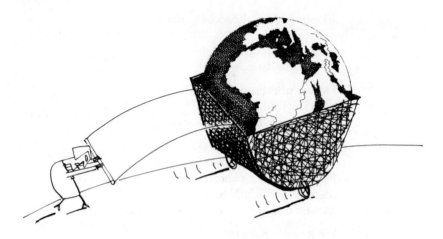

Mother Earth, 1982, by Paula Youens

JEAN BAKER MILLER (contemporary) American. Psychologist and psychotherapist. Sees as destructive the ways in which women and men have separated and so-called female characteristics have been underrated and male characteristics overrated. In the following extract she explores the implications of allowing such a separation.

Some of the things I have written may sound like things our grand-mothers would have told us: 'Men will be boys. We let them play their little games with each other. We know it isn't about the important things, but they think so. So we let them. We take care of them so that they can go on playing. Without us they couldn't.' But the games are not fun anymore, if they ever were. Many end in war games. What grandma did not tell us is that men are capable of something altogether different. (If they are not, then perhaps women had better take over completely!) But even though men are untapped wells of potential, they will not move forward if women continue to subsidise the status quo.

There has been a deluge of recent writing in many fields in the dominant culture bemoaning men's entrapment. These writings say that the goals held out to man create a person unable to arrive at satisfaction or even a sense of connection with what he is doing and those with whom he is doing it. Witness the stream of 'alienation' and 'failure of communication' literature. What this writing has not seriously considered is that these difficulties relate to the subjugation of women.

All social structures that male society has built so far have included within them the suppression of other men. In other ways, too, all of our society's advances are still a very mixed blessing. What a relatively few men in our advanced society have been able to build has been at the great expense of other men. Technologically advanced society has led to vast improvements for a small group of men and some improvements for a somewhat larger group – at the expense of misery for many and the destruction of whole cultures for others.

Toward a New Psychology of Women

CYNTHIA ENLOE (b. 1938) American. Writer, researcher and teacher. Active feminist and anti-militarist.

Between 1960 and 1978 the governments of Nato together spent 3.1 billion US dollars on military troops, equipment and research. The governments of the Warsaw Pact during the same 18 years spent $1.4 billion. In 1978 alone, Nato military expenditures totalled over $150 billion. In the 1980's analysts are predicting that military outlays by all the governments in the world will rocket upwards to the point where $600 billion is spent *annually* on militaries. Nato will be a major promoter of that non-productive spiral.

Military budgets never exist in splendid isolation. In each society in which women are battered, constrained by illiteracy, deprived of adequate health care, made to serve as cheap labour and reproducers of labour (including military labour), military budgets shape the rest of a government's public expenditures. Nato as an organisation cannot dictate military expenditures to any of its members, but it tries to impose a sense of *commitment* – 'don't let down our side' – and a sense of collective *fear* – 'the Soviets are getting ahead of us' – on each. . . .

As to military's presently popular claim – supported by many of its most avid legislative and cabinet supporters in annual budgetary debates – to being a promoter of industrial and technological development benefiting the entire society, this too is based on a fallacy. Defense critics such as Mary Kaldor in Britain and Emma Rothschild in the US have shown how in reality public spending on military weaponry strains – not boosts – the rest of the economy. One dollar spent on military industrial production creates *fewer* jobs than one dollar spent on civilian production. Often the dollars (or francs or pounds) spent on weaponry don't even go into the domestic economy; they are used to buy expensive equipment from abroad. In fact, Nato has operated for three decades as a sort of sales room for US defense contractors. Only since the mid-1970's have Nato's European governments been able to compete with the US, though not yet on an equal footing. This has turned Nato into an arena for fierce military-industrial rivalry.

Military equipment orders drain off engineers, scientists and skilled workers from civilian industry, where innovation is needed even more to help alleviate complex social problems. One of the favorite retorts by defenders of the military-industrial connection is that the whole society benefits from the 'spin-offs' of weapon research – 'Look at radar'; 'Look at laser beam surgery'. But this is certainly odd reasoning – if better medical technology is considered good for the community, then isn't it a wasteful detour to create a whole military-industrial complex to develop what could be produced far more directly in the civilian sector in the first place? . . .

Today women are acutely aware of the potency of officially sanctioned myths. Women therefore can be especially effective in challenging Nato. We can go beyond challenges to Nato's budget expectations and weapons strategies. We can question the basic assumptions about 'common interests', 'team-play' and 'threats' without which Nato would dissolve.

'The Military Model'

RUTH LEGER SIVARD (contemporary)

There is an unreality about the world military situation in 1979 that begins with its sheer size. Few of us can follow with interest the incredible numbers involved: millions of people in peacetime armies; trillions of dollars in wasted resources; nuclear overkill sufficient to destroy every city in the world many times over.

How much more difficult will it be for the historians of the future to find reality in this militarized world of 1979? How will their best computers deal with the balance of terror, the specialized language of the weaponeers, the gaming of megadeaths, the military grotesqueries of today?

What kind of world was it, they will try to imagine, that celebrated the Year of the Child while adding to a vast pool of deadly nuclear waste that would be its most long-lasting legacy to hundreds of generations to come?

Did their civil servants seriously play out war games that no one could win, but that required aggressor and defender alike to sacrifice hundreds of millions of their own people in nuclear deaths?

When nuclear weapons were developed and there proved to be no defense against them, was it self-deception or a sense of irony that led governments to rename their war ministries 'defense' ministries?

After the leading defense minister stated that nuclear war between the two superpowers would destroy in hours all that the two nations had built over centuries, where is the record of the public outcry against making even more such weapons?

How did the nuclear powers plan to control the prevailing winds over Europe to ensure that in event of war radioactive fallout would not blow back on their allies and themselves, killing them as freely as their enemies?

Who were the leaders who were prepared to march millions of young men against battlefield weapons that would blow them into radioactive dust?

Of course, the historians will conclude, it was not the real world of 1979; it was pure theater, global fantasy, a diversion no doubt from intractable social problems.

World Military and Social Expenditures, 1979

209

SCILLA McLEAN (b. 1944) British. Active member of Women's Peace Alliance.

During my teenage years I was oblivious to the menace of the cold war; I was 20 at the time of the Cuban Missile Crisis but hardly knew what was going on. During the years of the Aldermaston marches I was in South Africa, and wasn't particularly interested: the photos seemed to show a lot of anxious or odd-looking hippie-type people, sprinkled with some churchmen and academics with a very intense look about them. I was busy building a career for myself, and the worries they expressed simply didn't ring a bell with me.

Now I'm 38 and have a family, and I feel very differently. Not that having a family has everything to do with feeling differently – I'm trying to piece together why and how my mind and my feelings have changed.

[While running the French branch of the Minority Rights Group, she became involved in leading a Unesco research project on women in peace movements.]

The Unesco report was complete by the summer of 1980, in time for the United Nations Mid-Decade World Conference of Women in Copenhagen. I came away from the conference shocked: shocked at the way in which those vital issues which stunt the health and threaten the lives of millions of women all over the world had been shelved, in favour of wrangling over political rhetoric.

One thing happened, right at the beginning of the conference, which I shall never be able to forget. At the opening ceremony, with the plenary hall packed to the walls with delegates, press and observers, Queen Margarethe of Denmark and Kurt Waldheim having given their opening addresses, there was suddenly the kind of hush that makes you guess something unprogrammed is happening. Eight women wheeled in a wagon, loaded with paper, and walked in silence onto the rostrum. They represented those Scandinavian countries in which half a million petitions had been signed by women, calling for an immediate end to the arms race.

The petition had started six months before, when three housewives in Denmark were sitting round a kitchen table, confessing to one another their deep fears of nuclear war. When they first began to read newspaper articles, to pay attention, to watch films which gave them concrete information, they said they felt paralysed. Then they decided they must do something, even if it wasn't perfect.

Now they found themselves on this United Nations podium. **Bodil Graae** from Denmark spoke, and for less than a minute: **'We, half a million women from Northern Europe, ask you to stop the escalation of nuclear weapons. We call upon the United Nations to organise immediately negotiations which will lead to disarmament. We beg you in the names of ourselves and our children, to stop this madness.'** The tension-filled silence in the enormous plenary hall erupted into spontaneous and prolonged applause. Seasoned women diplomats said it was the one meaningful, moving moment in the entire conference.

'Odyssey for Peace: Women must take the Lead'

BRENDA THOMSON (b. 1937) British. Educationalist, peace worker and television broadcaster on multi-racial issues. Education Adviser, Bradford Metropolitan District.

As adults we are responsible for building alternative communities in which we ourselves do not use guns and bombs to settle disputes, nor any violent action to prove a point, nor yet use polarisation in argument to gain our ends. Adults can reduce the availability of war toys but they must at the same time reduce the availability of warlike models of behaviour. . . .

Why talk of war when we can speak of peace? Continued talk of war, war games, war toys, military might, may increase fears in the children that this world is an evil and dangerous place. It may thus increase the expression of their natural aggression in hostility. 'Wars will cease when men refuse to fight.' Instead of talking of banning war toys, why don't we promote toys that encourage creative imagination in their simplicity, toys that are designed for co-operative use or for competitive games of physical skill, toys that are sheer joy to use. Why *don't* we promote peace toys?

'Promote Peace Toys'

ANNE-MARIE FEARON (contemporary) British. Member of feminist non-violence study group who produced a special edition of *Shrew* from which this extract is taken.

In the process of bringing up my son, I have become convinced that there is a conspiracy (whether conscious or not) whereby men and older boys seek to initiate each new generation of little boys into the cult of 'maleness'.

This all-important process involves:

separating them from women, girls, babies
teaching them to fear and deny their own softer emotions
dulling the senses
teaching them to identify sexuality with violence, i.e. to prefer power
    to pleasure
making them compete with each other
getting them addicted to fear and tension

All this results, of course, in untold atrocities against women and girls, but I think we should remember that this process also does great violence to the psyche of the little boy. I don't mean by this that any woman should spend an ounce of energy on being sorry for the poor dears; men must now seek comfort from each other, not from women. But I think that when faced with a male chauvinist pig in all his glory, it could be helpful to hold onto the thought: 'he didn't want to be like this originally, he was bullied into it' or 'this noxious brute was once a tender, helpless baby'. It could make us feel stronger by making him seem less overwhelmingly powerful, and by reminding us that there is a part of him, however small and well-hidden, that is actually *on our side* – the side of freedom, pleasure, tenderness and fun.

'Come in Tarzan, Your Time is Up'

JANIS KELLY (b. 1948) American. Active in anti-war, gay liberation and feminist movements.

Ultimately what the army wants you to do is kill – on demand – unquestioningly – or to provide unquestioning support for others more directly involved in killing. Obedience is essential for that – and it requires the complete severing of an individual's responsibility for her acts. The dehumanisation inherent in military training works very well, as US atrocities in Viet Nam show. The young men who murdered and raped the Vietnamese did not start out as psychopaths. They started out as ordinary, naive, often poor, young men. . . . Those boys could not resist the dehumanising efficiency of the military machine . . . and young women will not be able to resist either.

'Women in the Military'

EILEEN FAIRWEATHER (contemporary) Irish. Writer, active feminist. This extract is about Northern Ireland in 1979.

In Turf Lodge, where a vast fort sits at the entrance to the estate, we witnessed for ourselves what army harrassment is like. The leader of one foot patrol swaggering through (and 'swaggering' is the only way to describe it) yelled at me, 'I'd like to slice out your guts.' I'd done and said nothing, was simply standing in the doorway, but he made it quite clear, through various obscene gestures, what he'd like to do to me. He then took my photograph. (The level of surveillance here is terrifying; the army computers contain information on every aspect of people's lives, from who their friends are, what time they go to work, right down to the colour of their toilet wallpaper.)

The woman of the house shouted something back, at which another soldier immediately bounded across. He hung over the gate for a full five minutes, shoving his huge gun at the dog and saying how one day soon it would end up as steak and kidney pie. Family pets have, before now, been found shot or hung from lampposts. Meanwhile other soldiers sat on a garden wall and began throwing milk bottles; three others stood in a woman's garden two doors down and yelled for her to come out – 'you whore'. The same woman once found a statue of the blessed Virgin Mary pinned to her door, red paint daubed around the crotch.

'Don't you Know There's a War on?'

LAUGHTER AND LIPSTICK

While women's recruitment material buries the function of the army under smiles and feminine imagery, recruitment material for men glorifies the machismo of the armed forces.

US Army

Laughter and Lipstick, Guns and Guts, 1981,

GUNS AND GUTS

'Humping joes...' 'if you've never felt invincible you've never ridden in a tank . . .' 'men who respect the tat-tat-tat of the machine guns...' 'our M60 monsters are things of beauty only to the guys who ride them . . .'

US Army

Neither men's nor women's recruitment material ever addresses the important questions of who controls the military and for what purposes it is used.

49

by Ine Megens and Mary Wings

DERRY RELATIVES' ACTION COMMITTEE Set up by Derry women in 1976 to campaign on behalf of political prisoners in Northern Ireland. This extract is from an interview with two of the founding members (Mary Neelis and Nina Hutchinson) and a supporter in London.

We have support from some women in England, who are socialists, and see what's going on over here. It's hard for us to understand mothers in England – they must be peculiar. Where is their sense of loyalty to their sons? Why don't they try to prevent their sons from coming over here, to be slaughtered, for what? So that England can maintain its control, and hold on to a small nation of a million and a quarter people. The war in Northern Ireland must be costing the English working class millions in terms of taxation. . . .

If they really care about their sons, they would put their feet down. I'm sure their sons don't join the army to oppress what English people are told, after all, are their 'own' people. They keep telling us that we are British subjects.

One point I'd like to make is that a few years ago, and recently too, members of the Relatives' Action Group in Belfast went to London and chained themselves to railings outside Downing Street. They were arrested and charged with entering the country *illegally*; now what I want to know is, how can you enter your own country illegally?

We do have many visitors and members of the relatives' groups who open their homes up to people from England, and other countries. We are continually looking after people who come to see for themselves what life is like. That, I think, is very important, and by doing that we have got to know many women from outside of the North, their ideas and politics. I think that meeting different women has affected our ideas a lot.

'Derry Relatives' Action'

JILL TWEEDIE (For biographical details, see p.153)

Recently, John Nott, our Minister of Defence, gave a bit of his own game away on a television programme and shivers hit my spine. He was talking, in general, about the proposals for a reduction of nuclear arms in Europe and he said the word 'emasculate', meaning, in general, that nations embarking upon unilateral disarmament would 'emasculate' themselves.

Oh, what Freudian mushroom clouds billow up there! Oh, what depths of male terror are thus revealed! I, a woman, one of half the world, have no part to play in this gig, consciously or unconsciously. I cannot 'emasculate' myself by so much as giving up my rolling pin, never mind a Cruise missile. That unguarded word that slipped out from Mr Nott means not only that he feels himself 'less of a man' confronted with disarmament, it has a clinical meaning, too. An emasculated man is castrated, he has lost his sexual potency, he has become that most despised of creatures among men – a eunuch, fit only for guarding female property against other men who are not the females' owners. The eunuch is a eunuch because he cannot penetrate, he is no threat, he can only defend.

How many other men, including those with their fingers on nuclear buttons, including our own Minister of Defence, unconsciously see nuclear weaponry as an integral part of their sexuality constantly under challenge from other male tribes? How many feel their virility dependent on aggression, their emasculation threatened by conciliation? Rape is grievous bodily harm under the guise of sex. Could nuclear war be planetary rape, sex under the guise of grievous bodily harm? Is it mere coincidence that missiles are phallic like the rockets of the space 'race'? Once upon a time, naked apes waggled their penises at each other in threatening gestures. Then they waggled guns, and now they waggle warheads.

Is the whole grotesque arms race, in some frighteningly subconscious way, a kind of world-wide cock-fight? Staged, you may well add, by too many men well past their potent prime?

'Mr Nott's Missile Machismo'

BUFFY SAINTE MARIE (contemporary) Native American. Singer and
songwriter.

Universal Soldier

He's five foot two and he's six feet four,
He fights with missiles and with spears,
He's all of thirty one and he's only seventeen,
Been a soldier for a thousand years.

He's a Catholic, a Hindu, an Atheist, a Jain,
A Buddhist and a Baptist and a Jew,
And he knows he shouldn't kill
And he knows he always will,
Killing for me my friend and me for you.

And he's fighting for Canada, he's fighting for France
And he's fighting for the U.S.A.
And he's fighting for the Russians and he's fighting for Japan,
And he thinks we'll put an end to war this way.

And he's fighting for Democracy, he's fighting for the Reds,
He says it's for the peace of all.
He's the one who must decide who's to live and who's to die
And he never sees the writing on the wall.

But without him how could Hitler have condemned him at Levalle,
Without him Caesar would have stood alone,
He's the one who gives his body as a weapon of the war,
And without him all this killing can't go on.

He's the Universal Soldier, and he really is to blame,
His orders come from far away no more,
They come from here and there and you and me,
And, brothers can't you see
This is not the way we put the end to war.

URSULA K. LE GUIN (b. 1929) American. Fiction writer. Organised and took part in non-violent demonstrations against atomic bomb testing and the war in Vietnam.

This is an extract from one of her many science-fiction novels. Shevek is the first traveller from Anarres, a moon settled 200 years previously by anarchist exiles, to visit Urras, the mother planet. Atro is a physicist on Urras.

Atro had once explained to him how this was managed, how the sergeants could give the privates orders, how the lieutenants could. give the privates and the sergeants orders, how the captains . . . and so on and so on up to the generals, who could give everyone else orders and need take them from none, except the Commander in Chief. Shevek had listened with incredulous disgust. 'You call that organization?' he had inquired. 'You even call it discipline? But it is neither. It is a coercive mechanism of extraordinary inefficiency – a kind of seventh-millennium steam engine! With such a rigid and fragile structure what could be done that was worth doing?' This had given Atro a chance to argue the worth of warfare as the breeder of courage and manliness and the weeder-out of the unfit; but the very line of his argument had forced him to concede the effectiveness of guerrillas, organized from below, self-disciplined. 'But that only works when the people think they're fighting for something of their own, you know, their homes, or some notion or other,' the old man had said. Shevek had dropped the argument. He now continued it, in the darkening basement among the stacked crates of unlabelled chemicals. He explained to Atro that he now understood why the army was organized as it was. It was indeed quite necessary. No rational form of organization would serve the purpose. He simply had not understood that the purpose was to enable men with machine-guns to kill unarmed men and women easily and in great quantities when told to do so. Only he still could not see where courage, or manliness, or fitness entered in.

The Dispossessed

Greenham Common Camp, 1982, by Penny Webb

'BRENDA THOMAS' From an interview with Susan Hemmings. 'Brenda Thomas's' husband is in the navy and was on an aircraft carrier in the South Atlantic during the conflict between Argentina and the UK in 1982.

I don't think of my husband or any of them as heroes. Does anyone come out of war a hero? What do you think about when you think you're going to be shot? Not your wife or your country, but your own survival, and that's basically what it's about. I'm not saying they aren't brave, but what it's down to is everyone for himself. Like throughout this whole crisis the only ones who really feel it are those who have actually lost someone or had someone injured. It just doesn't hit home with the rest of us, and that's the unpleasant reality – that's why they can all yell and cheer on the quayside.

So all this homecoming stuff is an awful fiasco. There's no glory to war, and despite what is being said about patriotism, really – what is there to be proud to be British about?

The Navy *still* haven't contacted me and I have no idea when he will get home, could be months. And that's so typical. Wives and families – the ones they say it's all for – have never been taken into consideration, and never will be. War is a man's job in a man's world.

'Falklands: "Brides and Sweethearts" Bite Back'

MARTA LOUISE MUNRO This poem was written when she was 15.

Not Allowed

We always played cowboys and Indians,
When we were young,
We always played commandos,
When we were young,
Hiding behind bushes and shooting our enemy.
I thought it was just children who play that.
They're not allowed to now,
Because the grown ups are playing it
But they really die.

ALIZA KHAN AND NIDAL (contemporary) Aliza is Israeli, Nidal is Lebanese. From an interview with Roisín Boyd.

Aliza: What Israel is doing now in the Lebanon is nothing new but an extreme part of its nature. Killing people barbarically, children, women, with poisoned gas and with cluster bombs. It's hard to imagine how human beings can do this. My mother, who emigrated to Israel from Germany, rang me two weeks ago and said that she is broken hearted because what Israel is doing now is what the Nazis did to her. There are a lot of people in Israel who supported Zionism moralistically but now slowly they are realising what it really means. Women must come out against it because our sisters are being murdered.

Nidal: Now, there is such a complete and utter isolation in Beirut. So complete, that was obvious from the phone call I got from my friend there. They are even cut off from the Palestinians and the Lebanese in the south. I asked her about lots of people and she said I can't see them. I felt so badly – was this the last time I'd speak to her? She told me, 'Tell the world what is happening'.

Aliza: It's because of the bloody Western countries that they are suffering. It's not just Israel. It's because of the West's interests that all those people died. I am calling you sisters, to come together against the holocaust of the Palestinian and Lebanese people. There is no way we can sit quietly and do nothing about it.

Letter from women in Israel. 'Once again the men have gone to battle. We are told that they want to defend us. The wives, daughters, sisters and mothers. We are supposed to wait with open arms for the return of the fighters. We shall not shut up. We shall not agree to be "purged" of the Palestinian people. Get out of Lebanon at once.' Women against the Invasion into Lebanon (published in Israeli papers)

'Women Speak out against Zionism'

HUMA IBRAHIM (contemporary) Pakistani.
This is an extract from a speech given in the USA in May 1981.

I am going to talk a little bit about what it means to be part of the Third World, in my case the country is Pakistan. . . .

It is extremely important for Americans to wake up not only to the atrocities happening in their own country, but also see the oppression of the Third World Peoples by your Government as a link in the whole war chain. A recent example is El Salvador. The way politics are developing most governments will be ruled by autocrats, military dictators, generals, and admirals for whom war is a normal extension of foreign policy. In such a case Nuclear Technology and weaponry becomes even more ominous.

It is clear that American concern in the Third World is imperialistic and not 'in order to keep the communists out' – though that is how it is presented to you – the public. The American Government would lose its strong hold on the consciousness of the American people if they learnt to think of communists as people just like us sitting here in this room today.

The employment of inhuman names for the so called 'enemy' is a way of making their elimination, their murder, their genocide, easy for ourselves. The Vietnamese were seldom referred to as a suffering people but were called 'gooks', 'zips', 'zipper heads', etc. . . . homicide began to sound like normal bureaucratic procedure.

We are in the hands of people like President Kennedy who was ready to start a thermo-nuclear war in 1962. If he had been 13 minutes late the world would be extinct today. We came that close. His brother the Attorney General asked him to consider whether the American Government or any government had the moral right to initiate thermo-nuclear war. The President said he had no time to consider theories when the country's *Manhood* was at stake. Not only is this concept of manhood demented but our trust in people like that is naive and equally misplaced.

Obviously we have to take responsibility for our own survival. . . .

Speech given in the United States

MIRIAM GALDEMEZ (contemporary) Salvadorean. Working in Europe representing the Revolutionary Democratic Front, major Salvadorean opposition force.

This is part of an interview she gave to Jenny Vaughan and Jane MacIntosh while in England for International Women's Day, 1981.

The social structure in El Salvador is inhuman. It's important to say this because, yes, machismo, is a real problem, but nothing's ever going to change until we have the basic necessities of life: economic security; housing; health and education. At the moment most people don't have either. And we're never going to get them until we change the whole power structure in El Salvador. We must join with our men who suffer too, as well as fight for our specific rights. That's why we set up the Association of El Salvadorean Women (AMES) on International Women's Day last year – to make sure women could do both these things. . . .

What people don't know is that the US has been intervening in El Salvador for years: training army officers in techniques of counter-insurgency; spying; imposing programmes of population control and sterilising women without their consent; dumping dangerous drugs which kill us. Many things. Had it not been for the US my people would have been at the door of their liberation many years before now.

'Women's Lives in El Salvador'

CLARIBEL ALEGRIA (contemporary) Salvadorean. One of her country's leading writers of both political and personal poems.

Small Country

Behind you
a riot of pallid orphans,
children with protruding bellies,
mendicant mothers
exhibiting their kids
full of flies,
tricky beggars

who pour their life
onto a clotted, scabby leg
and filthy bandages.
I stop and yell:
'The sky is falling!'
'Dear friends,'
the fat lady comments,
shuffling her cards,
'have your heard the latest?
They say the sky is falling.'
At three in the afternoon
the board meeting starts.
I rise and say:
'Gentlemen,
there's only one item
on the agenda today.
The sky is falling.'
The manager is upset.
'I propose,' he exclaims,
'the construction of a vault
under the earth.
We must protect our archives,
our valuables.'
The sentry reports the order
to the barracks.
'Have the troops fall out
in combat fatigues,'
screeches the general.
'Raise your rifles and bayonets,
hold up the sky.'
The day is overcast.
A normal quota of events
takes place.
Butchers sell 3/4s
to the housewives
and charge them for a kilo,
fat old maids vent their hatred
in classrooms,

Don Juans
peacock with their pals
while maids
ruin the meal
and contemplate abortion.
Soon the small tree by the café
will issue red cherries;
sugar cane, honey,
marching cotton
and meaty clouds
will turn into Cadillacs
on a casino night
upon renting a suite in Cannes.
I sit down at the table of intellectuals.
'What can we do?' I ask.
'The sky is falling.'
An old radical smiles.
He saw it coming twenty years ago.
'And if it's true,'
an angry student asks,
'what will we do?'
With a gesture appropriate
to the historical significance,
he pulls out a pen
and on the tablecloth
begins to compose a manifesto
by intellectuals and artists.
I don't go out for days.
The sky is not falling.
The politicians have said so,
the directors,
the generals,
even the beggars confirm it.
For every young lord
there's a knocked-up maid,
holding her own.

For every fat matron,
someone tubercular picking cotton,
for every politican
a blindman with a white cane.
Everything is licit, right.
My terror, infantile.
The public show
of anxiety
is bad for people,
is rotten for business,
scares children.
Tomorrow I'll go to the market.
The psychiatrist prescribed it.
I'll be in a position
to offer ten centavos to a beggar
and to feel compassion.

SUSAN BROWNMILLER (contemporary) American. Journalist and writer.
From *Against Our Will*, her study of rape.

It has been argued that when killing is viewed as not only permissible
but heroic behaviour sanctioned by one's government or cause, the
distinction between taking a human life and other forms of impermissi-
ble violence gets lost, and rape becomes an unfortunate but inevitable
by-product of the necessary game called war. Women, by this reasoning, are simply regrettable victims – incidental, unavoidable casualties
– like civilian victims of bombing, lumped together with children,
homes, personal belongings, a church, a dike, a water buffalo or next
year's crop. But rape in war is qualitatively different from a bomb that
misses its military target, different from impersonal looting and burning, different from deliberate ambush, mass murder or torture during
interrogation, although it contains elements of all of the above. Rape is
more than a symptom of war or evidence of its violent excess. Rape in
war is a familiar act with a familiar excuse.

War provides men with the perfect psychologic backdrop to give vent to their contempt for women. The very maleness of the military – the brute power of weaponry exclusive to their hands, the spiritual bonding of men at arms, the manly discipline of orders given and orders obeyed, the simple logic of the hierarchical command – confirms for men what they long suspect, that women are peripheral, irrelevant to the world that counts, passive spectators to the action in the centre ring.

Men who rape in war are ordinary Joes, made unordinary by entry into the most exclusive male-only club in the world. Victory in arms brings group power undreamed of in civilian life. Power for men alone. The unreal situation of a world without women becomes the prime reality. To take a life looms more significant than to make a life, and the gun in the hand is power. The sickness of warfare feeds on itself. A certain number of soldiers must prove their newly won superiority – prove it to a woman, to themselves, to other men. In the name of victory and the power of the gun, war provides men with a tacit licence to rape. In the act and in the excuse rape in war reveals the male psyche in its boldest form, without the veneer of 'chivalry' or civilization.

A simple rule of thumb in war is that the winning side is the side that does the raping. There are two specific reasons for this, one pragmatic and one psychologic, and neither has much to do with the nobility of losers or with the moral superiority of an heroic defence. First, a victorious army marches through the defeated people's territory, and thus it is obvious that if there is any raping to be done, it will be done on the bodies of the defeated enemy's women. Second, rape is the act of a conqueror. This is more than a truism. It helps explain why men continue to rape in war.

'To the victor belong the spoils' has applied to women since Helen of Troy, but the sheer property worth of women was replaced in time by a far more subtle system of values. Down through the ages, triumph over women by rape became a way to measure victory, part of a soldier's proof of masculinity and success, a tangible reward for services rendered. Stemming from the days when women were property, access to a woman's body has been considered an actual reward of war.

Against Our Will

ANNA ADAMS (contemporary) British. Poet. Author of poetry collection *A Reply to Interrupted Mail*.

Two Minutes' Silence

On Remembrance Day I remember
my father, the Unknown Civilian
who chose his age unwisely and
was eighteen in nineteen-fourteen.
The rest of his class volunteered
to die before Christmas, but he –
perceiving no sense in the war –
survived a snow-flurry of feathers
which wounded, but were not fatal.
His father had died of TB
on the very day war was declared;
from his sick-room, stinking of gangrene,
(his toes had already turned black),
he heard all London cheering
and said 'This will be a big thing:
a very big thing.' Then he died.
Coincidence One.
       Then my father,
declaring his war on death,
objected to being conscripted
to kill his fellow immortals,
and he was the very first conchie
exempted by Hampstead tribunal.
Good patriots hurled half-bricks
at his landlady's innocent windows
until he was safely arrested
for giving out pacifist leaflets.
He starved, and wrote Shelleyan verse
in a Dartmoor cell, until
a vacancy in the kitchens
allowed stolen bread to assuage
some of his backlog of hunger.
       Knutsford Jail was his college:

229

there he met most of my childhood's
honorary uncles.
        Unlike the dead, he succeeded
in saving his children's lives,
even cherishing them, until
his forty-third birthday, which fell
on the day the Second World War
was declared. Coincidence Two.
        Now that the whirlwind was raging
he joined the Home Guard, and kept watch
for invaders, out on the common,
which may not have been much use
to Democracy, but it served
for observing foxes and nightjars.
He found such absurd compensations
throughout a lonely life
of never quite belonging
to the remnants of his age-group.
At last, his longed-for retirement
from Fleet Street provoked his death-blow.
He sickened, almost at once,
and, after two years, he died.
He lay in the cancer-ward
and wept as, on hospital headphones,
he heard Britten's setting of Owen;
then died on Remembrance Sunday,
a week or so before Dallas.
Coincidence Three.
        None proves
that he was the Century's Man,
but all hint that One, alone,
who stands his inch of ground
may also be History's fulcrum
just as though he were Someone.

DOROTHEE SOELLE (contemporary) West German. Christian and pacifist.
This is an extract from a speech given at 'Waging Peace' conference in
Amsterdam in 1981.

. . . seriously to wage peace, we have to ask ourselves what is the price,
what is the risk? It's not simply to wait for a better balance, because this
whole doctrine of the balance of deterrence, or I like to say the balance
of terror, hasn't worked. It simply has not worked. It has exported the
wars into the Third World, and it has created enormous escalation. You
can't name an escalation a balance, it is no balance. It is an enormous
escalation, and it is more than preparation of war. I really think it is not
just preparation of war, it is war in which we live right now. We are
living in a merciless war of the rich against the poor, and our spending
for the military is the war against the poor, so the heroes who fall in this
battlefield (APPL) are the people who are starved to death in Calcutta,
and the people who are in El Salvador and other places in the Third
World. Our denial to help them, or our rejection, our death sentence
against them, that is the war we are leading in setting our priorities in
the death wish, and in death production.

Now if I talk about my own feelings in this whole question of the
arms race. I tell you I was reading during the last four months, during
the last fall and winter, a lot of peace research, and a terrible thing
happened to me, namely that I couldn't keep this in my mind, the
numbers just fell away, just dropped out of my head, and I couldn't get
it into a serious theoretical understanding. I felt all the time misled, my
good faith in science was misused, I felt confused, and I think the
simple explanation of that is my fear. I was so afraid to realise what is
going on, to think about it in clear consequences, that I couldn't keep it
in my mind, my mind couldn't really function in the way it otherwise
would function, because I do not want to see it and I do not want to
hear it, and I'm not better than my fathers and my mothers in Germany
who also told me when I asked them, 'we didn't know'.

I don't want this to happen again. I don't want my children coming
up to me and saying, now, what did you do, and me saying, I didn't
know.

Speech given in Amsterdam

HELEN CALDICOTT (b. 1939) Australian. Pediatrician. Campaigner to protect the environment and anti-nuclear activist since 1971 when she led opposition to French atomic testing in the South Pacific. Now resident in USA where she founded 'Physicians for Social Responsibility'.

What would happen if the world's nuclear arsenals were put to use?

Erupting with great suddenness, a nuclear war would probably be over within hours. Several hundred to several thousand nuclear bombs would explode over civilian and military targets in the United States (every American city with a population of 25,000 or more is targeted) and an equal or greater number of bombs would strike the principal targets in Europe, the Soviet Union, and China. Both major and minor population centers would be smashed flat. Each weapon's powerful shock wave would be accompanied by a searing fireball with a surface temperature greater than the sun's that would set firestorms raging over millions of acres. (Every 20-megaton bomb can set a firestorm ranging over 3,000 acres. A 1,000-megaton device exploded in outer space could devastate an area the size of six western states.) The fires would sear the earth, consuming most plant and wild life. Some experts believe that the heat released might melt the polar ice caps, flooding much of the planet. Destruction of the earth's atmospheric ozone layer by the rapid production of nitrous oxide would result in increased exposure to cosmic and ultraviolet radiation.

People caught in shelters near the center of a blast would die immediately of concussive effects or asphyxiation brought on as a result of oxygen depletion during the firestorms. Exposure to immense amounts of high-energy gamma radiation, anyone who survived near the epicenter would likely die within two weeks of acute radiation illness.

Those who survived, in shelters or in remote rural areas, would re-enter a totally devastated world, lacking the life-support systems on which the human species depends. Food, air, and water would be poisonously radioactive. Physical suffering would be compounded by psychological stress: For many, the loss of family, friends, and the accustomed environment would bring on severe shock and mental breakdown.

In the aftermath, bacteria, viruses, and disease-bearing insects – which tend to be thousands of times more radio-resistant than human beings – would mutate, adapt, and multiply in extremely virulent forms. Human beings, their immune mechanisms severely depleted by exposure to excessive radiation, would be rendered susceptible to the infectious diseases that such organisms cause: plagues of typhoid, dysentery, polio, and other disorders would wipe out large numbers of people.

The long-term fallout effects in the countries bombed would give rise to other epidemics. Within five years, leukemia would be rampant. Within 15 to 50 years, solid cancers of the lung, breast, bowel, stomach, and thyroid would strike down survivors.

Exposure of the reproductive organs to the immense quantities of radiation released in the explosions would result in reproductive sterility in many. An increased incidence of spontaneous abortions and deformed offspring, and a massive increase of both dominant and recessive mutations, would also result. Rendered intensely radio-active, the planet Earth would eventually become inhabited by bands of roving humanoids – mutants barely recognizable as members of our species.

What would be left? Experts have projected two possible scenarios. According to one, hundreds of millions of people in the targeted countries would die, but some might survive. According to the second, the synergistic ecological effects of thermal and nuclear radiation, long-term fallout, and exposure to increased cosmic radiation would make it doubtful that anyone could live for very long. Destruction would most likely be absolute. There will be no sanctuary.

Is it not remarkable how we manage to live our lives in apparent normality, while, at every moment, human civilization and the existence of all forms of life on our planet are threatened with sudden annihilation? We seem to accept this situation calmly, as if it were to be expected. Clearly, nuclear warfare presents us with the specter of a disaster so terrible that many of us would simply prefer not to think about it. But soothing our anxiety by ignoring the constant danger of annihilation will not lessen that danger. On the contrary, such an approach improves the chances that eventually our worst fears will be realized.

The United States and the Soviet Union already have enough firepower in their arsenals to destroy every city on earth seven times over. Still, the arms race continues, the weapons multiply and become more specialized, and the likelihood of their utilization grows. Why? Because both countries, driven by fear and a mutual distrust bordering on the pathological, are locked into a suicidal strategy calling, in the words of the Pentagon, for 'mutually assured destruction' (MAD) as the best deterrent to war. But 'arms for peace' and 'security through mass genocide' are strategies that defy logic and common sense. They epitomize our nuclear madness.

Nuclear disarmament is the first and foremost task of our time; it must be given absolute priority. It is increasingly urgent that we find a way to achieve this goal, for time is running out. Moreover, with nuclear reactors and thousands of containers of radioactive wastes vulnerable to attack around the world, all war – conventional or nuclear – is rendered obsolete.

Our environmental circumstances changed dramatically when the appearance of nuclear weapons forever altered the nature of war. If we are to survive, we must accept personal responsibility for war and peace. We cannot afford to delegate these responsibilities to generals, politicians, and bureaucrats who persist in the politics of confrontation and in outmoded ways of thinking that have always caused – and never prevented – wars. International disputes must now be settled by reason – not with weapons.

If the 1978 United Nations special session on disarmament proved anything, it is that existing approaches to arms control are inadequate – and that it is seemingly impossible to get governments to commit themselves to genuine disarmament. It is imperative, therefore, that a mass movement of concerned citizens around the globe take up this

(cont'd p. 236)

Crane of Peace, 1980, by Anne Lise Neckelmann

The woman holding the banner is Shizuko Tagaki. She is the General Secretary of the Women's Section of the Osaka Association of A-bomb victims. She was in Copenhagen in 1980 at a peace conference to speak on behalf of her best friend from the Association, Kazue Miura, who had died a few months before. (See the next piece.)

cause and compel our governments to make nuclear disarmament the central issue of national and international politics. Joining together in an enterprise that transcends national boundaries, we in the free world must take the initiative.

Only if we abolish nuclear weapons and permanently halt the nuclear power industry can we hope to survive. To achieve these ends, it is vital that people be presented with the facts. Today more than ever, we need what Einstein referred to as a 'chain reaction of awareness': 'To the village square,' he wrote in 1946, 'we must carry the facts of atomic energy.' Once presented, the facts will speak for themselves.

Out of the growing number of organizations opposed to nuclear power and nuclear arms must come a grass-roots movement of unprecedented size and determination. Its momentum, alone, will determine whether we and our children – and all future generations of humankind – will survive.

Nuclear Madness

KAZUE MIURA (1927–80) Japanese. Switchboard operator in the central telephone exchange at the time of the A-bombing of Hiroshima. One of the few people to survive in the innermost zone of the explosion.
This extract is part of her account of her life after the bomb.

In November, although I was still weak, I went to my two sisters in Osaka, carrying the ashes of our parents in an urn wrapped in cloth hanging from my neck. My sisters nursed me back to health. They introduced me to a good man, and we married in 1948.

My first baby was stillborn, as was the case with one of my older sisters who was A-bombed in Hiroshima. I was hesitant to have another, but we wanted children very badly. In 1950 I gave birth to a boy, and in 1953 I had a girl. My daughter, Maki, is troubled by anemia and low blood pressure.

As she grew older, Maki noticed the newspapers in the summer featured stories of the bombings and deaths of survivors. She came to hate all reminders of the bombing because of the pain it had caused me and her fear that I, too, would succumb. When she was fourteen she looked me in the face reproachfully and asked, 'Why did you give birth to me, Mom? You are a bomb victim, so you should not have brought me into the world.' I had long anticipated that question, but no amount of emotional preparation could have softened the blow of those few words. I told her that I had thought a lot before giving birth to her and didn't know whether she might get a bad disease, not wanting to mention leukemia. 'And what would you do if it happened to me?' she asked. What could I answer her? In painful honesty I told her that there was nothing we could do about it. That was the saddest and most heartbreaking moment of my life.

Maki is now married and has two children. She and the Women's Section members have been a constant source of help and encouragement to me, especially since my health has deteriorated. In late 1976, I began to suffer from symptoms of anemia, and a gynecological examination revealed myoma of the uterus (a fibro-muscular tumor). Now I had joined the ranks of the seriously ill *Hibakusha*, many of whom had been operated on for uterine cancer, myoma, or cystoma (ovarian cyst). Government benefits are often withheld and denied to *Hibakusha*, and it was only after this diagnosis that the government granted me 'Especially Serious Case' status. To my happiness, the Women's Section published my life story, *Survival At 500 Meters in Hiroshima*, in December 1979, and I hope that it may serve to prevent any other human being from experiencing the horrors of nuclear war. [Kazue Miura died on 25 April 1980 of stomach cancer.]

'Never again: the organization of women atomic bomb victims in Osaka'

NINA SWAIM (contemporary) American. Her active involvement in the anti-nuclear movement has included being co-author of *Ain't Nowhere We Can Run, A Handbook for Women on the Nuclear Mentality*, from which this extract is taken.

The nuclear industry is made up almost entirely of men – miners, construction workers, engineers, scientists, utility company officials, and government agents. Its structure is based on domination and

(cont'd p. 239)

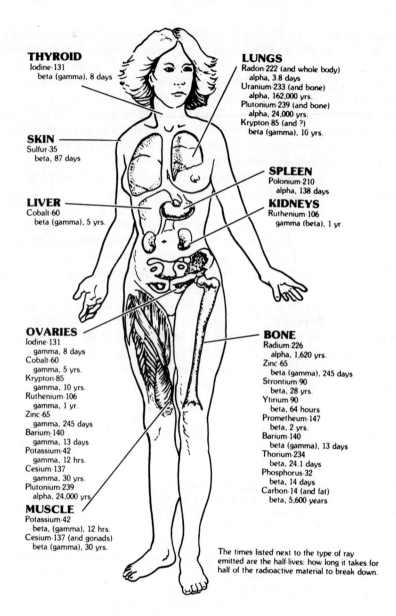

THYROID
Iodine-131
   beta (gamma), 8 days

SKIN
Sulfur-35
   beta, 87 days

LIVER
Cobalt-60
   beta (gamma), 5 yrs.

LUNGS
Radon-222 (and whole body)
   alpha, 3.8 days
Uranium-233 (and bone)
   alpha, 162,000 yrs.
Plutonium-239 (and bone)
   alpha, 24,000 yrs.
Krypton-85 (and ?)
   beta (gamma), 10 yrs.

SPLEEN
Polonium-210
   alpha, 138 days

KIDNEYS
Ruthenium-106
   gamma (beta), 1 yr.

OVARIES
Iodine-131
   gamma, 8 days
Cobalt-60
   gamma, 5 yrs.
Krypton-85
   gamma, 10 yrs.
Ruthenium-106
   gamma, 1 yr.
Zinc-65
   gamma, 245 days
Barium-140
   gamma, 13 days
Potassium-42
   gamma, 12 hrs.
Cesium-137
   gamma, 30 yrs.
Plutonium-239
   alpha, 24,000 yrs.

MUSCLE
Potassium-42
   beta, (gamma), 12 hrs.
Cesium-137 (and gonads)
   beta (gamma), 30 yrs.

BONE
Radium-226
   alpha, 1,620 yrs.
Zinc-65
   beta (gamma), 245 days
Strontium-90
   beta, 28 yrs.
Ytirium-90
   beta, 64 hours
Prometheum-147
   beta, 2 yrs.
Barium-140
   beta (gamma), 13 days
Thorium-234
   beta, 24.1 days
Phosphorus-32
   beta, 14 days
Carbon-14 (and fat)
   beta, 5,600 years

The times listed next to the type of ray
emitted are the half-lives: how long it takes for
half of the radioactive material to break down.

Radiation Diagram, 1980, by Val Page

exploitation within its own ranks (miners, fuel processing workers, and plant operators who are experiencing sharp increases in cancer). This same exploitation and domination extends beyond the present population and environment and into future generations. By centralizing power in a relatively few gigantic generators across the country, the industry ensures profit for a few (stockbrokers, banks, and industry officials) at the expense of the larger populace. Centralized energy production also ensures control over profit margins and energy policies. Because the nuclear industry is so closely bound to nuclear arms development, it is able to conceal its operations under the cloak of national security, as well as to intimidate the public into believing nuclear plants and nuclear arms development are in the nation's best interest. The 'Atoms for Peace' campaign following the devastation of Hiroshima and Nagasaki was very successful in assuaging any guilt for that act and subsequently in coercing the nation into an energy policy that is almost inextricably tied to nuclear development.

It should be clear that nuclear development affects all of us. A meltdown at a plant or a nuclear war will not discriminate among its victims. This centralized and lethal technology is unhealthy to all of life.

'The Effects of Nuclear Development on Women'

DENISE LEVERTOV (b. 1923) Born in England. Now American citizen. Poet and university teacher.

What It Could Be

Uranium, with which we know
only how to destroy,

lies always under
the most sacred lands –

Australia, Africa, America,
wherever it's found is found an oppressed
ancient people who knew

long before white men found and named it
that there under their feet
under rock, under mountain, deeper
than deepest watersprings, under
the vast deserts familiar
inch by inch to their children

lay a great power.
        And they knew the folly
of wresting, wrestling, ravaging from the earth
that which it kept
        so guarded.

Now, now, now at this instant,
men are gouging lumps of that power, that presence,
out of the tortured planet the ancients
say is our mother.
        Breaking the doors
of her sanctum, tearing the secret
out of her flesh.
But left to lie, its metaphysical weight
might in a million years have proved
benign, its true force being to be
a clue to righteousness –

showing forth
the human power
        not to kill, to choose
not to kill: to transcend
the dull force of our weight and will;

that known profound presence, *un*touched,
the sign
providing witness,
                occasion,
                ritual
for the continuing act of
non-violence, of passionate
reverence, active love.

WOMEN OPPOSE THE NUCLEAR THREAT (WONT)

The early months of 1980 were a spine-chilling beginning to the decade; NATO had decided to base Cruise and Pershing II missiles in Europe, Russia had invaded Afghanistan, the British Government published 'Protect and Survive' (Civil Defence pamphlet), the Cold War heated up again, and suddenly everyone was talking about nuclear war . . . not as a remote and horrific possibility, but as a likely event in the near future. The unthinkable was in everybody's minds . . . and particularly in our nightmares!

WONT began when two women who work together in Leeds started to talk about how worried we felt about the threat of nuclear war. We felt particularly upset at our own helplessness, we urgently wanted to 'do something' and argued that if we felt like this other women must do too. As feminists we were used to campaigning to take control of other aspects of our lives . . . what was the use of working for better health care, child care, education, etc. if the whole lot was to be blown up in a nuclear war?

Through a workshop at a local Women's Liberation Conference we drew together a small group of women who wanted to organise against nuclear weapons. Some of us had read of a petition of Scandinavian women that had collected half a million signatures to present to the UN Women's Conference; there were also women's campaigns in Greece, and in the US against conscription. Together with those women we saw our campaign as an international one, expressing our sisterhood, as against the male rivalries and mistrust that were leading the world to war again, this time with consequences too horrible to imagine. Many of us see war as a male activity, from which women suffer, and over which we have no control.

'Something in Common'

Mourning, 1981, by Paula Allan

Taken at the Pentagon Women's Action.

WOMEN'S PENTAGON ACTION Leaflet distributed by women taking part in protest against US arms spending (see next extract).

These are the frightening facts, and the hopeful ideas and feelings that are bringing women together. We invite you to read them.

We are gathering at the Pentagon on November 16 because we fear for our lives. We fear for the life of this planet, our Earth, and the life of the children who are our human future.

We are women who come in most part from the northeastern region of our United States. We are city women who know the wreckage and fear of city streets, we are country women who grieve the loss of the small farm and have lived on the poisoned earth. We are young and older, we are married, single, lesbian. We live in different kinds of households, in groups, families, alone; some are single parents.

We work at a variety of jobs. We are students-teachers-factory workers-office workers-lawyers-farmers-doctors-builders-waitresses-weavers - poets - engineers - homeworkers - electricians - artists - black-smiths. We are all daughters and sisters.

We have come here to mourn and rage and defy the Pentagon because it is the workplace of the imperial power which threatens us all. Every day while we work, study, love, the colonels and generals who are planning our annihilation walk calmly in and out the doors of its five sides. They have accumulated over 30,000 nuclear bombs at the rate of three to six bombs every day.

They are determined to produce the billion-dollar MX missile. They are creating a technology called Stealth – the invisible, unperceivable arsenal. They have revived the cruel old killer, nerve gas. They have proclaimed Directive 59 which asks for 'small nuclear wars, prolonged but limited.' The Soviet Union works hard to keep up with United States initiatives. We can destroy each other's cities, towns, schools, children many times over. The United States has sent 'advisors,' money and arms to El Salvador and Guatamala to enable those juntas to massacre their own people.

The very same men, the same legislative committees that offer trillions of dollars to the Pentagon have brutally cut day care, children's lunches, battered women's shelters. The same men have concocted the Family Protection Act which will mandate the strictly patriarchal family and thrust federal authority into the lives we live in our own homes. They are preventing the passage of ERA's simple statement and supporting the Human Life Amendment which will deprive all women of choice and many women of life itself.

We are in the hands of men whose power and wealth have separated them from the reality of daily life and from the imagination. We are right to be afraid.

At the same time our cities are in ruins, bankrupt; they suffer the devastation of war. Hospitals are closed, our schools deprived of books and teachers. Our Black and Latino youth are without decent work. They will be forced, drafted to become the cannon fodder for the very power that oppresses them. Whatever help the poor received is cut or withdrawn to feed the Pentagon which needed about $500,000,000 a day for its murderous health. It extracted $157 billion last year from our own tax money, $1,800 from a family of four.

With this wealth our scientists have been corrupted; over 40% work in government and corporate laboratories that refine the methods for destroying or deforming life.

The lands of the Native American people have been turned to radioactive rubble in order to enlarge the nuclear warehouse. The uranium of South Africa, necessary to the nuclear enterprise, enriches the white minority and encourages the vicious system of tacit oppression and war.

The President has just decided to produce the neutron bomb, which kills people but leaves property intact.

There is fear among the people, and that fear, created by the industrial militarists is used as an excuse to accelerate the arms race. 'We will protect you . . .' they say, but we have never been so endangered, so close to the end of human time.

We women are gathering because life on the precipice is intolerable.

We want to know what anger in these men, what fear which can only be satisfied by destruction, what coldness of heart and ambition drives their days.

We want to know because we do not want that dominance which is exploitative and murderous in international relations, and so dangerous to women and children at home – we do not want that sickness transferred by the violent society through the fathers to the sons.

What is it that we women need for our ordinary lives, that we want for ourselves and also for our sisters in new nations and old colonies who suffer the white man's exploitation and too often the oppression of their own countrymen?

We want enough good food, decent housing, communities with clean air and water, good care for our children while we work. We want work that is useful to a sensible society. There is a modest technology to minimize drudgery and restore joy to labour. We are determined to use skills and knowledge from which we have been excluded – like plumbing or engineering or physics or composing. We intend to form women's groups or unions that will demand safe workplaces, free of sexual harassment, equal pay for work of comparable value. We respect the work women have done in caring for the young, their own and others', in maintaining a physical and spiritual shelter against the greedy and militaristic society. In our old age we expect our experience, our skills, to be honored and used.

We want health care which respects and understands our bodies. Physically challenged sisters must have access to gatherings, actions, happy events, work. For this, ramps must be added to stairs and we must become readers, signers, supporting arms. So close, so many, why have we allowed ourselves not to know them?

We want an education for our children which tells them the true story of our women's lives, which describes the earth as our home to be cherished, to be fed as well as harvested.

We want to be free from violence in our streets and in our houses. One in every three of us will be raped in her lifetime. The pervasive power of the masculine ideal and the greed of the pornographer have come together to steal our freedom, so that whole neighborhoods and the life of the evening and night have been taken from us. For too many women the dark country road and the city alley have concealed the rapist. We want the night returned, the light of the moon, special in the cycle of our female lives, the stars and the gaiety of the city streets.

We want the right to have or not to have children – we do not want gangs of politicians and medical men to say we must be sterilised for the country's good. We know that this technique is the racist's method for controlling populations. Nor do we want to be prevented from having an abortion when we need one. We think this freedom should be available to poor women as it always has been to the rich. We want to be free to love whomever we choose. We will live with women or with men or we will live alone. We will not allow the oppression of lesbians. One sex or one sexual preference must not dominate another.

We do not want to be drafted into the army. We do not want our young brothers drafted. We want *them* equal with *us*.

We want to see the pathology of racism ended in our time. It has been the imperial arrogance of white male power that has separated us from the suffering and wisdom of our sisters in Asia, Africa, South America and in our own country.

Many North American women look down on the minority nearest them: the Black, the Hispanic, the Jew, the Native American, the Asian, the immigrant.

Racism has offered privilege and convenience; women often fail to see that they themselves have bent to the unnatural authority and violence of men in government, at work, at home. Privilege does not increase knowledge or spirit or understanding. There can be no peace while one race dominates another, one people, one nation, one sex despises another.

We must not forget that tens of thousands of American women live much of their lives in cages, away from family, lovers, all the growing-up years of their children. Most of them were born at the intersection of oppressions: people of colour, female, poor. Women on the outside have been taught to fear those sisters. We refuse that separation. We need each other's knowledge and anger in our common struggle against the builders of jails and bombs.

We want the uranium left in the earth and the earth given back to the people who tilled it. We want a system of energy which is renewable, which does not take resources out of the earth without returning them. We want those systems to belong to the people and their communities, not to the giant corporations which invariably turn knowledge into weaponry. We want the sham of Atoms for Peace ended, all nuclear plants decommissioned and the construction of new plants stopped. That is another war against the people and the child to be born in fifty years.

We want an end to the arms race. No more bombs. No more amazing inventions for death.

We understand all is connectedness. The earth nourishes us as we with our bodies will eventually feed it. Through us, our mothers connected the human past to the human future. We know the life and work of animals and plants in seeding, reseeding and in fact simply inhabiting this planet. Their exploitation and the organized destruction of never to be seen again species threatens and sorrows us.

With that sense, that ecological right, we oppose the financial connections between the Pentagon and the multinational corporations and banks that the Pentagon serves.

Those connections are made of gold and oil.

We are made of blood and bone, we are made of the sweet and finite resource, water.

We will not allow these violent games to continue. If we are here in our stubborn thousands today, we will certainly return in the hundreds of thousands in the months and years to come.

We know there is a healthy sensible loving way to live and we intend to live that way in our neighborhoods and our farms in these United States, and among our sisters and brothers in all the countries of the world.

Unity Statement

SUSAN PINES (contemporary) American. On the staff of War Resisters League. One of the organisers of the Women's Pentagon Action (see previous extract).

The Action at the Pentagon consisted of four stages, each stage signalled by a different 'larger than life' puppet. First, the white mourning puppet, accompanied by a slow, constant drum beat, moved around the parade grounds while women placed hundreds of tombstones in the ground to commemorate their sisters who had been victims of individual or state violence.

Then the red rage puppet rose and women's wailing and sorrow gave way to expressions of anger, yelling and chanting 'No More War', and 'We Will Stop You'.

The yellow puppet then came forward, signalling the beginning of the empowerment stage. The puppets led the women out of the parade grounds to encircle the Pentagon. As they walked, they wove a continuous braid, which was left, encircling the entire Pentagon.

As the defiance stage began, signalled by the black puppet, affinity groups blocked entrances to the Pentagon, many women weaving a web of brightly coloured yarn across doorways. At the end of the day 65 women were in custody. Sixty-two women were charged with obstruction of entrances and three were charged with defacement of federal property for marking the entrance of the building with blood. That night 43 women were sent to the Arlington County Jail, either sentenced to 10 days in prison or being held for trial.

In later trials women who were found guilty were sentenced to either 10, 15 or 30 days (30 days for second time offenders). In a statement written from jail and endorsed by many of the women who participated in the civil disobedience, Nesta King explained, '. . . we went to the Pentagon in an action which embodied our resistance to coercive authority. . . . The every day oppression of living in an increasingly authoritarian, militarised society is . . . a feminist concern. . . . We believe it is essential to resist directly. . . . Civil disobedience might help save our planet and usher in a free feminist future. That's why they put us here.'

'Women's Pentagon Action'

SUSANNAH YORK (contemporary) British. Actress, writer.

I am an actress and actresses, it is said, lead very sheltered lives. But one day on a film set somebody came by with a copy of Edward Thompson's pamphlet, *Protest and Survive*, and I discovered that I am one of millions in this country who haven't asked themselves the questions which that pamphlet raises – and by asking, confronted the one issue that today matters more than any other: the issue of war and nuclear armaments. The issue of world peace.

It is more than our birth-right, it is our birth-duty to question. We, the people, created the state, we set up our systems of government – and if we find that they have become foreign to us, we have not the birth-right to trust them blindly to act on our behalf. We have to break through the face they present to us, and come back to ourselves, to our own root beliefs; and we can only do so by asking the old-fashioned question: is this right? Are these actions which are being perpetrated in my name right by *me*? Do I actually believe that two-thirds of the world's population should be starved of food, housing, employment, medical help and education, so that governments and their military men may pursue their alien ends?

Do I indeed accept a society in which nice young people emerging from the universities may fairly seek advancement by finding ever new ways to destroy and kill? Do I believe in my own suicide, in that of the people I love? Is human destruction glorious, and is killing the purpose of society? And would *I* under any circumstances, push that button myself? For if I would not, how can I support the possible use of nuclear weapons by the people who act in my name? We have to ask ourselves: has the unacceptable become, after all, acceptable? For we condone these things with our silence, and that silence begins in our silence to ourselves.

'Can we Live with the Bomb?'

SUE BOND (b. 1950) British. Secretary of Burnley and Nelson Anti-Nuclear Alliance.

August 9th 1980

There was Vicki, Nicki,
Leon, Lauren,
David, Tania, Toby and others,
And my unborn child propping up one half of a banner.
As we walked
Stopping and starting
And more stopping,
Waiting.

The kids excited, impatient,
Holding brown sandwiches,
Jumping, dodging, trying to see round corners

(A flash far brighter than the sun
Mummy, my eyes, mummy.)

White cardboard mushrooms
Pushchairs draped with slogans,
Placards, badges, radiation suits,
The six year olds, blasé, reading the banners
'The last march was bigger'
'In London that was, on the train.'
Old campaigners.

(Skin peeling like fruit
From little faces, contorted.)

A long straight line of us
Cutting with care through the pallid city.
We look around,
High buildings stretch away down unfamiliar streets.
Glimpses of shops, now.
The kids are bored, complaining.

(The house cracks like a nut,
Screaming, their blood mingling with the debris.)

A policeman stands,
Face empty, boots shining like black knives,
Giving substance to his importance.
The shoppers wait to cross, patiently,
Eyes glazed with things to buy,
'Boots' then 'Woolworths', no, the Post Office
Before it closes.
We are not seen,
Just traffic passing.

(No air to breathe, the firestorm rages,
Bodies in charred heaps on twisted pavements.)

The square at last.
The kids tired, grumbling,
A little park, a few seats,
A bar of chocolate,
And they're gone.
Shouting, chasing, hiding,
Trampling the forbidden grass,
Pissing behind bushes,
Laughing.

(My little one,
Deformed, scarred, dying.)

Climbing the tall, grey cenotaph.
'Mum, look! Look what we've found.'
I looked,
Scruffy kids
Holding a bunch of scruffy flowers.
Three days old, left on the cenotaph.
'In memory of the children who died in Hiroshima 1945'
It said.
Fading.
'Put it back' I said.
Crying.

HOLLY NEAR (contemporary) American. Singer and songwriter. From 1978–80 travelled throughout USA 'on tour for a Nuclear Free Future'. All concerts were wheelchair accessible and had an interpreter for the hearing-impaired.

During a workshop before one of her performances, Holly talked about the need for a change in attitude:

We need to change the mentality, what is referred to as the nuclear mentality. It is the most highly technological version of oppression. Oppression has existed since early, early prehistoric times, whether it's child abuse, battered women, sexism, anti-gay attitudes, anti-semitism, class discrimination, racism, or disability discrimination. All of these things exist because a group of people can gain power and get tools by stepping on other people, abusing other people, using human life as a way to gain a position of power. The nuclear mentality and the nuclear madness is just the most technically advanced version of that which has been going on all along. We need to shut down the Seabrook nuclear power plant. But we can't just shut down Seabrook. We have to create good jobs for the workers at the plant and we have to deal with the attitude that allows a Seabrook to exist in the first place. This, to me, is where women come into play, where feminism has to be a leader in the work against the nuclear mentality. I think by virtue of our very oppression, strange as it may seem, we have been able to retain a kind of sensitivity to the life process that, had we been in a position of power over the last thousands and thousands of years, we might have lost. We don't know what women would have done with the same kind of power. It is nice to fantasize that we would have done a better job, but we don't know that, and by virtue of not having that kind of power in the past, we were able to develop certain skills, certain thought processes. We have been able to stay alive. We have to, as women, figure out what the best of that is, develop it, and take it further. We need to take that which is best of women, which includes the individual man. We need to take that woman who is a good mother and knows how to feed people because that has been her role, and allow her to move out and put herself in a position of leadership in the planet where she knows how to take care of Mother Earth, she knows the food process, and she knows the healing arts because she has been putting

(cont'd p. 254)

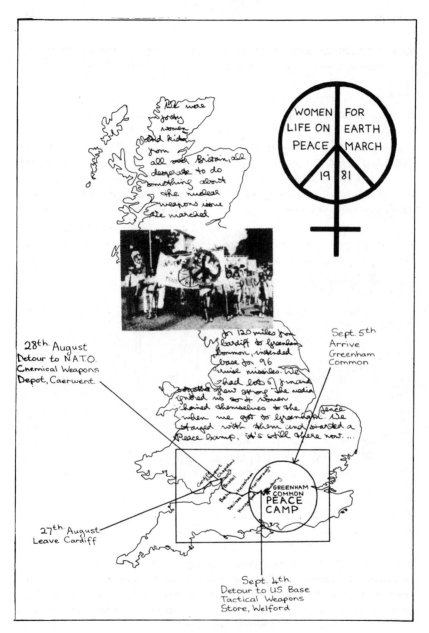

Map, 1981, by Evelyn Silver

mustard rubs on her kids' chests for years. She knows how to create a life which is liveable because her job throughout the generations has been to keep people alive.

I think it is terribly urgent, this issue of stopping nuclear power and nuclear madness. I don't think we have a lot of time. I also happen to be an optimist. I think that we can do it, because it is almost as if the urgency is finally going to push us off the fence and move us into a time when we in fact can give birth to something better. But in doing that I can't think of anybody I would rather have in a position of leadership than women who have been going through a feminist process in their own personal lives.

'Speaking Out'

LILIANE LIJN (contemporary) American. Sculptor, poet, writer.

. . . the act of receiving, the passive act, is in essence active the moment it is accomplished with awareness. It is this specific awareness which is the particular characteristic and moreover the function of the artist. Call it attention, care, love. I see it as a tenderness with which I perceive the world. In looking I am caressing what I see. I allow it to pass through my system carefully with regard for its every attribute. This is my intention and my pursuit. Is this feminine? It is the way of pleasure and feeling. I speak here of the way in: reception. I speak of a way of receiving which I consider whole. At once passive and active. Passive in that its receiving is an acceptance as opposed to a taking. Active in its attention and its ability to focus. Focussing is the most natural way to make choices.

'Receiving Change'

'PEACE SCHOLAR' Elise Boulding (see page 199) contacted women researchers on disarmament throughout the world. This piece comes from a reply by a scholar who is a specialist in non-violence.

I think research on nonviolent *alternatives* is crucial. When we have seriously explored some nonviolent alternatives, we may get some measure of disarmament. I don't think it will happen the other way around. By nonviolent alternatives I mean such things as nonviolent conflict resolution, nonviolent (civilian) defense, unarmed peacekeeping, etc. – but also economic structures that do not destroy, new kinds of social relationships, etc.

I also am not sure how much research we need in the conventional sense of that term. I think we need to *think*. I think we need to act creatively (which includes experimenting with alternatives). I think we need to understand better the ultimate sources of our anxieties and fears (which may involve some 'research'). But I happen not to think that we will be saved by 'social science' as that term is ordinarily construed.

We suffer mainly from a paralysis of will. Most people do not think we are capable of creating a relatively nonviolent world.

'Non-violent alternatives'

MANAMI SUZUKI (b. 1958) Japanese. Anti-nuclear campaigner and conservationist.

I was brought up in the Japanese countryside near the coast. My grandfather was a fisherman. I was a wild child and spent a lot of time swimming in the sea or climbing on the rocks. But when I was eight I had a great shock. My parents moved to Tokyo and I had to go to a school where the playground was covered in concrete and surrounded by traffic. I became very ill, but the doctors could not find any thing wrong with me. Then my father realised that it was the over-crowding of Tokyo which was affecting me, so he let me go to school in the country and I became well again. I started to do yoga and became more aware of the links between the spirit and the body and the environment.

Then I went to university in Tokyo and found out more about the importance of natural things and the need to conserve them. When I heard that Japan planned to start dumping nuclear waste in the Pacific in 1983 and realised that this would make the fish and other marine life radioactive, I started working in the anti-nuclear movement. I began to find out more about how the small islands of the Pacific are being

255

destroyed, not just by pollution but by the presence of the military. I visited the small island of Guam where a United States Airforce Base has taken all the good cultivable land and a submarine base has spoilt the fishing, so that the people are dependent on insecure jobs created by the military. I went to the Philippines and when I got to the airport saw many Philippino women standing there waiting for Japanese business men. They had been forced into prostitution because their land had been taken away by the military and by the big companies. The American soldiers father many illegitimate children which they abandon and they have encouraged the use of drink and drugs. Nuclear testing on other islands has made many people die of cancer.

In spite of all this suffering the Pacific Islanders possess a pure spirit. They have a calm and happy disposition and have a different concept of the universe than us. For the Japanese the sun is important, while for the Islanders it is the moon, the women's symbol, which is important. The flag of the island of Belau shows the yellow full moon in a blue ocean. The women on the islands not yet dominated by the West are very powerful and, unlike the men, think of their ancestors and their children, not just of the present. In Belau the women have been instrumental in the island's struggle to remain independent of the United States. The United States wants the island for military purposes and so has tried to persuade the Islanders to vote in a referendum, in favour of closer ties between the two countries. The women realised what that would mean and so they, especially the mothers, went around explaining what the referendum meant and why everyone should vote against it. The United States held a referendum four times but each time it was defeated by the action of the women.

But the people of the Pacific are too few and too poor to withstand the militarisation of their islands and sea without the help of people in other countries. Now I am travelling around Europe and the United States explaining why everyone should work together for a Nuclear Free Pacific.

Nuclear Free Pacific

JOAN CAVANAGH (b. 1955) American. Member of Steering Committee of the New Haven Feminist Union. 'Founding Mother' of Anti-Nuclear task force 'Sisters Opposed to Nuclear Genocide'. Has served many jail sentences for acts of civil disobedience.

I am a Dangerous Woman

I am a dangerous woman
Carrying neither bombs nor babies
Flowers or molotov cocktails.
I confound all your reason, theory, realism
Because I will neither lie in your ditches
Nor dig your ditches for you
Nor join your armed struggle
For bigger and better ditches.
I will not walk with you nor walk for you,
I won't live with you
And I won't die for you
But neither will I try to deny you
Your right to live and die.
I will not share one square foot of this earth with you
While you're hell-bent on destruction
But neither will I deny that we are of the same earth,
born of the same Mother
I will not permit
You to bind my life to yours
But I will tell you that our lives
Are bound together
And I will demand
That you live as though you understand
This one salient fact.

I am a dangerous woman
because I will tell you, sir,
whether you are concerned or not,
Masculinity has made of this world a living hell
A furnace burning away at hope, love, faith, and justice,
A furnace of My Lais, Hiroshimas, Dachaus.
A furnace which burns the babies

You tell us we must make,
Masculinity made Femininity
Made the eyes of our women go dark and cold,
sent our sons – yes sir, *our* sons –
To War
Made our children go hungry
Made our mothers whores
Made our bombs, our bullets, our 'Food for Peace,'
    our definitive solutions and first strike policies
Yes sir
Masculinity broke women and men on its knee
Took away our futures
Made our hopes, fears, thoughts and good instincts
'irrelevant to the larger struggle.'
And made human survival beyond the year 2000
An open question.
Yes sir
And it has possessed you.

I am a dangerous woman
because I will say all this
lying neither to you nor with you
Neither trusting nor despising you.
I am dangerous because
I won't give up, shut up, or put up
    with your version of reality.
You have conspired to sell my life quite cheaply
And I am especially dangerous
Because I will never forgive nor forget
Or ever conspire
To sell yours in return.

PETRA KELLY (b. 1948) West German. Chairperson of the German Green (Ecologist) Party, 1981–2.

While women have increasingly discovered their own oppression in Western Europe, in the USA, in Australia and elsewhere, they have also learned to organise themselves and speak out against the oppression of others. There has been much consciousness raising. Political issues have become personal – and personal issues political. . . .

I have hope for the world although it is 10 minutes before Doomsday – because women all over the world are rising up, infusing the anti-nuclear, peace and alternative movements with a vitality and creativity never seen before.

Women stand up in courtrooms and explain the differences between natural and artificial radiation; they stand up at demonstrations and non-violent occupations of nuclear sites because *they* are the genuine ombudsmen of children to come; they, like Dr Helen Caldicott, a children's doctor from Australia, firmly believe that each of us must accept total responsibility for the earth's survival. . . .

Women who have opposed the military base enlargement in Larzac, women who do not buy toy guns at Christmas, women who are in solidarity with their sons who are war resisters and who resist the movement to try to draft women (as is the case in Germany) *know* that the accumulation of weapons today constitutes much more a *threat* than a protection. There have been over a thousand nuclear explosions on the surface of the earth (till end of 1980) and it is estimated that the number of soldiers in the world today is twice the number of teachers, doctors and nurses. . . .

We are often told, especially in the atomic age, that the experts, that the big firms in charge of nuclearising and militarising, do not know how to deal with the problems that now threaten worldwide disaster – 'that all the facts are not in', that more research must be done and more reports written. This has become an excuse for endlessly putting off action. We already know enough to *begin* to deal, as George Wald states, with all our major problems: nuclear war, overpopulation, pollution, hunger, the desolation of the planet, the inequality among peoples.

The present crisis is a crisis, *not* of information, but of *policy*. We cannot cope with all the problems that threaten us, while maximising profits. And societies that insist above all else on maximising profits for the few thereby threaten disaster for all.

As things stand now, the people, especially women and children of the Third World are to perish first. . . .

In the last few years, I have also observed that women, through their downgrading have sought to raise their status at times by becoming part of the masculine world (cf. Mrs Thatcher and Indira Gandhi). When women fight for equal status with men, the danger is that one day they may become four star generals, build death technology, and join the front ranks in times of war.

So conditioned by male and masculine values are some of us, that we have made the mistake of imitating and emulating men at the cost of our own feminism.

Coming to terms with and relating to the masculine within ourselves is a crucial part of our development as women, both collectively, and individually. When I assess the world of male values it is clear to me that I do not wish to stand equally beside men.

Policies are *so divorced* from current needs. Half the world's expenditure on scientific research and development is on military projects. . . .

Women must lose all their fears in speaking up, in demanding what is *theirs* and their children's. Only if we begin to rediscover our own nature, can we forge new ways, ways of wholeness, balance, de-centralisation, preservation, mutual inter-dependence, co-operation, gentleness, non-possessiveness and soft energies.

For me, the words 'feminine' and 'masculine' do not denote sexual divisions of women and men, but are rather the energies belonging to both women and men. Although feminine principles and the unconscious originally predominated, as the ego became less and less dependent upon the unconscious, humanity moved into an era of patriarchy, in which the masculine – with its attachment to the ego – is the predominant principle. With this change came masculine material-ism, waste, alienation, domination, possession, and the relationship with nature was broken.

Thus, in order to stop living *against* the earth, in order to create technology that serves us and does not enslave us, we must reassert feminine values of wholeness, balance and harmony. It must become *impossible* for a small ruling class to monopolise the wealth from world resources, while transferring the social costs to the people in the form of poisoned air, water, soil and cells.

One of my greatest hopes is that men would *recover* the affective and nurturing roles with children and other people historically denied to them . . . and which has repressed the gentle humane side of males and shaped the male personality into that hyper-aggressiveness and

(cont'd p. 261)

Shibokusa Mothers' Committee, Japan

Shibokusa Mothers' Committee staging a sit-in on former agricultural land on the north face of Mount Fuji that Japanese military are using for firing practice.

Barricade of Greenham Common Air Base, March 1982, by Paula Allan

antagonistic combativeness. A richer pattern of friendship could also develop in an ecological society, diffusing the often over-exclusive nature of the nuclear marriage that makes two married adults each other's sole personal nurturer of personal intimacy over a lifetime.

And a society no longer bent on conquering the earth, no longer bent on having the largest trade balances and the largest guns and tanks, could bring about more time for contemplation, for creativity, for affirmation of others and of one's self for which there is no time in the here and now.

'Women and the Future'

THE WOMEN AT GREENHAM COMMON In September 1981, women and children marched 120 miles from Cardiff to Greenham Common and set up a Peace Camp outside the US air base there.

This extract comes from an open letter inviting women to come to an international celebration and protest in December 1982; 30,000 women were present.

Dear women,

The US air base at Greenham Common in Berkshire is the first place in Europe where 96 Cruise missiles are to be sited in December 1983. Since September 1981 women have been camping outside the main gate of the air base, protesting against this decision which has been taken without consulting the people of this country.

The women who set up the Peace Camp have made personal sacrifices because they feel so strongly about this issue. They have left their families and friends, and given up jobs to live in tents and borrowed caravans without electricity or heating throughout the severe cold of last winter. They have already faced 2 evictions and some of them have spent time in prison – but they are still here and will continue to stay and make a peaceful stand. We all feel that we cannot rely on those in power to protect our lives. The women who have left their families feel that they are taking the greatest responsibility in caring for their children by stopping Cruise missiles coming to this country. We are all individuals with a responsibility to sustain and nurture life – something we can do together, with mutual support.

The Peace Camp has been a women's initiative. Reversing traditional roles, women have been leaving home for peace, rather than men leaving home for war. The camp involves women of different ages and backgrounds. Some have never taken part in any political action before; others have been members of the Labour Party or women's groups, but all feel the urgency of the nuclear threat and are determined not to remain silent. As women we have been actively encouraged to stay at home and look up to men as our protectors. But we reject this role. We cannot stand by while others are organising to destroy life on our earth. It is not enough to go on demonstrations. We must find other ways of expressing the strength of our opposition to this madness. We have one year left in which to reverse the Government's decision about Cruise missiles. There is still time to stop them.

With peace and love, from the women at Greenham Common.

Open Letter

SUE KINGZETT (b. 1967) British. Wrote the poem when she was 14 to express her feelings about nuclear war.

The Six Minute Warning

Ladies and Gentlemen on the third stroke it'll be
The last time you hear me from studio three,
Although this is strange you must understand,
That in six minutes' time the rockets will land,
So unplug your telly and put out your cat,
Find anything strong like a knife or a slat,
Assemble your family and close all the doors,
Then go through your pantry to add to your stores,
Turn out your lights to save on the bill,
Then phone up your lawyer to check on your will,
Bring out your phone book to read while inside,
And to ring up your friends to see who's survived,
March out your children in line to your hut,
After checking your windows are all tightly shut,
Cancel the papers, the milk and the bread,
And make sure the goldfish is automatically fed,

(cont'd p. 265)

Angela and Helen at Molesworth Peace Camp, 1981, by Paula Allan

Dispose of the elders beyond eighty-two,
And any big animal send to the zoo,
Take all your jewellery and things that you cherish,
As anything left is certain to perish,
With two minutes gone and four minutes left,
Please lock all your doors to insure against theft.
Read all the instructions on page twenty-three,
Of the booklet on how to survive world war three,
Read very carefully and inwardly digest,
Then sit in your shelter for a one minute test,
Then strap all your seat belts and block all your ears,
As now flying above is the height of your fears,
No stepping outside for the next 90 weeks,
Or you'll be exposed to radiation leaks,
I think that is all on this nuclear list,
Good luck for the future if a future exists.

HELEN YOUNG (contemporary) British. Set up Molesworth Peace Camp, December 1981, with Angela Needham and Jean Hutchinson.

Most people feel that there is nothing they can do to stop the armaments race, and believe that nuclear war is highly likely. This is a self-fulfilling prophecy because if we do nothing nuclear war is highly likely. So let's start with the belief that nuclear war will not happen and that disarmament will soon start. How will this happen?

On July 9 the United Nations Second Special Session on Disarmament ended in disarray. It is 37 years since the dropping of the first atomic bomb on Hiroshima, yet the nuclear arms race and the proliferation of these insane weapons escalates. Politicians and those who hold power seem powerless to stop it, unless of course for some insane reason they actually want to destroy the world.

What about us – the people in the world who do not want nuclear war, and would rather be fed, housed, educated and allowed to live – not spending our resources on weapons of mass destruction? If we are the ones who want nuclear disarmament, we are the ones to take on ourselves responsibility for it. We need to match the tremendous energy going into the arms race (largely paid for with our money) with a greater energy into the race for peace. Bridgend Peace Camp succeeded when the council realised that the peace campers were willing to put themselves at risk by staying in the shutters while liquid concrete was poured on them. This was a real commitment and I believe history shows that most people are capable of such commitment. But how do people come out of their apathy to make such a commitment? By taking one step at a time, and by doing what they can from where they are. After each step, the next is easier.

When we started the Molesworth camp in the depth of winter, in snow, we got two very different reactions. From many supporters: 'How brave', 'What commitment', 'I couldn't do it myself', etc. – and on the other hand: 'layabouts living off the state', 'we'll listen to you, when you can do an honest day's work', etc. The truth is that we are neither heroes nor parasites but ordinary people who were in a position to be able to take a step towards a goal we felt to be important – life without the threat of nuclear war. Taking that step was difficult – it seemed absurd at Christmas to take a tent into the middle of Cambridgeshire, and go and live in it. It was so absurd that even to talk about it was embarrassing. But it was for me at that time the right thing to do, and once the step was taken, I felt a great relief, and the freedom I have gained over the months from taking that first step has been tremendous; and I shall be able, and have indeed been able, to take the next steps. What are the next steps for the peace movement to take?

One of the next steps we could take is to encourage some kind of continuous protest which everyone can take part in. We are doing a continuous protest at the peace camps, but obviously this is only for the few. But everyone could protest every month for ten minutes wherever they were in some way. As a start members of the Peace Camp blockaded the American base at Alconbury for ten minutes on Hiroshima Day. We just walked across the road, sat down for ten minutes and then left. We had told them before, and we were watched by police, but we were allowed to do it. We plan to have another protest on the 6th of every month. If you are at work you can stop work and explain your reasons, emphasising what particular aspect of peace you are most keen on: multilateralism, unilateralism, disarm for development, etc. If you are unemployed you can do it together in towns. If you are into direct action you can sit on zebra crossings for ten minutes or just walk to and fro stopping traffic. The general aim would be to stop everything for ten minutes as the protest escalates over the months. The particular aim is to give people the confidence to protest and the feeling of a nonviolent way that can achieve success. Even if you are in a job where you are not allowed to take part in demonstrations, there would be some way of doing something within your job showing your colleagues that you have some freedom to express your views.

This would be a first step towards making a greater commitment. That first step is so difficult, because so much is done for us that we are apt to say; 'It's nothing to do with us, it's their fault.' But it's up to us. And what have we to lose? – everything we love and care for, if we don't at least try and take more steps from where we are.

'A Continuous Protest for Peace'

ANN NICOL (b. 1943) British. Author of children's books. Active in Youth CND in the 1960s. Currently involved in the peace movement, member of Friends of the Earth and the Life Style Movement.
    This is a letter she wrote to *Peace News* in 1982.

I would like to suggest ways in which everyone can campaign for peace on their own without necessarily being in an organised group. Recently I decided that since 'the journey of a thousand miles begins with a single step', I would try to take one step for peace, however small, every day. The things I have done have ranged from writing letters to the press, to simply leaving a leaflet on the post office counter while signing my child benefit book. Here are some other ideas:

leaving *PN* in doctors' waiting rooms;
always carrying a few leaflets to leave in banks, libraries, phone
    booths, toilets, etc;
displaying posters at home;
persuading church or library to take a poster;
having peace symbols on everything: car, bike, pram, shopping bag,
    self, envelopes;
talking to friends or workmates and encouraging them not to feel
    powerless;

Anyone, no matter how housebound or short of time, can use this method to back up the work of more active people and to make sure that disarmament is an issue that people in their area are aware of. Yours for peace,

'Campaigning in Isolation'

JUDY CHICAGO (b. 1939) American. Feminist artist.

Untitled Poem

And then all that has divided us will merge
And then compassion will be wedded to power
And then softness will come to a world that is harsh and unkind
And then both men and women will be gentle
And then both women and men will be strong
And then no person will be subject to another's will
And then all will be rich and free and varied
And then the greed of some will give way to the needs of many
And then all will share equally in the Earth's abundance
And then all will care for the sick and the weak and the old
And then all will nourish the young
And then all will cherish life's creatures
And then all will live in harmony with each other and the Earth
And then everywhere will be called Eden once again

DANIELLE GRÜNBERG (b. 1940) British. Theatre director. In 1981 she became the national co-ordinator of the Women's Peace Alliance. She was the only English peace worker to participate in the Nordic Peace March in 1982.

Why should three hundred people, most of them women, spend the best part of their summer holiday marching 3,000 miles, from Stockholm to Minsk?

The answer goes back to last summer, when a group of Scandinavian women had the idea for a Peace March from Copenhagen to Paris.

Nordic Peace March, 1982, by Danielle Grünberg

Critics then said: 'Why are you marching in the West? You should be going to Moscow.' This was the start of Peace March 82, organised by Women for Peace from Scandinavia, a three week long journey by foot, boat and train from Stockholm to Minsk.

This was an historical occasion. The first time the slogans 'No to Nuclear Weapons in Europe, East and West', 'No to Nuclear Weapons in the World' and 'Yes, to Disarmament and Peace' would be carried by West Europeans in Russia.

'The main idea behind the march', said Eva Nordland, one of the chief organisers, 'is that we are marching against the suicide weapons to raise the consciousness in ourselves and everyone else of the need to fight against destruction. We are *not* marching against NATO *or* the Warsaw Pact.'

This message was not a difficult one to put across to the Russian people. During the marches through Leningrad, Moscow and Minsk many women watching cried. The memory of twenty million dead in World War II is still very close to their hearts and there is a real fear of another war – and of the United States.

Altogether the march left a cobweb of impressions. Spontaneous meetings with Russian people in Leningrad. Short marches and tight security in Moscow. Much singing and dancing in Minsk, all accompanied by a tight schedule of sightseeing and factory visits.

There were frustrations but the march was a success as it held out a hand of friendship with no strings attached. Above all, it showed once again the leading role women are playing in the struggle for peace and disarmament.

Nordic Peace March, 1982

MURIEL RUKEYSER (For biographical details, see p.198.)

Peace the Great Meaning

Peace the great meaning has not been defined.
When we say peace as a word, war
As a flare of fire leaps across our eyes.
We went to this school. Think war;
Cancel war, we were taught.
What is left is peace.
No, peace is not left, it is no canceling;
The fierce and human peace is our deep power
Born to us of wish and responsibility.

Chronology

1793	*'When we carry our eyes back through the long records of our history we see wars of plunder, wars of conquest, wars of religion, wars of pride, wars of succession, wars of idle speculation, wars of unjust interference, and hardly among them one war of necessary self-defence in any of our essential or very important interests.'* – Anna Laetitia Barbauld
1803	Britain declares war on France.
1805	War of the Third Coalition (Napoleonic Wars). Britain, Austria, Russia and Sweden against France.
1815	Congress of Vienna ends Napoleonic Wars. New York Peace Society founded.
1816	London and Massachusetts (later American) Peace Societies founded.
1820	Female Peace Society founded in Cincinnatti. From the 1830s, a number of other peace societies formed.
1830	July Revolution in Paris. Charles X replaced by Louis Philippe.
1837	Boston Women's Peace Association founded.
1838–42	First Afghan War.
1843	The first of many Universal Peace Congresses held. Women allowed to attend but not to speak.
1848	Revolutionary activity in France, Germany, Austria, Italy and Ireland.
1853	Russo–Turkish War starts.
1854–6	Crimean War. Britain, France and Turkey against Russia.
1854	Quaker delegation visits Czar Nicholas I in attempt to stop war. *'Won't the world come to think with us [Quakers] some day?'* – Caroline Fox *'Separately we are weak and can achieve only a little but if we extend our hands around the whole world, we should be able to take the earth in our hands like a child.'* – Frederika Bremer
1858–9	Wars in China and India. France and Piedmont at war with Austria.
1861–5	American Civil War.
1863	Russia invades Poland and 600 French women sign a petition to the Emperor in protest. British women petition Queen Victoria.

1867	International League for Peace and Liberty founded at Geneva.
1869	American Woman Suffrage Association formed.
1870	Franco–Prussian War. Paris besieged and France defeated.

'While rendering all honour to the noble efforts now being made for the relief of the wounded, we, women of England, desire also to aid the still nobler work . . . the extinction of war . . . [and] a general disarmament.' – The Englishwoman's Review

1871	Commune of Paris. Radicals take control of Paris, then suppressed.
1877	43,000 British women sign petition against imminent Russo–Turkish war.
1878	Women at Paris Peace Conference ask for equal places for women on councils of arbitration.

'The Peace party in the country would have received a larger augmentation of force if women equally with men possessed the authority of citizens to elect their governor.' – The Englishwoman's Review

1880	From *c.*1880 British military spending increases sharply and more military contracts given to private companies. More peace societies established in Europe and women become increasingly active. In 1880 the Universal Alliance of Women for Peace founded in France and British women publish pamphlet called 'How to organise a local peace association in your neighbourhood'.
1882	Priscilla Peckover starts journal *Peace and Goodwill*.
1893	First women get vote in parliamentary elections (New Zealand).
1894	War between China and Japan.
1896	International Congress in Berlin debates 'Women's part in the Peace Movement'.
1898	Swedish Women's Peace Association started. US at war with Spain over Cuba.
1899	Hague Peace Conference inaugurated. Does not succeed in limiting arms race but sets up Permanent Court of Arbitration at The Hague.
1899–1902	Boer War between Britain and South Africa. Women in Europe protest.
1901	First woman delegate to International League for Peace and Liberty.
1903	Women's Social and Political Union founded in Britain.
1904	International League for Woman Suffrage formed.
1905	Bertha von Suttner first woman to be awarded share of Nobel Peace Prize.
1906	Dreadnought battleship building starts in Britain and naval arms race intensifies.
1907	First woman MP (Sweden).
1913	Hague Peace Palace dedicated.
1914–18	First World War.

1914	*'Even when women possess the right to vote, centuries will probably pass before humanity will be able to contain war-like madness, by reasonable measures.'* – Ellen Kay In July manifesto published by International Woman Suffrage Alliance calls on governments to prevent war. In August war begins. Women in suffrage movement split over whether to support war.
1915	Women's Peace Party formed in USA. International Congress of Women assembles at The Hague, *'to protest against war and to suggest steps which may lead to warfare becoming an impossibility.'* – Aletta Jacobs The Congress sends women to visit heads of state of fourteen European countries in attempt to stop war. International Committee of Women for Permanent Peace set up.
1916	Easter Rising in Dublin. *'. . . the aspiration after liberty cannot be quelled by shot or shell.'* – Hannah Sheehy Skeffington. Conscription introduced to Britain, where Rosa Waugh makes a peace pilgrimage and is imprisoned. Women are active in anti-conscription campaigns.
1917	Revolution in Russia. USA enters First World War and starts conscription.
1918	British women over 30 get vote.
1919	Women's International League for Peace and Freedom set up.
1919–20	Paris Peace Conference.
1920	League of Nations established. American women get vote. Conscription ends in Britain.
1921	Germany ordered to pay £6,600,000,000 war reparations.
1922	The fascists march into Rome. Jane Addams publishes *Peace and Bread in Time of War*.
1924	First woman ambassador, Alexandra Kollontai, from USSR to Norway.
1928	After much campaigning for peace, fifteen countries sign the Kellogg-Briand Pact, calling for a renunciation of war. British women over 21 get the vote.
1929	Wall Street Crash (crisis in US banking and stockmarket). Poverty in USA, USSR and Europe between First and Second World Wars.
1931	American women collect over 3 million signatures for a disarmament conference. Jane Addams awarded share in Nobel Peace Prize and gives the money to WILPF.
1936	Germany invades the Rhineland. Civil war in Spain.
1936–8	Purges in USSR under Stalin.
1938	Germany invades Austria. *'Where are the mothers of the world? Farewell to you all! What may be coming tomorrow?'* – Czech member of WILPF *'It is a tragic dilemma that the world is in: to acquiesce is moral suicide and perhaps ultimately war.'* – Emily Balch

1939–45	Second World War. Conscription re-introduced to Britain. *'There's never been a lack of men willing to die bravely. The trouble is to find a few able to live sensibly.'* – Winifred Holtby
1941	Japan attacks Pearl Harbor. USA enters Second World War.
1943	In Britain 90 per cent of single women and 80 per cent of married women work outside their homes. (In 1982, 39 per cent of married women work outside the home.)
1945	On 6 August, the USA drops an atomic bomb on Hiroshima, killing 160,000 people. In Czechoslovakia, of 15,000 children who had passed through Terezin concentration camp, about 100 return home.
	United Nations set up.
1946	Emily Balch awarded share in Nobel Peace Prize.
1947	State of Israel established.
	Simone de Beauvoir publishes *The Second Sex* – *'the men with the most scrupulous respect for embryonic life are also those who are most zealous when it comes to condemning adults to death in war.'*
1949	India wins independence from Britain after a long campaign of passive resistance.
	NATO is established.
1950	Accumulation of nuclear weapons and Cold War. In USA communists and socialists persecuted by State (McCarthyism). USA announces decision to develop H-bomb. Over one million British sign petition for world to ban nuclear weapons.
1953	International exchange of children's drawings arranged by American women; 20,000 pictures circulating in 32 countries.
1951	President Eisenhower announces strategy of more A-bomb power, less man power. Inhabitants of two Pacific islands (Rongelup and Utirik) contract radiation sickness from US nuclear testing.
1955	Warsaw Pact set up (East European equivalent to NATO).
1956	B47 plane crashes at Lakenheath air-base in Britain, causing fire in weapons store containing three nuclear bombs.
	Britain's first nuclear power station, Calder Hall (now Sellafield) opens. It produces plutonium which may be used in manufacturing nuclear weapons.
1958	Campaign for Nuclear Disarmament begins in Britain. First Aldermaston march.
	1,000 scientists from 43 countries petition for international treaty to ban nuclear testing.
1959	USSR proposes conference to draw up general Peace Treaty.
1960	President de Gaulle announces plans for French nuclear strike force.
1961	Berlin Wall built. In North Carolina, USA, a B52 bomber with two nuclear weapons on board crashes. Spilled uranium contaminates land to depth of fifty feet.

1962   USSR and USA conflict over storage of Soviet missiles in Cuba.
        Britain gets Polaris submarines.
1963   USA tests first neutron bomb. USSR makes SS8 ICBM operational.
        Partial test ban treaty states nuclear testing can only be carried out
        underground or in the sea. France continues atmosphere tests
        until 1975.
        CND becomes less active.
1964   Betty Friedan publishes *The Feminine Mystique*. Civil rights
        movement and women's movement begin to develop in USA.
        Escalation of US troops in Vietnam.
        *'If you kill inside your country you get in trouble. If you kill outside the
        country, right time, right season, latest enemy, you get a medal.'* – Joan
        Baez
        In Maryland USA, a B52 with two weapons on board crashes.
        Both are recovered 'relatively intact'.
mid-1960s Mutual Assured Destruction (MAD) i.e. US and USSR now each
        capable of destroying the other, even if not the first to attack.
1967   Outer Space Test Ban Treaty bans placing of weapons of mass
        destruction in earth's orbit.
1968   Radical student demonstrations in USA and Western Europe,
        especially in Paris.
        Sweden rejects nuclear weapons and Alva Myrdal appointed
        Minister for Disarmament.
        Underground nuclear test in Nevada, USA, breaks through
        surface and releases radiation into atmosphere.
        6,400 sheep killed in Utah, USA, by escaping nerve gas.
        USSR enters Czechoslovakia.
1969   British army in Northern Ireland; CS gas used.
        Women in New York destroy draft (conscription) files as protest
        against Vietnam War.
        Leaks of nerve gas at Okinawa in Pacific permanently harm 25 US
        servicemen and 100 children.
        USSR tests SS12 missiles.
1970s   Recession worsens women's economic position but women's
        movement continues to grow.
1972   First Strategic Arms Limitation Talks (SALT). Arms proliferation
        continues.
1974   In USA Karen Silkwood dies under suspicious circumstances on
        her way to give crucial evidence about negligence at nuclear
        power station.
1976   Peace marches in Northern Ireland.
1977   Mairead Corrigan and Betty Williams share Nobel Peace Prize for
        peace work in Northern Ireland.
        80,000 Australians march against uranium mining.
1978   Demonstration against building of Torness nuclear power station
        in Britain.

1979　　In spite of much protest NATO agrees to site Cruise missiles in
　　　　Europe.
　　　　USSR enters Afghanistan and some Soviet women protest.
　　　　US Congressional Report says Bikini Island might not be safe for
　　　　100 years as result of US testing.
　　　　Serious accident at Three Mile Island nuclear power plant, USA.
　　　　Radiation released and children and pregnant women evacuated.
　　　　Movement against nuclear power becomes stronger.

1980　　World spends well over $400 billion on arms, i.e. nearly a million
　　　　dollars a minute.
　　　　World has over 40,000 nuclear warheads, many much bigger than
　　　　bomb dropped on Hiroshima. At least 6 countries possess nuclear
　　　　weapons: USA, USSR, China, Britain, France and India. 40 more
　　　　countries have enough knowledge to produce nuclear weapons in
　　　　the 1980s.
　　　　Action Man voted toy of the decade.
　　　　Peace movement gains momentum. Large anti-nuclear
　　　　demonstrations in Europe, USA and Japan in early 1980s.
　　　　Peace Tax campaign launched in Britain.
　　　　Zimbabwe gains independence.

1981　　Reagan cuts public spending but defence spending planned to rise
　　　　from 24 per cent to 31 per cent of Federal Budget.
　　　　Greenham Common and Molesworth Peace Camps set up in
　　　　Britain.

1982　　United Nations Special Session on Disarmament is inconclusive.
　　　　Britain and Argentina fight over Falklands/Malvinas.
　　　　Mothers for Peace arrange for group of Soviet and American
　　　　women to make joint tour of Britain.
　　　　30,000 women gather at Greenham Common Peace Camp and
　　　　encircle the base in protest against siting of Cruise missiles there.
　　　　*'Traditionally in our society women leave the actions to men. We need to
　　　　mobilise women and show women we can do things.'*

Biographical Details of Artists

ALLAN, PAULA (b. 1957). American. Photographer and journalist, became active in Peace Movement while covering Women's Pentagon Action in 1981. In England in 1982 she was involved in the Greenham Common Peace Camp.

ANDRIESS, EMMY (1914–53). Dutch. Photographer. Brought up by relatives after mother's death in 1928. While studying at the Academy of Art in The Hague she lived in a communal house which was unusual for that time. She belonged to a group of avant-garde left-wing photographers working in Holland.

AUCLERT, HUBERTINE. French. Prominent suffragist. Started suffragist newspaper *La Citoyenne* (the 'Woman Citizen') and edited it from 1881–91.

BODY, MARY ANN (b. 1780).

COKE, DOROTHY (b. 1897). British. Studied at the Slade School of Art. Appointed official war artist in 1940. She concentrated on painting the women's services.

CONNELLY, FRANCES (b. 1953). British. Member of the Cambridge Women's Peace Collective.

DUER MILLER, ALICE (1874–1942). American. Novelist and poet.

FLORIKA (contemporary). Born in Rumania. Lives in America.

GRÜNBERG, DANIELLE (b. 1940). British. Theatre director. In 1981 she became the national co-ordinator of the Women's Peace Alliance. She was the only English peace worker to participate in the Nordic Peace March in 1982.

KNIGHT, LAURA (1877–1970). British. Painter. Worked as an official artist during Second World War. Published her autobiography, *The Magic of the Line*, 1965.

KOLLWITZ, KÄTHE (1867–1945). German. Artist and sculptor. Political and social content of her work led to the Kaiser vetoing gold medal awarded for her prints and in 1930s Hitler ordered her works to be removed from public display. A son was killed in First World War and her grandson in Second World War.

LANGE, DOROTHEA (d. 1965). American. Photographer. Particularly known for recording the situation of poor Americans in 1930s. Hired by the War Relocation Authority of Federal Government to take the series of photographs from which the one reproduced comes.

McGREGOR, JESSIE (1853–1919). British. Student at the Academy schools where she won a medal in 1872. Exhibited at the Royal Academy and in later life worked also as an illustrator.

McIAN, FANNY (1814–97). Scottish. Exhibited at the Royal Scottish Academy and was the first woman artist to be made an honorary member in 1854. She was the director of the first 'Female School of Art' which met in Somerset House.

MEGENS, INE and WINGS, MARY (contemporary). Both work in the Netherlands.

MERRITT, ANNA LEA (1844–1930). Born in America. Artist. Largely self-taught although she received some tuition in Paris in 1871. Exhibited at the Royal Academy.

MITHILA WOMEN (contemporary). Indian (Bihar). Traditionally, it is only women in the region that produce these paintings. The forms have existed for centuries with little change. Painted on mud floors and walls, the designs are frequently changed due to the impermanence of the materials or the need to celebrate a new occasion. The paintings all have some religious significance.

MODERSOHN-BECKER, PAULA (1876–1907). German. Painter. Trained in painting in England and Germany. From 1897 lived for some time in the rural artists' colony in Worpswede where great emphasis was placed on the landscape and the life of the peasants. She also worked frequently in France. She died a few days after giving birth to a daughter.

MUDIE-COOKE, OLIVE (1890–1925). British. Painter.

NECKELMANN, ANNE LISE (b. 1921). Danish. Antique dealer and photographer. Involved in the women's movement.

SILVER, EVELYN (contemporary). British. Went on the original march to Greenham Common air base in 1981. Works with Sister Seven, a group of women artists who concentrate on issues like nuclear war.

THOMPSON, ELIZABETH (LADY BUTLER) (1846–1933). British. Painter. Trained at the Kensington School of Art and in Italy.

WEBB, PENNY (contemporary). British. Photographer.

YOUENS, PAULA (b. 1953). British. Cartoonist. Her cartoons have been published as *Lone Thoughts from a Broad*, Women's Press, London, 1981. This cartoon was drawn for this anthology.

List of Sources

ADAMS, A., 'Two Minutes' Silence', in *Stand*, vol. 22, no.3, 1981, p.28.

ADDAMS, J., 'Account of her interview with the Foreign Ministers of Europe', speech published in *The Survey*, New York, 17 July 1915.

AIKIN, L., 'Necessity', in *Epistles on Women, Exemplifying their character and condition in various ages and nations, with Miscellaneous Poems by Lucy Aikin*, J. Johnson, London, 1810, p.137.

ALEGRIA, C., 'Small Country', Editorial Universitaria, Universidad de El Salvador, in *A Book of Women Poets from Antiquity to Now*, ed. and tr. Barnstone & Barnstone, Schocken Books, New York, 1980, pp.279–81.

AL-KHANSÂ, 'For her Brother', tr. E. Powys Mathers, *Anthology of World Poetry*, 1928, in *Penguin Book of Women Poets*, ed. Cosman *et al.*, Penguin Books, Harmondsworth, 1978, pp.65–7.

ANDRIESS, E., *Photographs 1944–52*, pub. Rijksmuseum Vincent Van Gogh, Amsterdam, 1975.

ANON., 'Shule Agra', in *The Cruel Wars, 100 Soldiers' Songs from Agincourt to Ulster*, compiled K. Dallas, Wolfe Music, 1972.

ARMSTRONG, M., *Fanny Kemble; a Passionate Victorian*, Macmillan, London, 1938, p.336.

ARROWSMITH, P., 'Greenhouse', in *On The Brink*, CND publications, London, 1981, p.3.

ASQUITH, Lady C., *Diaries 1915–18*, Hutchinson, London, 1918, p.327.

ATHILL, D., *Instead of a Letter*, Chatto & Windus, London, 1963, pp.140–1.

AUCKLAND, Mrs, Address to Peace Society Meeting, in *The Englishwoman's Review*, London, 15 June 1880, p.274.

AUSTRALIAN WOMEN'S WEEKLY, from the editorial of 7 October 1939, quoted in C. Shute, 'From balaclavas to bayonets: women's voluntary war work 1939–41', *Hecate*, vol.6, no.1, Brisbane, 1980.

BACHMANN, I., 'Every Day', tr. M. Hamburger, in *Penguin Book of Women Poets*, ed. Cosman *et al.*, Penguin, Harmondsworth, 1978, p.219.

BAGNOLD, E., *A Diary Without Dates*, Virago, London, 1978, p.90.

BAKER MILLER, J., *Toward a New Psychology of Women*, Beacon Press, Boston, 1976; Pelican, Harmondsworth, 1978, pp.80–1.

BARBAULD, ANNA LAETITIA, *The Works of Anna Laetitia Barbauld*, with a Memoir by Lucy Aikin, Longman, London, 1825, vol II, p. 107.

BEAUVOIR, S. de, *Memoirs of a Dutiful Daughter*, 1st pub. Paris, 1958; tr. J.

Kirkup, André Deutsch and Weidenfeld & Nicolson, London, 1959, pp.64–5.

BEAUVOIR, S. de, Introduction to *Djamila Boupacha*, by de Beauvoir and Halimi, G., first pub. Paris, 1962; tr. P. Green, André Deutsch, London, 1962, pp.19–21.

BEHN, A., 'The Golden Age', from *Poems Upon Several Occasions*, 1684, in *A. Behn, Collected Works*, 6 vols, ed. M. Summers, Heinemann, London, 1915, vol. VI, pp.138–41.

BERNHARDT, S., *My Double Life; Memoirs of Sarah Bernhardt*, Heinemann, London, 1907, pp. 151–2.

BLATCH, H. STANTON, *Mobilising Women-Power*, The Women's Press, New York, 1918, p.184.

BOND, S., 'August 9th 1980', in *Peace News*, no.2139, 20 February 1981.

BOULDING, E., 'Women and Peace Work', in *Women in the 20th Century World*, Halstead Press, John Wiley, New York, 1977, p.167.

BRADDON, M. E., from 'After the Armistice, 1859', *Garibaldi and Other Poems*, Bosworth & Harrison, London, 1861, pp.312–13.

BRAZIL, A., *A Popular Schoolgirl*, Blackie, Glasgow, 1920, quoted in Gillian Freeman, *The Schoolgirl Ethic*, Allen Lane, London, 1976, p.96.

BRONTË, C., *The Brontës and their Circle*, selected and ed. C. Shorter, J. M. Dent, London, 1896; repr. 1914, pp.245–6.

BROWNMILLER, S., *Aginast Our Will*, Simon & Schuster, New York, 1975; Penguin, Harmondsworth, 1976, pp.32–3, 35.

BUCK, P., *Of Men and Women*, Methuen, London, 1942, pp.155–6.

BURNEY, F., *Fanny Burney's Diary; a Selection from the Diary and Letters*, ed. J. Wain, The Folio Society, London, 1961, pp.289–90.

BUSSEY, G. and TIMS, M. *Pioneers for Peace. Women's International League for Peace and Freedom 1915–1965*, Allen & Unwin, London, 1965, p.116: p.30; p.132: p.167.

BUTLER, J., *Our Christianity Tested by the Irish Question*, Fisher Unwin, London, 1887, pamphlet, Fawcett Library.

CALDICOTT, H., *Nuclear Madness*, 1st pub. Methuen, Sydney, 1979; Bantam, London and New York, 1980, pp.65–8.

CALL TO A NATIONAL DELEGATION OF AMERICAN WOMEN FOR PEACE, 1950, pamphlet, Fawcett Library.

CATT, C. C., *Carrie Chapman Catt*, by M. G. Peck, H. W. Wilson, New York, 1944, p.82: p.213; p.115: p.301.

CAVANAGH, J., 'I am a Dangerous Woman', c/o 32 Stevens St., New Haven CT 06519, USA.

CAVENDISH, M., Duchess of Newcastle, *CCXI Sociable Letters*, 1st pub. London, 1664; facsimile ed. Scolar Press, Menston, England, 1969, pp.26–8.

CHESNUT, M., *Mary Chesnut's Civil War*, ed. C. Vann Woodward, Yale University Press, New Haven, 1981, p.172.

CHICAGO, J., Untitled poem in *The Dinner Party, A Symbol of our Heritage*, Anchor Press, New York, 1979, p.256.

CH'IU CHIN, Untitled Poem, tr. K. Rexroth and Ling Chung, in *The Orchid Boat*, McGraw Hill, New York, 1972, p.153.

CLAIRMONT, C., *The Journals of Claire Clairmont*, ed. M. Kingston Stocking, Harvard University Press, Cambridge, Mass., 1968, p.358.

CRAIK, D., 'Guns of Peace', in *Poems*, Sampson Low, Marston, Low & Searle, London, 1872, p.90.

DAVIS, R. H., 'The Civil War', in *Bits of Gossip*, Archibald Constable, London, 1904, pp.125–6.

DAVYS, M., 'To Artander' in *Familiar Letters betwixt a Gentleman and a Lady. The Works of Mrs Davys*, H. Woodfall, London, 1725, vol.II, p.272.

DAY, D., *Loaves and Fishes*, Gollancz, London, 1968, p.80.

DEMING, B., *We Cannot Live without our Lives*, Grossman, New York, 1974, pp.176–7.

DÉRAISME, M. *et al.*, Address to the President of France, in *The Englishwoman's Review*, London, 5 January 1884, pp.35–6.

DERRY RELATIVES' ACTION COMMITTEE, 'Derry Relatives' Action', in *Women in Collective Action*, ed. A. Curno *et al.*, Association of Community Workers in U.K., London, 1982, pp.37–8.

DICKINSON, E., *The Letters of Emily Dickinson*, ed. Thomas H. Johnson and Theodora Ward, Cambridge, Mass., The Belknap Press of Harvard University Press, 1958; letter quoted in *The Life of Emily Dickinson* by R. Sewall, 2 vols, London, Faber & Faber, 1976, vol.II, p.536.

DROITS DES FEMMES [Women's Rights], 13 and 20 July 1870, in *The Englishwoman's Review*, London, 11 August 1870, no.11, pp.248–9.

DUFF, P., *Left, Left, Left. A Personal Account of Six Protest Campaigns*, Allison & Busby, London, 1971, pp.267–71.

DUFFY, M., *Capital*, Cape 1975; Penguin, Harmondsworth, 1978, pp.175–6.

EASTMAN, C., 'Suggestions to the American Union against Militarism for 1916–17', in *Crystal Eastman on Women and Revolution*, ed. B. W. Cook, Oxford University Press, New York, 1978, pp.250–1.

EASTMAN, C., 'A Program for Voting Women', Pamphlet, Women's Peace Party of New York City, March 1918, in *Crystal Eastman on Women and Revolution*, ed. B. W. Cook, Oxford University Press, New York, 1978, pp.266–7.

EDGEWORTH, M., *The Life and Letters of Maria Edgeworth*, ed. A. J. C. Hare, 2 vols, Edward Arnold, London, 1894, vol.I, p.188.

EICHER, M. F., 'Personal End of a War', in *Peace is our Profession*, ed. J. Barry, East River Anthology, New Jersey, 1981, p.77.

ELIAS, G., 'Poverty, politics, and mental health', in *Medical World*, London, December, 1974, p.146.

EMERSON, G., *Winners and Losers*, Harcourt Brace Jovanovich, New York and London, 1971, pp.329–32.

ENLOE, C., 'The Military Model', in *Loaded Questions, Women in the Military*, ed. W. Chapkis, Transnational Institute, Amsterdam, 1981, pp.26, 27 and 53.

FAIRWEATHER, E., 'Don't you Know There's a War on?', *Spare Rib*, London, no.78, January 1979, p.20.

FEARON, A.-M., 'Come in Tarzan, Your Time is Up', *Shrew*, Summer 1978, pub. by Women and Non Violence Study Group, c/o Jenny Jacobs, 2 College Close, Buckleigh, Westward Ho!, Devon EX9 1BL.

FENELON, F., *The Musicians of Auschwitz*, Michael Joseph, London, 1977, pp.74–5.

FINCH, A., 'The Soldier's Death', 1st pub. *c.*1691; in *The Albatross Book of Living Verse*, ed. L. Untermeyer, Collins, London, 1933, p.244.

FISHER, M. and WILLIAMS, E., 'Quaker Women', quoted from *Quaker Women 1650–1690*, by M. Richmond Brailsford, Duckworth, London, 1915, pp.100–1.

FLORENCE, L. S., *We did not Fight 1914–1918. Experience of War Resisters*, ed. J. Bell, Cobden-Sanderson, London, 1935, pp.119–21.

FLORIKA, Sisterhood is Powerful, in *Sisterhood is Powerful*, ed. R. Morgan, Random House, New York, 1970, nr p.54.

FOAKES, G., *Between High Walls – A London Childhood*, Shepheard-Walwyn, London, 1972, p.63.

FRANK, A., *The Diary of Anne Frank*, 1st pub. Amsterdam, 1947; trans. B. M. Mooyaart-Doubleday, Vallentine Mitchell, 1953; Pan Books, London, 1954, pp.179–80, 186–7.

FRY, RUTH, *Emily Hobhouse, A Memoir*, Jonathan Cape, London, 1929, pp.60–70.

GALDEMEZ, M., 'Women's Lives in El Salvador', *Spare Rib*, London, no.106, May 1981.

GASKELL, E., *The Letters of Mrs Gaskell*, ed. J. A. V. Chapple and A. Pollard, The University Press, Manchester, 1966, pp.655–6.

GAUL, A., 'The War Wife', song, H. W. Gray, New York, 1916.

GELLHORN, M., *The Face of War*, Hart-Davis, London, 1959, pp.6–8.

GOLDMAN, E., *Living my Life*, Alfred Knopf, New York, 1931; Dover Publications, New York, 1970, p.73: vol.I, pp.226–7; p.89: vol.II, pp.556–7; p.100: vol.II, pp.600–1.

GROTE, H., 'The War from an Unpopular Point of View', in *Collected Papers in Prose and Verse, 1842–62*, John Murray, London, 1862, pp.257–8.

GRÜNBERG, D., Nordic Peace March 1982, pub. as 'Swedes' peace march to Soviet', *Undercurrents*, 55/56, September 1982, p.5.

H., M. M., 'Florence Nightingale and the English Soldier', *The English Woman's Journal*, vol.I, no.2, April 1858, pp.74–5.

HAMILTON, H., 'The Jingo-woman', first appeared in *Napoo!*, Blackwell, Oxford, 1918; *Scars Upon My Heart*, sel. C. Reilly, Virago, London, 1981, pp.47–9.

HAWKES, J., 'Women against the Bomb', *Twentieth Century*, no.978, August 1958, pp.185–8.

HEINOVA, R., *from . . . I never saw another butterfly . . ., Children's Drawings and Poems from Theresienstadt Concentration Camp 1942–1944*, ed. Volavkova, details compiled by J. Weil, McGraw Hill, New York, 1964, p.38.

HOBHOUSE, M., Letter to Jack, in *Margaret Hobhouse and her Family*, by her son Stephen Hobhouse, Stanhope Press, Rochester, 1934 (280 copies), p.242.

HOWE, JULIA WARD, 'Battle Hymn of the Republic', first appeared in *The Atlantic Monthly*, 1862; 'Peace Appeal', September 1970, quoted in chapter, 'Women in the Fight for Peace', in *The Fight for Peace*, by Devere Allen, Macmillan, New York, 1930; repr. as *The Peace Movement in America*, Jerome Ozer, New York, 1972, pp.277–8.

HUTCHINSON, D., 'Opportunities Masquerade as Problems', *Pax et Libertas* (now *Peace and Freedom*), Aldsworth, Glos., vol.32, no.2, 1967.

IBRAHIM, H., Speech given in the United States (unpublished).

IRISH WOMEN'S INTERNATIONAL LEAGUE, *A New Way*, Dublin, 1917, Irish International Library.

JACKSON, H. H., *A Century of Dishonour: A Sketch of the United States Government's Dealings with some of the North American Tribes*, Chatto & Windus, London, 1881; ed. A. F. Rolle, Harper Torchbooks, New York, 1965, pp.298–9, 337.

JAMESON, S., *Challenge to Death*, Constable, London, 1934, p.20.

JAMESON, S., *Journey from the North*, Collins, London, 1970, vol.2, p.27.

JEBB, LADY, Extract from *Journal*, quoted in M. R. Bobbitt, *With Dearest Love to All*, Faber & Faber, London, 1960, p.47.

JORDAN, R., *George Sand, a Biography*, Constable, London, 1976, pp.263–4.

KARTINI, R. A., *Letters of a Javanese Princess*, first published in Dutch in 1911; tr. A. L. Symmers, Charles Scribner's Sons, New York, 1921; Oxford University Press, Jakarta, 1976, p.21.

KELLY, J., 'Women in the Military', *'Off Our Backs'*, Washington, DC, April 1980.

KELLY, P., 'Women and the Future', in *Undercurrents*, 55/56, London, September 1982, pp.29–31.

KEMBLE, F. A., *Journal of a Residence on a Georgian Plantation in 1838–1839*, first pub. London and New York, 1863; Jonathan Cape, London, and Alfred A. Knopf, New York, 1961, p.215.

KHAN, A. and NIDAL, Interview, *Spare Rib*, London, August 1982.

KING, C., Statement at WILPF Conference, *Pax et Libertas* (now *Peace and Freedom*), Aldsworth, Glos., vol.33, no.2, 1968.

KINGZETT, S., 'The Six Minute Warning', *The Winners and Runners-Up*, The English Programme Poetry Competition, 1982, Thames Television, London, 1982, p.13.

KLANZINGA, Mrs, in *The Brunt of the War*, coll. and pub. Emily Hobhouse, London, 1902.

KOLLONTAI, A., *Love of Worker Bees*, 1st pub. Russia, 1923: 1st complete English tr., C. Porter, Virago, London, 1977, p.21.

KOLLWITZ, K., *The Diary and Letters of Kaethe Kollwitz*, ed. H. Kollwitz, trans. R. and C. Winston, Henry Regnery, Chicago, 1955, pp.88–9.

KOLLWITZ, K., *Käthe Kollwitz, Graphics, Posters, Drawings*, Elefanten Press, 1979, ed. R. Hinz, trans. R. and R. Kimber, Writers and Readers Publishing Co-operative, London, 1981, plates 89, 102, 132.

LADY, A, *An Examination of the Principles which are Considered to Support the Practice of War*, by a Lady. Tract no. VIII of the Society for the Promotion of Permanent and Universal Peace, first published in *The Herald of Peace*, 1823; Thomas Ward, London, 1840, pp.12, 25–6.

LANGE, D., *Executive Order 9066* H. and R. Conrat, California Historical Association, M.I.T. Press, Cambridge, Mass., 1972, p.53.

LAST, N., *Nella Last's War. A Mother's Diary 1939–45*, ed. R. Broad and S. Fleming, Falling Wall Press, Bristol, 1981, pp.228, 256–7.

LEE, G. M., 'The Cow and Calf', *War Toys*, Peace Pledge Union, London, 1980.

LE GUIN, U. K., *The Dispossessed*, Gollancz, 1974; Granada Publishing, St Albans, 1974, p.253.

LEVERTOV, D., 'What It Could Be', in *Candles in Babylon*, New Directions, New York, 1982.

LIJN, L., 'Receiving Change', in *Resurgence*, Bideford, Devon, no.86, May–June 1981.

LONSDALE, K., *Removing the Causes of War*, The Swarthmore Lecture, Allen & Unwin, London, 1953, pp.67–70.

LUXEMBURG, R., 'Prison letter to Sophie Liebknecht' in *Letters from Prison*, 1st tr. Eden and Cedar Paul, 1923; Independent Labour Party/Square One Pamphlets, London, 1972, p.22.

LYSISTRATA PETITION, 'We will not die with you', *Shrew*, Summer 1978, pub. by Women and Non Violence Study Group, c/o Jenny Jacobs, 2 College Close, Buckleigh, Westward Ho!, Devon EX39 1BL.

McLEAN, S., 'Odyssey for Peace; Women must take the Lead', *Women Speaking*, vol.5, no.10, London, April–June 1982.

MACKENZIE, D., Letter to Bertrand Russell, in *Autobiography of Bertrand Russell (1914–1944)*, Allen and Unwin, London, 1968, vol. 2, p.77.

MANDELSTAM, N., *Hope Against Hope: A Memoir*, tr. M. Hayward, Collins and Harvill Press, London, 1971, p.297.

MANNES, M., *Out of my Time*, Gollancz, London, 1972, p.236.

MANSFIELD, K., *Letters and Journals of Katherine Mansfield* ed. C. K. Stead, Penguin Books, Harmondsworth, 1977, p.131.

MARTINEAU, H., *British Rule in India*, Smith, Elder, London, 1857, pp.301–14.

MATSUOKO, Y., *Daughter of the Pacific*, Harper, New York, 1952, pp.178–9.

MAYHEN, B. T., 'To My Black Sisters', *Up from Under*, vol.1, no.3, New York, 1971, p.44.

MEAD, M., 'Warfare is only an Invention – not a Biological Necessity', reprinted from *Asia*, vol.40, 1940, in *War*, ed. L. Branson and G. Goethals, Basic Books, New York, 1964, pp.273–4.

MEGENS, I. and WINGS, M., *Loaded Questions*, ed. W. Chapkis, Transnational Institute, Amsterdam/Washington, 1981, pp.48–9.

'MILL', 'A Place called Waterloo; Experiences of a Soldier's Wife',*The English Woman's Journal*, vol.13, August 1864, pp.269–71.

MILLETT, K., *Flying*, Granada, New York, 1975; Paladin, Granada Publishing, St Albans, 1975, pp.566–8.

MIURA, K., 'Never Again', in Bruin and Salaff, 'Never again: the organisation of women atomic bomb victims in Osaka', *Feminist Studies*, vol.7, no.1, New York, Spring 1981, p.13.

MODERSOHN-BECKER, P., in *Paula Modersohn-Becker, her Life and Work*, by G. Perry, Women's Press, London, 1975, p.35.

MONSTROUS REGIMENT, *Scum*, transcript of play from Monstrous Regiment, 4 Elder Street, London E1 6BT.

MONTAGU, M. WORTLEY, *Woman not Inferior to Man*, 1st pub. 1739 as 'by SOPHIA a Person of Quality'; facsimile reprint by Bentham Press, London, 1975, p. 49–56.

MORGAN, E., *The Descent of Woman*, Souvenir Press, 1972; Corgi, London, 1974, pp.218–19.

MORGAN, LADY, *France, 1817: the Aftermath of War* (4th ed., 1818). Quoted in *Lady Morgan in France*, ed. E. Suddaby and P. J. Yarrow, Oriel Press, Newcastle, 1971, pp.49–50.

MORGAN, R., 'The Vigil', from 'Four Visions on Viet Nam', in *Monster*, Random House, New York, 1961.

MUGABE, S., 'My life in the struggle', interview by Abigail Urey Ngara, *Africa Woman*, no.25, London, January, 1980.

MUNRO, M. L., 'Not Allowed', *War Toys*, Peace Pledge Union, London, 1980.

NEAR, H., 'Speaking Out', in *Aint Nowhere We Can Run, A Handbook for Women on the Nuclear Mentality*, Koen, Swaim & Friends, Box 801, Norwich, VT 05055, USA, 1980, pp. 57–8.

NDAAYA, C., 'Kàsàlà', *Classiques Africains*, distr. Armand Colin, Paris; tr. J. Gleason, *Penguin Book of Women Poets*, ed. Cosman *et al.*, 1980, pp.307–8.

NHAT CHI MAI, 'One who burns herself for Peace', in *On Being Female*, ed. B. Stanford, Simon & Schuster, New York, 1974, p.233.

NICOL, A., 'Campaigning in Isolation', *Peace News*, Nottingham, 15 October 1982.

NIGHTINGALE, F., Letter, May 1855, quoted in *Florence Nightingale 1820–1910*, by C. Woodham-Smith, Constable, London, 1950, p.238.

OKIMOTO, T., quoted in *Children of the A-Bomb*, compiled by A. Osada, Tokyo, 1959; tr. J. Dan and R. Sieben-Morgan, Peter Owen, London, 1963, pp.98–100.

PALEY, G., 'In These Times', in *Ain't Nowhere We Can Run, A Handbook for*

Women on the Nuclear Mentality, Koen, Swaim & Friends, Box 801, Norwich, VT 05055, USA, 1980, pp.41–2.

PANKHURST, A., 'I Didn't Raise my Son to be a Soldier' (banned under 1915 War Precautions Act), song, first quoted L. L. Robson, *The First AIF Melbourne*, MUP, 1970, p.101.

PANKHURST, E., 'WSPU Circular Letter August 13, 1914', in *Women at War 1914–1918*, ed. A. Marwick, Fontana, London, 1977, pp.28–9.

PANKHURST, S., *The Suffragette Movement: an Intimate Account of Persons and Ideals*, Longmans, Green, London, 1931, pp.592–3.

PANKHURST, S., *The Worker's Dreadnought*, vol.IV, no.20, 11 August 1917, p.824, City of London Museum.

PASTON, M., 'Letter to John Paston', in the *Paston Letters*, 1st pub. London 1787–1823; in *Paston Letters*, ed. N. Davis, Oxford University Press, London, 1971, vol.I, pp.329–31.

PAWELCZYNSKA, A., Introduction to *Values and Violence in Auschwitz. A Sociological Analysis*, Warsaw, 1973; tr. C. Leach, University of California Press, Berkeley, 1979, p.5.

'PEACE SCHOLAR', 'Non-violent alternatives', from 'Women Researchers on Disarmament, National Security and World Order', ed. E. Boulding, *Women's International Quarterly*, Pergamon Press, Oxford, 1982.

PECKOVER, P., 'Peace To-day', Paper read at the Mutual Instruction Meeting at Norwich, 25 April 1900. Printed by request of the Norfolk, Cambridgeshire and Huntingdonshire Quarterly Meeting of the Society of Friends.

PEEL, C. S., *How We Lived Then, 1914–18*, Bodley Head, London, 1929, p.85: p.39; p.112: p.137.

PETHICK-LAWRENCE, E., *My Part in a Changing World*, Gollancz, London, 1938, pp.322–3.

PETITION in favour of Lilburne's release, quoted in *Women, Resistance and Revolution*, by S. Rowbotham, Penguin Books, Harmondsworth, 1972, p.16.

PINES, S., 'Women's Pentagon Action', *War Resisters International Newsletter*, London, no.186, February 1982.

PISAN, C. de, *The Book of Peace. The Livre de la Paix of Christine de Pisan*, ed. C. C. Willard, Mouton, The Hague, Netherlands, 1958, pp.61–3. Tr. for this book by P. Rickard, E. J. Rickard and C. Naughton.

RICE, V. G., *Call to Women*, mid-March 1967, p.1, Fawcett Library.

RICH, A., 'Splittings', in *The Dream of a Common Language*, W. W. Norton, New York, 1978, pp.10–11.

RICHARDSON, D., *Pilgrimage*, Duckworth, London, 1919; Virago, London, 1979, vol.II, p.75.

ROBINSON, Miss, 'War in the Nineteenth Century', Lecture given at Southport in October 1889; printed in *The Women's Penny Paper*, 2 November 1889, no.54, vol.II, p.18, Fawcett Library.

ROYDEN, A. M., *The Great Adventure: The Way to Peace*, London, 1915, pp.11–16.

RUKEYSER, M., 'This Morning', 1st pub. *Selected Poems 1973*, in *A Book of Women Poets from Antiquity to Now*, ed. Barnstone and Barnstone, Schocken Books, New York, 1980, pp.498–9.

RUKEYSER, M., 'Peace the Great Meaning', *Collected Poems*, McGraw Hill, New York; in *Peace is our Profession*, ed. J. Barry, East River Anthology, New Jersey, 1981, p.134.

RUSSELL, D., *The Right to be Happy*, George Routledge & Sons, London, 1927, pp.294–5.

RUSSELL, D., *Call to Women*, May–August 1977, Fawcett Library.

SACHS, N., 'Chorus of the Rescued', tr. M. Roloff, in *Penguin Modern European Poets: Kovner and Sachs*, Penguin, Harmondsworth, 1971, pp.85–6.

SAINTE MARIE, B., 'Universal Soldier', Southern Music Publishing Co., London.

SANGER, M., *Woman and the New Race*, Blue Ribbon Books, New York, 1920, pp.159–66.

SAPPHO, Untitled poem, tr. W. Barnstone, *Greek Lyric Poetry*, 1962; in *A Book of Women Poets from Antiquity to Now*, ed. Barnstone and Barnstone, Schocken Books, New York, 1980, pp.31–2.

SCARLETT, D., *Window onto Hungary*, Broadacre Books, Bradford, 1958, pp.306–7.

SCHREINER, O., *Woman and Labour*, T. F. Unwin, London, 1911; Virago, London, 1978, pp.170, 173, 178.

SÉVIGNÉ, Mme de, Letter, 9 August 1675, tr. for this book by Judith Hayward from *Lettres Choisies de Madame de Sévigné*, Dent, London, 1912.

SEWALL, M. W., *Women, World War and Permanent Peace*, John J. Newbigin, San Francisco, 1915.

SH'ARAWI, H., Petition to the British High Commissioner, in *Middle Eastern Muslim Women Speak*, ed. E. Fernea and B. Q. Bezirgan, University of Texas Press, Austin and London, 1977, p.196.

SINCLAIR, M., *A Journal of Impressions in Belgium*, Hutchinson, London, 1915, pp.61–2.

SIVARD, R. L., *World Military and Social Expenditures, 1979*, World Priorities, Virginia, 1979, p.15.

SKRJABINA, E., *Siege and Survival. The Odyssey of a Leningrader*, tr. and ed. by N. Luxenburg, Southern Illinois University Press, Carbondale and Edwardsville, 1971, pp.41–3.

SMITH, S., 'In the Beginning of the War' (1942), in *Me Again*, Virago, London, 1981, pp.28–30; and 'The Poets are Silent', in *The Collected Poems of Stevie Smith*, prepared by J. MacGibbon, Allen Lane, London, 1975, p.208.

SNOAD, W., 'A Woman's Creed', in *Shafts*, London, 12 November 1892, vol.I, no.2, p.31, Fawcett Library.

SOELLE, D., Speech given in Amsterdam (unofficial transcript).

SORABJI, C., 'The International Mind in Individuals', speech from The Prevention of the Causes of War Conference, 2–8 May 1924, International Council of Women, Aberdeen.

SPEAR, L., 'An Event in Asia and Shaker Heights', in *Peace is our Profession*, ed. J. Barry, East River Anthology, New Jersey, 1981, p.77.

STANTON, E. C., GAGE, M. J., and ANTHONY S. B., eds, *History of Woman Suffrage*, 3 vols, Fowler and Wells, New York 1882, vol.II, pp.2; 87–9.

STEIN, G., *Everybody's Autobiography*, Heinemann, London, 1938, p.113.

SUTTNER, B. von, *Lay Down Your Arms; the Autobiography of Martha von Tilling*, 1st pub. in German, 1885; English ed., tr. T. Holmes, Longmans Green & Co., London, 1908, pp. 3–4.

SUTTNER, B. von, *Memoirs of Bertha von Suttner; the records of an eventful life*, Ginn, London and Boston, 1920, vol. II, pp.34–6.

SUTTNER, B. von, *Man's Noblest Thought* (a novel), Berlin, 1911, in *Suffragette for Peace – A Life of Bertha von Suttner*, by Beatrix Kempf, tr. R. W. Last, Oswald Wolff, London, 1972, p.79.

SUZUKI, M., Nuclear Free Pacific, unpublished communication.

SWAIM, N., 'The Effects of Nuclear Development on Women', in *Ain't Nowhere We Can Run, A Handbook for Women on the Nuclear Mentality*, Koen, Swaim & Friends, Box 801, Norwich, VT 05055, USA, 1980, p.20.

SWANWICK, H., *The Roots of Peace*, Cape, London, 1938, pp.181, 183–4.

SYNKOVA, A., 'I'd Like to Go Alone', in . . . *I never saw another butterfly . . .*, *Children's Drawings and Poems from Theresienstadt Concentration Camp 1942–1944*, ed. Volavkova, details compiled by J. Weil, McGraw-Hill, New York, 1964, p.38.

TEASDALE, S., 'There Will Come Soft Rains', in *Scars Upon My Heart*, sel. C. Reilly, Virago, London, 1981, pp.110–11.

ST TERESA OF AVILA, *The Interior Castle*, written c.1588, tr. a Benedictine of Stanbrook, Thomas Baker, London, 1906, p.117.

'THOMAS, BRENDA', 'Falklands: "Brides and Sweethearts" Bite Back', *Spare Rib*, no.121, London, August, 1982.

THOMSON, B., 'Promote Peace Toys', *War Toys*, Peace Pledge Union, London, 1980.

THOMPSON, F., *Lark Rise to Candleford*, Oxford University Press, 1939; Penguin, Harmondsworth, 1972, p.247.

TREVELYAN, K., *Fool in Love*, Gollancz, London, 1962, p.90.

TS'AI YEN, 'Eighteen Verses Sung to a Tartar Reed Whistle', tr. K. Rexroth and Ling Chung, *The Orchid Boat*, 1972; in *The Penguin Book of Women Poets*, ed. Cosman *et al.*, Penguin Books, Harmondsworth, 1978, p. 49.

TSHEBRIKOVA, 'Open letter to the Czar', *The Times*, London, 11 March 1890.

TWEEDIE, J., *In the Name of Love*, Cape, London, 1979, pp.51–4.

TWEEDIE, J., 'Mr Nott's Missile Machismo', *Sanity*, CND, London, December/January 1981/2, p.22.

VICTORIA, QUEEN, quotation from her *Journal*, in C. Woodham-Smith, *Queen Victoria, her Life and Times*, Hamish Hamilton, London, 1972, vol. I, p.354.

WALKER, C., Advertisement in *The Cambridge Intelligencer*, no.404, 11 April 1801.

WARD, M., *England's Effort: Six letters to an American friend*, Smith, Elder & Co., London, 1916, pp.41, 79–80.

WEETON, E., *Journal of a Governess*, 1st pub. Oxford University Press, 1936; David & Charles, Newton Abbott, Devon, 1969, vol.1, pp.10–11.

WITTIG, M., *Les Guérillères*, Editions de Minuit, Paris, 1969, trans., D. Le Vay, Peter Owen, London, 1971, pp.127–8.

WOLF, C., *The Quest for Christa T.*, Halle, East Germany, 1968; tr. C. Middleton, Virago, London, 1982, pp.19–20.

WOLLSTONECRAFT, M., *A Vindication of the Rights of Women*, J. Johnson, London, 1792; Pelican, Harmondsworth, 1975.

WOLLSTONECRAFT, M., Letter to Ruth Barlow, in *Collected Letters of Mary Wollstonecraft*, ed. R. Wardle, Cornell University Press, Ithaca, New York, 1979, p.257.

THE WOMEN AT GREENHAM COMMON, 'Open Letter', c/o 01-274 6653.

WONT, 'Something in Common', *European Nuclear Disarmament Bulletin*, no.3, Bertrand Russell Peace Foundation, Nottingham, 1980.

WOMEN OF ENGLAND'S ACTIVE SERVICE LEAGUE, *What Greater Glory?*, ed. Caws and Watts, Blackie, London, p.8.

WOMEN'S GROUP OF THE CAMPAIGN FOR NUCLEAR DISARMAMENT, Press statement published in *Daily Worker* (now *Morning Star*), London, 30 June 1958.

WOMEN'S PENTAGON ACTION, 'Unity Statement', c/o 1638 R St.NW, Washington, DC, USA.

WOOLF, V., *Three Guineas*, 1st pub. Hogarth Press, London, 1938; Penguin, Harmondsworth, 1977, p.24.

WOOTTON, B. F., *In a World I Never Made*, Allen & Unwin, London, 1967, p.50.

WORDSWORTH, D., *Journals of Dorothy Wordsworth*, 1st ed. E. de Sélincourt, 2 vols, Macmillan, London, 1941; this text available in paperback as *Home at Grasmere*, ed. C. Clark, Pelican, Harmondsworth, 1960, p.190.

WRIGLEY, Mrs, *Life as We Have Known It*, by Co-operative Working Women, intro. V. Woolf, ed. M. Llewelyn Davies, Virago, London, 1977, p.65.

YIM, L., *My Forty Year Fight for Korea*, Gollancz, London, 1952, pp.210–11.

YORK, S., 'Can we Live with the Bomb?', *Cosmopolitan*, London, January 1981, pp.99, 137.

YOUNG, H., 'A Continuous Protest for Peace', *Peace News*, 2178, Nottingham, 17 September 1982.

YÜ HSÜAN-CHI, 'To the Minister Liu', tr. G. Waters, in *A Book of Women Poets from Antiquity to Now*, ed. Barnstone and Barnstone, Schocken Books, New York, 1980, p.126.

ZETKIN, C., *The Toilers Against War*, Modern Books, London, 1934, pp.110–11.

ZIMROTH, E., 'Planting Children: 1939', *Women's Studies*, Flushing, New York, vol.7, no.3, 1980.

Further Reading and Resources

Books

Entries marked with an asterisk are particularly important texts.
*BLATTER, JANET and MILTON, SYBIL, *The Art of the Holocaust*, Pan Books, London, 1981. Contains over 350 works of art created in ghettos, concentration camps and in hiding, 1933–45.
BOSANQUET, HELEN, *Free Trade and Peace in the Nineteenth Century*, Publications de l'Institut Nobel Norvegien, vol.6, H. Aschehoug, Kristiania, Denmark, 1924.
BRIDENTHAL, RENATE and KOONZ, CLAUDIA (eds), *Becoming Visible: Women and European History*, Houghton Mifflin, New York, 1977.
DEGEN, MARIE LOUISE, *The History of the Woman's Peace Party*, Johns Hopkins University Press, Baltimore, 1939.
*DEMING, BARBARA, *Remembering Who We Are*, Pagoda, USA, 1982; distributed in UK by Naiad Press. A study of the relationship between feminism, non-violence and the Left; includes letters from women in revolutionary parties on the subject.
*DWORKIN, ANDREA, *Our Blood*, Women's Press, London, 1982. A prophetic and visionary study of sexual politics and rape.
*FEMINISTS AGAINST NUCLEAR POWER, *Nuclear ReSisters*, published by Feminists against Nuclear Power, London, 1981. Informal investigations into dangers of nuclear power. Available from alternative bookshops.
*GEARHART, SALLY MILLER, *The Wanderground: Stories of the Hill Women*, Persephone Press, Waterdown, Mass., 1979. Collection of stories about women living in a women's culture separate from men and their values.
*GRIFFIN, SUSAN, *Pornography and Silence: Culture's Revenge Against Nature*, Harper & Row, New York, 1981; Women's Press, London, 1981. The relation between the horror of pornography and divisions in society.
GYORGY, ANNA and FRIENDS, *No Nukes: Everyone's Guide to Nuclear Power*, South End Press, Boston, 1979.
*KALDOR, MARY, *The Baroque Arsenal*, André Deutsch, London, 1982. Technical description of arms industry and its effect on the economy.
*JONES, LYNNE, *Keeping the Peace: Women's Peace Handbook*, Women's Press, London, 1983. An action guide to women and the Peace Movement.
* LE GUIN, URSULA K., *The Word for World is Forest*, Berkely Publishing,

New York, 1976; Gollancz, London, 1977; Granada, London, 1980. Science fiction story which shows the conflict between a peace-loving and an aggressive culture.

*LESSING, DORIS, *The Children of Violence,* a sequence of 5 novels, the fifth of which, *The Four-Gated City* (1969), Granada, London, 1972, includes discussion of the 1960s Peace Movement and a vision of the future.

*LESSING, DORIS, *The Marriages between Zones Three, Four and Five,* Jonathan Cape, London, 1980; Granada, London, 1981. A fictional description of the damage done by polarising male and female 'qualities', with a dream about the possible ways forward.

*McALLISTER, PAM (ed.), *Reweaving the Web of Life: Feminism and Non-Violence,* New Society Publishers, Philadelphia, 1982. An anthology of contemporary women's writing.

*MERRILL, JUDITH, *That Only a Mother,* 1st pub. 1948; reprinted in *Women of Wonder,* ed. Pamela Sargent, Penguin, Harmondsworth, 1978. A science fiction story about atomic war.

MORRISON, SYBIL, *I Renounce War: The Story of the Peace Pledge Union,* Sheppard Press, London, 1962.

*MURPHY, DERVLA, *Race to the Finish? The Nuclear Stakes,* John Murray, London, 1981. Guide to nuclear power and weapons for non-specialists.

MYRDAL, ALVA, *The Game of Disarmament: How the United States and Russia Run the Arms Race,* Pantheon Books, New York, 1976; Manchester University Press, Manchester, 1977; Spokesman, Nottingham, 1980.

*PARTRIDGE, FRANCES, *A Pacifist's War,* Hogarth Press, London, 1978. An account of the thoughts and feelings of a committed pacifist during the Second World War.

PHELPS, CHRISTINE, *The Anglo–American Peace Movement in the Mid-Nineteenth Century,* Columbia University, New York, 1930.

*RAVEN, SUSAN and WEIR, ALISON, *Women in History: Thirty Five Centuries of Feminine Development,* Weidenfeld & Nicolson, London, 1981. Biographies of interesting women.

*ROWBOTHAM, SHEILA, WAINRIGHT, HILARY and SEGAL, LYNNE, *Beyond the Fragments,* Merlin Press, London, 1980. On the relationship between the Women's Movement and the Left.

*SHEEHY SKEFFINGTON, HANNAH, *British Militarism as I Have Known it,* Donnelly Press, New York, 1917. Description of British Army in Ireland during First World War. Book was banned in England when first published.

*SIGMUND, ELIZABETH, *Rage against the Dying: Campaign against Chemical and Biological Warfare,* Pluto Press, London, 1980. Good easy-to-read summary of the dangers of chemical and biological weapons.

*THOMPSON, DOROTHY (ed.), *Over Our Dead Bodies,* Virago, London, 1983. A selection of theoretical and personal articles on the bomb.

*TINKER, IRENE and BRAMSON, MICHELLE BO, *Women and World Development,* Overseas Development Council, Washington, 1976. A collection of essays exploring global attempts to resolve urgent problems of equality and growth.

WASSERMAN, URSULA, *I was an American*, Bodley Head, London, 1955. One woman's growing awareness of the importance of peace, her involvement with the United Nations and the problems she faced under McCarthyism.

*WEIL, SIMONE, *The Need for Roots: Prelude to a Declaration of Duties towards Mankind*, Paris, 1949; Routledge & Kegan Paul, London, 1952. Translated by A. F. Wills. Written during German occupation of France by a religious thinker analysing ways to establish just and stable French government.

WOLF, CHRISTA, *A Model Childhood*, Berlin, 1976; Virago, London, 1982. Translated by Ursule Molinaro and Hedwig Rappolt. An autobiographical novel which confronts the issue of complicity with Nazism through the leading character's relationship with her child.

Films and Video

CALDICOTT, HELEN, *Critical Mass*, 1980 (video).
CALDICOTT, HELEN, *If You Love This Planet*, 1982 (video).
DURAS, MARGUERITE, *Hiroshima, Mon Amour*, France, 1959 (film).
FIELD, CONNIE, *Rosie the Riveter*, USA, 1981 (film).
KIRK, GWYN, *Common Sense* (working title) Britain, 1983 (film and video).
SANDERS BRAHMS, HELMA, *Germany Pale Mother*, Germany, 1980 (film).

Useful Information Sources

Fawcett Library, City of London Polytechnic, Old Castle Street, London E1. 01-283 1030.
Friends Library, Friends House, Euston Road, London NW1. 01-387 3601.
Imperial War Museum, Lambeth Road, London, SE1 6HZ. 01-735 8922.
Tom Harrisson Mass-Observation Archive, Arts Building D, University of Sussex, Brighton, BN1 9QN. 0273 606755 ext. 1054.
University of Bradford, School of Peace Studies, Bradford, West Yorks, BD7 1DP.
Women's Research and Resources Centre, 190 Upper Street, London N1. 01-359 5773.

Information and Study Packs

'The Peace Pack', New Internationalist Publications, 42 Hythe Bridge Street, Oxford, OX1 2EP.
'The Trade Game', OXFAM, 274 Banbury Road, Oxford.
'War Toys', Peace Pledge Union, 6 Endsleigh Street, London, WC1. 01-387 5501.

'Dove Pax', Teachers for Peace, CND, 11 Goodwin St, London, N4. 01-263 0977.
'Study Kit on Feminism and Non-Violence', War Resisters International League, 55 Dawes Street, London, SE17. 01-703 7189.
'Peace Movement Kit', Women's Peace Alliance, Box 240, *Peace News*, 8 Elm Avenue, Nottingham.
'Piecing It Together: Feminism and Non-violence', c/o Jenny Jacobs, 2 College Close, Buckleigh, Westward Ho!, Devon EX39 1BL.

Publications

Peace Education Newsletter, 9 Coombe Road, New Malden, Surrey, KT3 4QA.
Peace News (fortnightly), 8 Elm Avenue, Nottingham. 0602 53587.
Sanity (monthly), CND, 11 Goodwin Street, London, N4. 01-263 0977.
Spare Rib (monthly), 27 Clerkenwell Close, London, EC1R 0AT. 01-253 9792.

Peace Organisations

In Britain

Bertrand Russell Peace Foundation, Bertrand Russell House, Gamble Street, Nottingham.

Campaign Against Arms Trade, 5 Caledonian Road, London, N1 9DX. 01-278 1976.

CND (Campaign for Nuclear Disarmament), 11 Goodwin Street, London, N4 3HQ. 01-263 0977.

END (European Nuclear Disarmament), 227 Seven Sisters Road, London N4. 01-272 1236.

Peace Camps Information. Phone (Mon.–Sat. 4.30–6.30 p.m.) 01-274 6655.

Peace Pledge Union, 6 Endsleigh Street, London WC1. 01-387 5501.

Peace Tax Campaign, 26 Thurlow Road, Leicester, LE2 1YE.

War Resisters International, 55 Dawes Street, London SE17. 01-703 7189.

WILPF (Women's International League for Peace and Freedom), 29 Great James Street, London, WC1N 3ES. 01-242 4817 (Mondays).

Women's Peace Alliance, Box 240, *Peace News*, 8 Elm Avenue, Nottingham.

WONT (Women Oppose the Nuclear Threat), Box 600, *Peace News*, 8 Elm Avenue, Nottingham.

International Groups

American Friends Service Committee, 1501 Cherry Street, Philadelphia, PA 19102, USA.

Campaign for a Nuclear Free Pacific, Pacific Concerns Resources Centre, PO Box 27692, Honolulu, Hawaii 96827, USA.

Friends Society, Dorothea Woods, 32 Rue de Vermont, CH-Geneva 1201, Switzerland.

International Feminist Network, Via S. Maria dell'Anima 30, Rome, Italy (06/58 08 231) and OP50 (Cornavin), 1211 Geneva 2, Switzerland (022/33 67 46).

SIPRI (Peace Research), Maria Lunderius, Sveavägen 166, S-113, 46 Stockholm, Sweden.

Transnational Institute, Feminism Project, Paulus Pottersraat 20, Amsterdam, Netherlands.

War Resisters League, 339 Lafayette Street, New York, NY 10027, USA.

Women's International Democratic Federation, Unter den Linden 13, 1080 Berlin, German Democratic Republic.

Women's Research Centre, 252 Bloor Street West, Toronto, Ontario, Canada.

Acknowledgments

The Collective and Publishers gratefully acknowledge the following for granting permission to reproduce material in copyright:

ANNA ADAMS 'Two Minutes' Silence' is reprinted from *Stand*, vol.22, no.3 (n.d., 1981?), by permission of the Editor.

JANE ADDAMS the extract from an Account of her Interview with the Foreign Ministers of Europe is reprinted by permission of the Swarthmore College Peace Collection, Pennsylvania.

CLARIBEL ALEGRIA 'Small Country', from *A Book of Women Poets from Antiquity to Now*, edited by A. and W. Barnstone, and published by Schocken Books Inc., is reprinted by permission of Editorial Universitaria, Universidad de El Salvador.

AL-KHANSÂ 'For her Brother', translated by E. Powys Mathers, is reprinted by permission of Houghton Mifflin Company and Boni Publishing Company.

MARGARET ARMSTRONG the extract from *Fanny Kemble; a Passionate Victorian* is reprinted by permission of Macmillan, London and Basingstoke.

LADY CYNTHIA ASQUITH the extract from *Diaries 1915–1918*, published by Hutchinson, is reprinted by permission of the publisher and the literary agent, Joan M. Ling.

DIANA ATHILL the extract from *Instead of a Letter* (Reprint Society edition, 1965) is reprinted by permission of André Deutsch Ltd.

AUSTRALIAN WOMEN'S WEEKLY extract reprinted by permission of the Editor.

INGEBORG BACHMANN 'Every Day', originally published in her collection *Die Gestundete Zeit* by R. Piper & Co. Verlag, Munich, is reprinted by permission of the translator, Michael Hamburger Copyright © 1978 Michael Hamburger, and R. Piper & Co. Verlag.

ENID BAGNOLD the extract from *A Diary Without Dates* is reprinted by permission of William Heinemann Ltd and Little, Brown & Co.

SIMONE DE BEAUVOIR the extract from *Memoirs of a Dutiful Daughter*, translated by James Kirkup and published by André Deutsch and Weidenfeld & Nicolson, Copyright © The World Publishing Company. The extract from the Introduction to Simone de Beauvoir and Gisele Halini's *Djamila Boupacha*, translated by Peter Green, published by André Deutsch, is reprinted by permission of André Deutsch Ltd.

SUE BOND 'August 9th 1980' from *Peace News*, no. 2139 (Feb. 1981), is reprinted by permission of *Peace News*, 8 Elm Avenue, Nottingham.

ELISE BOULDING the extract from her paper, 'Women and Peace Work', in *Women in the Twentieth Century World,* published by Halstead Press, is reprinted by permission of the author and Sage Publications Inc.

ANGELA BRAZIL the extract from *A Popular Schoolgirl* is reprinted by permission of Blackie & Son Ltd.

SUSAN BROWNMILLER the extract from *Against Our Will* copyright © 1975 by Susan Brownmiller, is reprinted by permission of Secker & Warburg and Simon & Schuster, a Division of Gulf and Western Corporation.

PEARL S. BUCK the extract from *Of Men and Women* is reprinted by permission of Methuen London Ltd.

GERTRUDE BUSSEY and MARGARET TIMS the extracts from *Pioneers for Peace – Women's International League for Peace and Freedom, 1915–1965,* reissued by WILPF in 1980, are reprinted by permission of WILPF and the authors.

HELEN CALDICOTT the extract from *Nuclear Madness: What you can Do* is reprinted by permission of Autumn Press, Inc., Copyright © 1978, 1980, by Helen M. Caldicott.

CARRIE CHAPMAN CATT the extracts from *Carrie Chapman Catt: a Biography,* by Mary Grey Peck, are reprinted by permission of H. W. Wilson & Company, New York.

JOAN CAVANAGH 'I am a Dangerous Woman' reprinted by permission of the author.

MARY CHESNUT the extract from *Mary Chesnut's Civil War,* edited by C. Vann Woodward, published by, and reprinted by permission of, Yale University Press, Copyright © 1981 by C. Vann Woodward, Sally Bland Metts, Barbara G. Carpenter, Sally Bland Johnson, and Katherine W. Herbert.

JUDY CHICAGO Untitled Poem from *The Dinner Party* by Judy Chicago, Copyright © 1979 by Judy Chicago. Reprinted by permission of Doubleday & Company, Inc.

CH'IU CHIN Untitled Poem, translated by Kenneth Rexroth and Ling Chung, from *The Orchid Boat* published by McGraw-Hill, reprinted by permission of Seabury Press, New York.

CLAIRE CLAIRMONT the extract from *The Journals of Claire Clairmont,* edited by Marion Kingston Stocking, reprinted by permission of Harvard University Press, © 1968 by the President and Fellows of Harvard College.

DAILY WORKER the Press Statement of the Women's Group of the Campaign for Nuclear Disarmament, originally published in the *Daily Worker,* is reprinted by permission of the *Morning Star* (formerly *Daily Worker*).

DOROTHY DAY the extract from *Loaves and Fishes* is reprinted by permission of Harper & Row, Publishers, Inc.

BARBARA DEMING the extract from *We Cannot Live without our Lives* is reprinted by permission of Grossman Publishers, a division of The Viking Press, New York and the author.

DERRY RELATIVES' ACTION COMMITTEE the extract 'Derry Relatives'
Action' in *Women in Collective Action*, edited by Ann Curno *et al.* and
published by the Association of Community Workers, is reprinted by
permission of the Association.

EMILY DICKINSON the extract from *The Letters of Emily Dickinson*, edited by
Thomas H. Johnson and Theodora Ward, and published by The Belknap
Press, is reprinted by permission of Harvard University Press, © 1958 by
the President and Fellows of Harvard College.

PEGGY DUFF the extract from *Left, Left Left. A Personal Account of Six Protest
Campaigns* is reprinted by permission of Allison & Busby.

MAUREEN DUFFY the extract from *Capital* is reprinted by permission of
Jonathan Cape Ltd and George Braziller Inc.

CRYSTAL EASTMAN the extracts from 'Suggestions to the American Union
against Militarism for 1916–17' and 'A Program for Voting Women' are
reprinted by permission of the Swarthmore College Peace Collection and
the WILPF, US Section.

MARGARET FLANAGAN EICHER 'Personal End of a War' from *Peace is our
Profession*, edited by Jan Barry, is reprinted by permission of the Editor and
the author.

GERTRUDE ELIAS the extract from 'Poverty, Politics and Mental Health',
first published in *Medical World* (Dec. 1974), is reprinted by permission of
the author.

GLORIA EMERSON the extract from *Winners and Losers: Battles, Retreats,
Gains, Losses and Ruins from a Long War* Copyright, and reprinted by
permission of, Alfred A. Knopf, Inc.

CYNTHIA ENLOE the extracts from 'The Military Model', in *Loaded
Questions, Women in the Military*, edited by Wendy Chapkis, are reprinted
by permission of the Transnational Institute, Amsterdam.

EILEEN FAIRWEATHER the extract from 'Don't you Know There's a War
on?' in *Spare Rib*, no.78 (June 1979), is reprinted by permission of the author
and the *Spare Rib* Collective.

ANNE-MARIE FEARON the extracts from 'Come in Tarzan, Your Time is
Up', from *Shrew* (Summer 1978), published by Women and Non-violence
Study Group, are reprinted by permission of the Group.

FANIA FENELON the extract from *The Musicians of Auschwitz* is reprinted by
permission of Michael Joseph and Opera Mundi.

GRACE FOAKES the extract from *Between High Walls* is reprinted by
permission of Shepheard-Walwyn (Publishers) Ltd.

ANNE FRANK the extract from *The Diary of a Young Girl*, translated by B. M.
Mooyaart-Doubleday, is reprinted by permission of Vallentine Mitchell &
Co.

MIRIAM GALDEMEZ the extract from the interview with Jenny Vaughan
and Jane MacIntosh, 'Women's Lives in El Salvador', in *Spare Rib*, no.106
(May 1981), is reprinted by permission of Miriam Galdemez, the
interviewers and the *Spare Rib* Collective.

MRS GASKELL the extract from *The Letters of Mrs Gaskell*, edited by J. A. V. Chapple and A. Pollard, © 1966 Manchester University Press, reprinted with their permission.

MARTHA GELLHORN the extract from *The Face of War*, originally published by Rupert Hart-Davis, is reprinted by permission of the author.

EMMA GOLDMAN the extracts from *Living my Life*, Copyright, and reprinted by permission of, Alfred A. Knopf, Inc.

THE WOMEN AT GREENHAM COMMON the 'Open Letter' is reprinted by permission of the Greenham Common Women's Peace Camp.

DANIELLE GRÜNBERG 'Nordic Peace March, 1982', from *Undercurrents*, no.55/56 (Sept. 1982), reprinted by permission of the Editor.

JACQUETTA HAWKES the extract 'Women against the Bomb', from *The Twentieth Century Magazine*, is reprinted by permission of the author.

MARGARET HOBHOUSE the extract from *Margaret Hobhouse and her Family*, by Stephen Hobhouse, is reprinted by permission of Paul Hobhouse.

DOROTHY HUTCHINSON the extract from her article in *Pax et Libertas* (international newsletter of WILPF), vol.32, no.2 (April–June 1967), is reprinted by permission of the Women's International League for Peace and Freedom, Geneva.

HUMA IBRAHIM the extract from her speech is reprinted by permission of Women against Militarism.

STORM JAMESON the extract from *Challenge to Death* is reprinted by permission of Constable Publishers. The extract from *Journey from the North* is reprinted by permission of Collins Publishers and A. D. Peters & Co. Ltd.

LADY JEBB the extract from her Journal, quoted in *With Dearest Love to All: Letters and Journals of Lady Caroline Jebb*, edited by Mary Reed Bobbitt, is reprinted by permission of Faber & Faber.

RUTH JORDAN the extract from *George Sand, a Biography*, published by Constable, is reprinted by permission of the author.

RADEN ADJENG KARTINI the extract from *Letters of a Javanese Princess: Raden Adjeng Kartini*, translated by Agnes Louise Symmers, is reprinted by permission of Charles Scribner's Sons.

JANIS KELLY the extract from 'Women in the Military', in *Off our Backs* (April 1980), is reprinted by permission of the author.

PETRA KELLY the extract from 'Women and the Future' from *Undercurrents*, no.55/56 (Sept. 1982), is reprinted by permission of the Editor.

FRANCES ANNE KEMBLE the extract from *Journal of a Residence on a Georgian Plantation in 1838–1839*, edited by John A. Scott, Copyright, and reprinted by permission of, Alfred A. Knopf, Inc.

ALIZA KHAN and NIDAL the extracts from their interview with Roisín Boyd, 'Women Speak out Against Zionism', in *Spare Rib*, no.121 (Aug. 1982), are reprinted by permission of the interviewees, Roisín Boyd and the *Spare Rib* Collective.

CORETTA KING the extract from her article in *Pax et Libertas* (international newsletter of WILPF), vol.33, no.2 (April–June 1968), is reprinted by permission of the Women's International League for Peace and Freedom, Geneva.

SUE KINGZETT 'The Six Minute Warning' from *Thames TV English Programme Poetry Competition*, is reprinted by permission of the author.

ALEXANDRA KOLLONTAI this extract is taken from *Love of Worker Bees* by Alexandra Kollantai, translated by Cathy Porter, which is published by Virago Press, London.

NELLA LAST the extract from *Nella Last's War; A Mother's Diary, 1939–45*, edited by Richard Broad and Suzie Fleming, is reprinted by permission of Falling Wall Press and The Tom Harrisson Mass-Observation Archive Trustees, University of Sussex. (The Archive contains many women's and men's diaries for the Second World War period.)

GILLIAN MARY LEE 'The Cow and Calf' from *War Toys Bulletin*, published by the Peace Pledge Union, is reprinted by permission of the author.

URSULA K. LE GUIN the extract from *The Dispossessed* is reprinted by permission of Harper & Row, Publishers, Inc. and Victor Gollancz Ltd.

DENISE LEVERTOV 'What It Could Be', from *Candles in Babylon*, Copyright © 1982 by Denise Levertov, is reprinted by permission of the author and New Directions Publishing Corporation.

LILIANE LIJN the extract from 'Receiving Change', published in *Resurgence* (May–June 1981), is reprinted by permission of the author.

KATHLEEN LONSDALE the extract from *Removing the Causes of War* is reprinted by permission of George Allen & Unwin.

LYSISTRATA PETITION reprinted by permission of the Editor of *Shrew*.

DOROTHY MACKENZIE the extract from *Autobiography of Bertrand Russell*, volume 2, is reprinted by permission of George Allen & Unwin.

NADEZHDA MANDELSTAM the extract from *Hope Against Hope*, translated by Max Hayward, Copyright © 1970 by Atheneum Publishers; English translation Copyright © 1970 by Atheneum Publishers. Reprinted with the permission of Atheneum Publishers.

MARYA MANNES the extract from *Out of My Time* is reprinted by permission of Victor Gollancz Ltd and David J. Blow.

KATHERINE MANSFIELD the text of the extract from *The Letters and Journals of Katherine Mansfield: a Selection*, edited by C. K. Stead and published by Penguin Books, was originally in *Journal of Katherine Mansfield*, by Katherine Mansfield Copyright 1927 by Alfred A. Knopf, Inc. and renewed 1955 by J. Middleton Murry. Reprinted by permission of the publisher.

YOKO MATSUOKA the extract from *Daughter of the Pacific* is reprinted by permission of Harper & Row, Publishers, Inc.

BETTY THOMAS MAYHEN 'To My Black Sisters', from *Up from Under*, vol.1, no.3 (Jan.–Feb. 1971), is reprinted by permission of the Editor.

SCILLA McLEAN the extract from 'Odyssey for Peace' in *Women Speaking*, vol.5, no.10 (Apr.–June 1982), is reprinted by permission of the Editor.

MARGARET MEAD the extract from 'Warfare is only an Invention – not a

Biological Necessity', in *War,* edited by Leon Branson and George W.
Goethals and published by Basic Books, Inc., is reprinted by permission of
Catherine Bateson.

JEAN BAKER MILLER the extract from *Toward a New Psychology of Women* by
Jean Baker Miller Copyright © 1976 by Jean Baker Miller. Reprinted by
permission of Beacon Press, Richard Scott Simon Ltd and Georges
Borchardt Inc.

KATE MILLETT the extract from *Flying* is copyright, and reprinted by
permission of, Alfred A. Knopf, Inc., and Granada Publishing Limited.

KAZUE MIURA the extract from 'Never Again: the Organization of Women
Atomic Bomb Victims in Osaka', reprinted with changes from *Feminist
Studies,* vol.7, no.1 (Spring 1981), pp.15–18, by permission of the publisher,
Feminist Studies, Inc. Copyright © 1981 by Feminist Studies, Inc.

MONSTROUS REGIMENT the extract from *Scum* is reprinted by permission
of the Collective and Mary McCusker.

ELAINE MORGAN the extract from *The Descent of Woman,* copyright © 1972
by Elaine Morgan, is reprinted by permission of Souvenir Press Ltd and
Stein & Day Publishers.

ROBIN MORGAN 'The Vigil' from 'Four Visions on Vietnam' in her
collection, *Monster,* published by Vintage Books, New York, A Division of
Random House, is copyright, and reprinted by permission of, Random
House, Inc., New York and the author.

SALLY MUGABE the extract from *Africa Woman* magazine, no.25 (Jan.–Feb.
1980), is reprinted by permission of the Managing Editor.

MARTA LOUISE MUNRO 'Not Allowed' from *War Toys Bulletin,* published
by the Peace Pledge Union, is reprinted by permission of the author.

CITÈKÙ NDAAYA 'Ndaaya's Kàsàlà', translated by Judith Gleason, is
reprinted by permission of Classiques Africains, and Judith Gleason
Copyright © 1978 Judith Gleason.

HOLLY NEAR 'Speaking out' in *Ain't Nowhere we can Run: Handbook for
Women on the Nuclear Mentality,* by Susan Koen and Nina Swaim, is
reprinted by permission of the author and WAND (Box 801, Norwich, VT
05055, USA).

NHAT CHI MAI 'One who Burns Herself for Peace', from *On Being Female,*
edited by Barbara Stanford, is reprinted by permission of the Editor.

ANN NICOL 'Campaigning in Isolation', a letter published in *Peace News* (15
Oct. 1982), is reprinted by permission of the author.

TAKAKO OKIMOTO the extract from *Children of the A-Bomb: the Testament of
the Boys and Girls of Hiroshima,* compiled by Arata Osada, and translated by
Jean Dan and Ruth Sieben-Morgan, is reprinted by permission of Peter
Owen and Uchida Rokakuho Publishing House, Tokyo.

GRACE PALEY the extracts from 'In These Times' in *Ain't Nowhere we can
Run: Handbook for Women on the Nuclear Mentality,* by Susan Koen and Nina
Swaim, is reprinted by permission of the authors and WAND (Box 801,
Norwich, VT 05055, USA).

ADELA PANKHURT 'I Didn't Raise my Son to be a Soldier', from *The First AIF* by L. L. Robson, is reprinted by permission of the author and Melbourne University Press.

SYLVIA PANKHURST the extract from *The Suffragette Movement: an Intimate Account of Persons and Ideals* is reprinted by permission of Longman Ltd.

ANNA PAWELCZYNSKA the extract from the Introduction to *Values and Violence in Auschwitz* is reprinted by permission of Polish Scientific Publishers, Warsaw.

MRS C. S. PEEL the extracts from *How We Lived Then, 1914–1918* are reprinted by permission of The Bodley Head.

EMMELINE PETHICK-LAWRENCE the extract from *My Part in a Changing World* is reprinted by permission of Victor Gollancz Ltd.

SUSAN PINES the extract from 'Women's Pentagon Action', in *WRI Newsletter*, no.186 (Feb. 1982), is reprinted by permission of the author and War Resisters' International.

CHRISTINE DE PISAN the extract from *Le Livre de la Paix* [*The Book of Peace*], edited by Charity Cannon Willard and translated by Peter Rickard, Elizabeth Jane Rickard and Carol Naughton, is reprinted by permission of Mouton & Co., The Hague.

VERA G. RICE the extract from the editorial in *Call to Women*, no.50 (March 1967), is reprinted by permission of the current Editor and the author.

ADRIENNE RICH 'Splittings' is reprinted from *The Dream of a Common Language, Poems, 1974–1977*, by Adrienne Rich, Copyright © 1978 by W. W. Norton & Company Inc.

DOROTHY RICHARDSON the extract from volume II of *Pilgrimage* is reprinted by permission of Virago Press, London, and Mark Paterson and Associates on behalf of Sheena Odle.

MURIEL RUKEYSER 'This Morning', from *Selected Poems*, published by New Directions, is reprinted by permission of International Creative Management, New York. 'Peace the Great Meaning', from *Collected Poems*, published by McGraw-Hill, is reprinted by permission of International Creative Management, New York.

DORA RUSSELL the extract from *The Right to be Happy* is reprinted by permission of Routledge & Kegan Paul Ltd and Harper & Row, Publishers, Inc. The extract from Dora Russell's letter to *Call to Women* (May–Aug. 1977) is reprinted by permission of the Editor and the author.

NELLY SACHS 'Chorus of the Rescued' tr. M. Roloff, is reprinted by permission of Jonathan Cape Ltd and Suhrkamp Verlag, Frankfurt am Main.

BUFFY SAINTE MARIE the song 'Universal Soldier' is reprinted by permission of the Peer-Southern Organisation and Caleb Music Inc., Los Angeles, © Copyright 1963 by Woodmere Music, North Woodmere, New York, USA and Southern Music Publishing Company Limited, 8 Denmark Street, London WC2.

MARGARET SANGER the extract from *Woman and the New Race*, originally published by Blue Ribbon Books, New York, is reprinted by permission of Doubleday & Company Inc.

SAPPHO Untitled Poem, from *Greek Lyric Poetry*, translated by W. Barnstone, is reprinted by permission of Schocken Books Inc.

DORA SCARLETT the extract from *Window onto Hungary* is reprinted by permission of Broadacre Books Ltd.

HUDA SH'ARAWI the petition to the British High Commissioner, quoted in *Middle Eastern Muslim Women Speak*, edited by Elizabeth Warnock Fernea and Basima Qattan Bezirgan, is reprinted by permission of The University of Texas Press, Copyright © 1977 by The University of Texas Press.

MAY SINCLAIR the extract from *A Journal of Impressions in Belgium* is reproduced by permission of Curtis Brown, London, on behalf of the Estate of May Sinclair.

RUTH LEGER SIVARD 'World Military and Social Expenditures, 1979', from *World Military and Social Expenditures 1981*, by Ruth Sivard, Copyright © World Priorities, Leesburg, VA 22075, USA.

ELENA SKRJABINA the extract from *Siege and Survival. The Odyssey of a Leningrader*, by Elena Skrjabina Copyright © 1971 by the Southern Illinois University Press. Reprinted by permission of the Southern Illinois University Press.

STEVIE SMITH the short story 'In the Beginning of the War' is reprinted from *Me Again* by permission of Virago Press, London and Farrar, Straus & Giraux Inc. 'The Poets are Silent', from *The Collected Poems of Stevie Smith*, published by Allen Lane, is reprinted by permission of James MacGibbon, Stevie Smith's executor.

DOROTHEE SOELLE the extract from her speech given at the 'Waging Peace' conference is reprinted by permission of the Author.

CORNELIA SORABJI the extract from 'The International Mind in Individuals', in *The Prevention and Causes of War*, published by the International Council of Women, is reprinted with their permission.

LAUREL SPEAR 'An Event in Asia and Shaker Heights', from *Peace is our Profession*, edited by Jan Barry, is reprinted by permission of the Editor and the author.

GERTRUDE STEIN the extract from *Everybody's Autobiography*, published by William Heinemann Ltd, is reprinted by permission of David Higham Associates Ltd.

BERTHA VON SUTTNER the extract from *Man's Noblest Thought*, translated by R. W. Last, is quoted in *Suffragette for Peace* by Beatrix Kempf, and is reprinted by permission of Oswald Wolff Publishers Ltd.

MANAMI SUZUKI 'Nuclear Free Pacific' is published by permission of the author.

NINA SWAIM the extract 'The Effect of Nuclear Development on Women', in *Ain't Nowhere we can Run: Handbook for Women on the Nuclear Mentality*, by Susan Koen and Nina Swaim, is reprinted by permission of the author and WAND (Box 801, Norwich, VT 05055, USA).

HELENA M. SWANWICK the extracts from *The Roots of Peace* are reprinted by permission of Jonathan Cape Ltd.

ALENA SYNKOVA 'I'd Like to Go Alone', from . . . *I never saw another butterfly* . . ., compiled by Jiri Weil and published by McGraw-Hill, is reprinted by permission of Artia, Prague, and the Editor Helena Volavková.

SARA TEASDALE 'There Will Come Soft Rains', from *A Treasury of War*, 2nd series, edited by G. H. Clarke, and published by Houghton Mifflin Company, is reprinted by permission of Macmillan Publishing Company.

ST TERESA OF AVILA the extract from *The Interior Castle*, translated by a Benedictine of Stanbrook, originally published by Thomas Baker, was reprinted in *A Book of Comfort*, compiled by Elizabeth Goudge, and published by Michael Joseph Ltd.

'BRENDA THOMAS' the extracts from her interview with Susan Hemmings, 'Falklands: "Brides and Sweethearts" Bite Back', in *Spare Rib*, no.121 (Aug. 1982), are reprinted by permission of 'Brenda Thomas', Susan Hemmings, and the *Spare Rib* Collective.

FLORA THOMPSON the extract from *Lark Rise to Candleford* is reprinted by permission of Oxford University Press.

BRENDA THOMSON the extract from 'Promote Peace Toys', from *War Toys Bulletin*, published by the Peace Pledge Union, is reprinted by permission of the author.

KATHARINE TREVELYAN the extract from *Fool in Love*, published by Victor Gollancz Ltd is reprinted by permission of Anthony Sheil Associates Ltd, Copyright © Katharine Trevelyan 1962.

TS'AI YEN lines from 'Eighteen Verses Sung to a Tartar Reed Whistle', translated by Kenneth Rexroth and Ling Chung, from *Women Poets of China*, copyright © 1972 by Kenneth Rexroth and Ling Chung. Reprinted by permission of New Directions Publishing Corporation.

JILL TWEEDIE the extract from *In the Name of Love* is reprinted by permission of Jonathan Cape Ltd and Pantheon Books Inc. The extract from her article, 'Mr Nott's Missile Machismo', in *Sanity* (Dec.–Jan. 1981/82), is reprinted by permission of CND Publications.

QUEEN VICTORIA the extract from her journal, quoted in *Queen Victoria: her Life and Times*, volume 1, *1819–1861*, by Cecil Woodham-Smith, copyright, and reprinted by permission of, Alfred A. Knopf, Inc., and Hamish Hamilton Ltd.

ELLEN WEETON the extract from *Journal of a Governess* is reprinted by permission of Oxford University Press.

MONIQUE WITTIG the extract from *Les Guérillères*, translated by David Le Vay, and published by Peter Owen Ltd, London, is reprinted with their permission and that of Les Éditions de Minuit.

CHRISTA WOLF the extract from *The Quest for Christa T.*, translated by Christopher Middleton, is reprinted by permission of Farrar, Straus & Giroux Inc., Virago Press, London, and Mitteldeutscher Verlag, Halle.

MARY WOLLSTONECRAFT the extract from *Collected Lettters of Mary*

Acknowledgments

Wollstonecraft, edited by Ralph M. Wardle, copyright, and reprinted by permission of, Cornell University Press.

WOMEN'S PENTAGON ACTION the extract from the Unity Statement is reprinted by permission of the Women's Pentagon Action Group.

WONT the extract from the article 'Something in Common: Women Oppose the Nuclear Threat', from *END Bulletin*, no.3 (1980), published by the Bertrand Russell Peace Foundation, is reprinted by permission of the Foundation and the Leeds WONT Group.

VIRGINIA WOOLF the extracts from *Three Guineas* are reprinted by permission of the Author's Literary Estate and The Hogarth Press, and Harcourt Brace Jovanovich, Inc., New York.

BARBARA FRANCES WOOTTON the extract from *In a World I Never Made* is reprinted by permission of George Allen & Unwin.

DOROTHY WORDSWORTH the extract from *Journals of Dorothy Wordsworth*, edited by E. de Sélincourt, is reprinted by permission of Macmillan, London and Basingstoke.

LOUISE YIM the extract from *My Forty Year Fight for Korea*, fourth edition 1967, pages 209–10, 310 words. Publisher: International Culture Research Center, Chung-Ang University, Seoul, Korea.

SUSANNAH YORK the extract from 'Can we Live with the Bomb?' is reprinted by permission of *Cosmopolitan*.

HELEN YOUNG 'A Continuous Protest for Peace', from *Peace News*, no.2178 (Sept. 1982), is reprinted by permission of *Peace News*, 8 Elm Avenue, Nottingham.

YÜ HSÜAN-CHI 'To the Minister Liu', translated by Geoffrey Waters, from *A Book of Women Poets from Antiquity to Now*, edited by A. & W. Barnstone, reprinted by permission of Schocken Books and the translator.

EVAN ZIMROTH 'Planting Children: 1939', originally published in *Women's Studies: an Interdisciplinary Journal*, vol.7 (1980), is reprinted by permission of the author.

Every effort has been made to trace copyright holders of material in this book; unfortunately, in some cases, this has proved impossible. The Collective and Publishers would be glad to hear from any copyright holders they have been unable to approach, and to print due acknowledgments at the earliest opportunity.

306